D0078219

CHICAGO PUBLIC LIBRARY

R00745 95297

CLAUSAL FORM
LOGIC

INTERNATIONAL COMPUTER SCIENCE SERIES

Consulting editors   **A D McGettrick**   University of Strathclyde
                        J van Leeuwen   University of Utrecht

SELECTED TITLES IN THE SERIES

CLAUSAL FORM LOGIC

An Introduction to the Logic of Computer Reasoning

Tom Richards

La Trobe University

ADDISON-WESLEY
PUBLISHING
COMPANY

Sydney · Wokingham, England · Reading, Massachusetts
Menlo Park, California · New York · Don Mills, Ontario
Amsterdam · Bonn · Singapore · Tokyo · Madrid · San Juan

REF
QA
76.76
.E95
R53
1989

© 1989 Replee Pty Ltd.

All rights reserved. No part of this publication may be reproduced, stored in a retrieval system, or transmitted in any form or by any means, electronic, mechanical, photocopying, recording or otherwise, without prior written permission of the publisher.

Many of the designations used by manufacturers and sellers to distinguish their products are claimed as trademarks. Addison-Wesley has made every attempt to supply trademark information about manufacturers and their products mentioned in this book. A list of the trademark designations and their owners appears on page xiv.

Cover designed by Crayon Design of Henley-on-Thames and printed by The Riverside Printing Co. (Reading) Ltd.
Typeset by the AMS from the author's T$_E$X files.
Printed in Great Britain by The Bath Press, Avon.

First printed 1989.

British Library Cataloguing in Publication Data
Richards, Tom
  Clausal form logic   :   an introduction to the logic of computer reasoning. —
  (International computer science series).
  1.   Computer systems.   Programming.
  Applications of mathematical logic
  I.   Title   II.   Series
  005.13'1

  ISBN 0–201–12920–5

Library of Congress Cataloging in Publication Data
Richards, Tom.
  Clausal form Logic.
  (International computer science series)
  Bibliography: p.
  Includes index.
  1.   Expert systems (Computer science)   2.   Artificial
intelligence.   3.   Logic, Symbolic and mathematical.
4.   Reasoning.   I.   Title.   II.   Series.
QA76.76.E95R53   1989   006.3   88–26280
ISBN 0–201–12920–5 (U.S.)

Preface

Aims and objectives

This is an introductory book about an increasingly important type of formal logic called Clausal Form Logic (CFL). It is a very simple type of logic; all its statements are of the form *if something then something*. It lacks the usual apparatus of quantifiers (for all x, there is an x) and connectives (and, or, not, if and only if) which are normally associated with logical systems. Yet, despite this apparent poverty, it has as much power as a logic with all of these devices, both to represent statements and to carry out reasoning on them.

This simple if-then format of statements in CFL makes it ideally suited for computer-based reasoning systems, and for this reason it has come into much prominence lately. It is not too much to say that nearly all computational logic systems in current use employ CFL in one guise or another. Possibly the best-known example is the artificial intelligence programming language PROLOG, whose statements are more or less the if-then statements of CFL, and which works more or less in the way that CFL does. (The 'more or less' here hides a lot of interesting problems, as later chapters in this book will discuss.)

There are now many computing-oriented books on PROLOG and computational logic, but coherent introductory accounts of CFL *as a logic* are rather scarce. While much can be found on the computational algorithms for executing CFL reasoning on a machine, along with their heuristics, denotational semantics and implementation problems, there is less on CFL just as a system of symbolic logic.

In this book I try to fill that gap, by describing CFL as a symbolic system, with rules for expressing statements in it, rules for effecting proofs in it, and traditional, formal, truth-theoretical semantics for it. As such, the book functions rather as an arithmetic text does with respect to implementing arithmetic on a computer. Computational arithmetic is designed to approximate ordinary arithmetic; it is only if you have learned ordinary arithmetic that you can see, by contrast, where the computer approximation falls down.

The same is true of logic. The CFL described here is the ideal that computer reasoning systems approximate to, and as with arithmetic, fall short of, by trying to imitate with finite resources a process that can always exceed any finite bound. This is the logician's CFL, not the computer user's reasoning software.

Approach

The book begins not with CFL, but with an interesting diagrammatic way of representing statements and reasoning about them. This is semantic nets, also widely used in computer reasoning. These, though graphical in nature, bear a strong underlying resemblance to CFL. Their study helps a reader to grasp the idea of visual representation of abstract structure, and the manipulation of that visual representation to effect reasoning on the abstractions. That is the *pons asinorum* over which all must travel if they are to grasp the fundamental idea of symbolism and its power.

Semantic nets also provide an understanding of the fundamental parts, components and construction rules for CFL, presented in a visual way. This allows an abstraction to the more symbolic and less diagrammatic approach to reasoning found in CFL. Even there though, another layer of abstraction must be tackled: seeing the symbols as abstractions from their typographical representations on paper, seeing the marks on paper (or bits in a computer, also physical symbols) and their manipulation as finite approximations to a fully abstract intellectual process that exceeds any finite bounds.

At the end of the book is an Appendix explaining the 'usual' type of logic: first-order predicate calculus (PC). The Appendix also shows how to translate PC into CFL, so that what you find in a 'usual' logic book you can transplant to the CFL realm of if-then statements or to the semantic net diagrams. The practical importance of that exercise, is to warp the 'usual' wisdom on logic over to the computer-compatible format.

Readership

The book will be of interest to anyone who wants to understand the logic underlying computer reasoning systems. That logic is not obvious from learning a computer reasoning system such as PROLOG; in fact one is likely to be thoroughly misled about how intuitive logical ideas such as truth and modelling the world apply to these systems.

The book is aimed at **computer scientists** working in other parts of the field; at computer science **students** (all of whom need to know this sort of logical system these days); at **philosophers** and **logicians** (and their students) who want to study the newer approaches to symbolic logic; and at anyone with a lively intellectual curiosity about the abstractions of pure human reason. It will particularly interest the aficionados of artificial intelligence.

If you want to read this book solo, you certainly can. It presupposes only a well-trained mind, and it provides many examples and worked exercises to involve you in active thinking. Further Reading sections at the end of each of the four parts will help you get back to the history and sideways to parallel accounts.

For students in classes, a high-school acquaintance with mathematics is really desirable; not because the book presupposes any algebra or such things, but because the understanding of symbols and the art of symbol manipulation is a desirable background attainment. The chapters can be given to good classes at the rate of about one per lecture, plus tutorials, so a typical 26-lecture component size would suffice. The level of the book is suitable for good first-year students, and right on up to Honours classes. Tutorials are recommended, but parallel laboratory work with PROLOG might confuse because of differences not just of notation, but of expressive power and deductive technique. Students who already know PROLOG will find the book illuminating; those who will later learn it will find their PROLOG fits readily into new conceptual niches, enriching their understanding of it.

Using the book

Like most technical books, you will need to work through the examples thoroughly. In the text **bold font** is used to mark new concepts and terminology, *italic font* as usual means emphasis, sans serif font is used for semantic net symbolism, and `typewriter font` for CFL symbolism.

You will find exercises throughout the text. They are designed partly as reinforcement and practice of what you have learned; but mainly to introduce new concepts and techniques in an environment where you do the work. If you omit the exercises, you will rapidly get lost. So please always do them. You can always solve them on the basis of what you know, but in solving them and in comparing your answer with the one given, you are likely to learn quite a lot. Answers are given at the end of the book.

Each chapter has a summary at the end of it, to recapitulate the main concepts and terminology of the chapter. Sometimes the entry for a term in the summary may clarify or restate matters from a different angle. Most of the notes are rather loose and informal. Much of the early terminology is redefined more formally later in the book, when the precision becomes desirable.

Related material

A computer assisted learning program on this CFL is available, for IBM-PC type machines, from Dr Diego Latella, Via E. Basile 113/E, 00128, Roma, Italy. It includes English to CFL translation exercises and an intelligent assistant to help the user find CFL deductions. Preorder enquiries should be directed to him before placing orders.

Acknowledgements

The book has been long in preparation, growing out of invited lectures at an international conference on logic and computation in Melbourne in 1984. See *Logic and Computation, Proceedings of a Conference*, vols. 1 and 2, J.N. Crossley and J. Jaffar, eds.; Monash University, Computer Science Department, Clayton, Vic. 3168, Australia. Numerous students suffered and helped with early lectures. My department, Computer Science at La Trobe University in Melbourne, has provided a great working environment and splendid support. I would thank especially Steven Bodnar for his technical help with TₑX, in which this book is typeset. I wrote the TₑX macros, and could have finished the book a year earlier if I had not been so foolish as to use TₑX. Thanks too, to Manfred von Thun and Ross Brady of the Philosophy Department for reading early versions, and especially to the anonymous referees who did an excellent and thorough job. I am also grateful to Addison-Wesley's editors, notably Lynne Balfe and Stephen Troth, and to Malcolm Clark of TₑXpert Systems for manipulating the TₑX macros. All these people made the book twice as good as it would have been. Errors and stupidity are all my fault.

But most of all I want to thank Lyn, Naomi and Marshall, a long-suffering family who have not had the husband and father they deserved in the last couple of years. The book is dedicated with affection to Emeritus Professor of Philosophy George Hughes, of Victoria University of Wellington, who showed me the exhilaration of high-grade thinking.

Tom Richards

La Trobe University
September 1988

Contents

Trademark notice
micro-PROLOG™ is a trademark of Logic Programming Associates Ltd.
IBM™ is a trademark of the International Business Machines Corporation.
T$_E$X™ is a trademark of the American Mathematical Society.
UNIX™ is a trademark of A T & T.

Part I
LOGIC IN DIAGRAMS

Chapter 1
Logic: reasoning about reasoning

This chapter introduces you to the fundamental ideas of logic:

- Logic is a method of reasoning correctly.
- Logical reasoning is performed by calculating with symbols according to the rules of logic.

Since logical reasoning is calculating with symbols, we shall see that computers can be programmed to do logic – known as **logic programming**.

We shall also solve a couple of small logic puzzles to become familiar with the way logical reasoning works.

1.1   Reasoning about problems

We begin with a problem, since logic is about reasoning, and problems are supposed to be solved by reasoning.

1.1.1   A problem

We will call the problem (P1):

> Smith, Brown and Jones were sitting around a table.   (1)
> Their occupations were butcher, baker, and candlestick-maker,
> but not necessarily in that order.   (2)
> Smith was shorter than the candlestick-maker,   (3)
> the baker was Smith's best customer,   (4)
> and the candlestick-maker owed Brown $5.00.   (5)

Who was whom?

Problems like this are solved using logical reasoning. Reasoning is the art of finding out what information follows from what other information, of finding out what information is consistent with what other information, of what information is needed to answer a problem, and how to derive that answer.

The study of how to reason correctly is called **logic**. As a discipline, it goes back over two millennia to Plato and Aristotle, who – as Euclid did with geometry – laid down enduring foundations that students still learn today. There was much progress in Roman and Medieval times, but it was not until the late nineteenth century that the powerful types of logic we use today began to be developed.

In the seventeenth century, the great German philosopher and mathematician Leibniz argued that the aim of logicians should be to turn their art into a science along the lines of mathematics; then instead of debating a problem we would all be able to calculate the answer. His ideas about how to turn logic into a system of calculation are less significant than the suggestion itself, which has been taken up vigorously in the last twenty years or so, by computer scientists and logicians concerned with the problem of processing information.

What concerns these scientists is not **data processing** – how to store and retrieve data. In data processing we do not try to get the computer to reason with that data, but to put it away economically and then find it efficiently. If, for instance, a data processing computer is storing personnel records, we could ask it to retrieve for us everyone on a salary of under $20 000 who has been on the payroll for over five years. But if we stored in that computer the information in (P1) above, we would not expect it to be able to tell us who is whom.

But suppose we had a computer that could reason. Could it find the answer to our request in (P1)? Yes it could. Then how can it do so? The principles involved are the subject of this book.

We call this sort of computing ability **knowledge processing**, to distinguish it from data processing. Knowledge processing is a branch of the wider and very fascinating study of artificial intelligence. **Artificial intelligence** (AI) is concerned with trying to make computers carry out the really tough, hard-to-understand, intellectual processes such as understanding language, visual recognition of people and places, and commonsense reasoning. It is not concerned with the easy-to-understand processes such as doing arithmetic, however hard *you* might find that skill.

1.1.2   Trial-and-error solutions

How could we solve problem (P1)? The reason for playing with such puzzles is that if we think about how we actually solve them, that might give us the clues to the principles of reasoning. (Thinking about our thinking, reasoning about our reasoning – that is what logic is about.)

The most obvious solution method is to invent a possible solution and see if it fits the data. Try it for yourself, now, with this possible solution:

Brown is the butcher.
Jones is the baker.
Smith is the candlestick-maker.

Did it work?

Using this trial-and-error method might not seem very logical, because you did not try to reason to the answer from the data. (It is certainly inefficient, since there are six possible solutions to test.) But you used the cornerstone of logical reasoning in your thinking, the **Principle of Inconsistency**:

• If something is inconsistent with your data, it is false (provided you accept your data as true, of course).

Now try this possible solution:

Smith is the butcher.
Brown is the baker.
Jones is the candlestick-maker.

You should have been able to figure out that this solution *could be* correct, unlike the earlier one. That is, you should have been able to figure out that it is *consistent with* the data. But maybe there are other possible solutions that are also consistent with the data. (You have four more to check out.)

We are up against another logical principle here (the Non-principle of Consistency?):

- Just because something is consistent with your data, that does not mean it follows from the data.

So we are still looking for a more 'logical' method of solving problems, one which:

- reasons from data to solution, rather than testing guesses, and
- shows that its solution is *the* correct one, and not merely a situation consistent with the data.

1.1.3   A reasoned solution

Let us try a more sophisticated line of reasoning, forwards from the data until we deduce the solution, rather than backwards from a guess at the solution. The reasoning is set out below, step by step. On each line we write down a new item of information that we can deduce, and on the left we note the already-known items from which we inferred it. On the right, each item of information is given a reference number, as we did for the information in the statement of (P1). The three results we want are at lines (8), (10) and (11):

From (3)	Smith is not the candlestick-maker.	**(6)**
From (5)	Brown is not the candlestick-maker.	**(7)**
From (6) and (7)	Jones is the candlestick-maker.	**(8)**
From (4)	Smith is not the baker.	**(9)**
From (6) and (9)	Smith is the butcher.	**(10)**
From (8) and (10)	Brown is the baker.	**(11)**

This approach has some advantages over the trial-and-error method. It is far more efficient for one thing, and for another it shows that the solution is unique. By the time we get to line (8), for example, we know that it is Jones and only Jones who makes candles.

The disadvantage of the method is that it does seem to require some creative thinking and planning from the problem-solver; for at each stage of that piece of reasoning, it was never fixed and definite about what to do next. Why, for instance, did we choose first to make those inferences in lines (6) and (7) about who is *not* the candlestick-maker? Because in that way we could determine quickly who *was*. That was a much better way to begin than by trying to find the butcher, which would not have led anywhere.

Exercise 1.1 Start on this horse-race problem: There were three horses in a race, Gay Deceiver, Deety, and Black Hat. The information available is:

Ralph rode Black Hat.	(1)
Colonel Mustard's horse finished immediately behind Deety.	(2)
Piggy rode the last placed horse.	(3)
Merridew rode Miss Scarlett's horse.	(4)
Mrs White did not own the horse Piggy was riding.	(5)

Which horse got which place, and who owned and who rode each of them?

The derivation of the answer was quite short for the size of the problem, and each step is quite plainly correct. But it was far from obvious how to choose each step, as you no doubt realized when you did it. That is one of the serious difficulties facing logicians in their attempts to mechanize reasoning. The task of choosing the next step in a reasoning process seems, from this exercise, to be intuitive and creative rather than mechanical; an art not a science.

Another serious difficulty is that the derivation of the answer relied on a great many assumptions and on items of information that were not stated in (1) to (5) of the exercise. Some of them are so banal that we forget that they *are* assumptions, for example, we assumed that to reach (6), a jockey rides only one horse in a race. (If you want to track down your assumptions, it helps to imagine that a computer is carrying out the reasoning, and that it has no information except what we specifically program into it.) Other assumptions are that Mrs White owns one of the horses, that the three horses are indeed *three* horses, not one horse known by three names, that the owners are not jockeys, and so on.

It is apparent that reasoning, even in an antiseptic little puzzle like the horse-race one, is a very complicated activity. One of the triumphs of modern logic has been to reduce that complex activity to a small number of simple basic ingredients – like a chemist showing how the huge variety of molecules in the world are made up of a few simple types of atom.

1.2 Reasoning with symbols

Plato and Aristotle, long before Leibniz, provided the basic approach needed for computer-based reasoning. And that was to devise a way of representing knowledge in **symbols**, and doing the reasoning about that knowledge by manipulating those symbols in various ways. Symbols can be marks on paper, counters in a game, or bit patterns in a computer memory.

In arithmetic, the symbolic approach is second nature to most people, enshrined in rules like the Sign Rule:

Change sign when you shift a term from one side of an equation to the other;
so that when we are given the symbols:

$$a - x = b$$

we know we can juggle them using the sign rule to get:

$$a = b + x.$$

Modern mathematics has been made possible largely by finding good ways to symbolize mathematical concepts, which allow us to carry out meaningful manipulations. (Think, for instance, of the difficulty of multiplying XCVI by LIX.)

The same is true of modern **symbolic logic**, logic done by symbol manipulation. The symbol system of Aristotelian logic, like arithmetic based on Roman numerals, was too clumsy and restrictive to survive, and has been replaced by a number of modern systems.

We will look at only two such systems in this book, chosen because they are in fairly widespread use in computer-based reasoning.

(1)   **semantic nets** are a way of drawing knowledge and concepts as a type of network. They provide a powerful diagrammatic way of representing knowledge; but the manipulation of them, which represents the reasoning, can get a bit clumsy. Their virtue is their easily understood graphical way of representing information and linking it all together.

(2)   **Clausal form logic** has symbols that look more like algebra than network diagrams, but it has many structural similarities to semantic nets. It is more flexible in its ability to represent knowledge, and easier to manipulate (reason with) than semantic nets.

In addition to these two types of logic, there is the most common variety of all, which is the sort discussed in nearly every modern logic textbook. Called **predicate calculus**, it is more flexible than the other two, and uses an algebraic type of symbolism. Its very richness of devices for expressing logical concepts, and its numerous manipulation rules, make it the most congenial for humans to use. Predicate calculus (of which there are many varieties and extensions) is the normal type of logical symbolism used by logicians, mathematicians, and philosophers. But its very richness makes it more complicated for computers to handle, compared to the very simple manipulation methods of clausal form logic. Because of this, and because it is so widely discussed, we will not look at it in this book.

1.2.1   Computer reasoning

Computers are supposed to be good at manipulating data. To get computers to reason, then, the obvious approach is to encode the rules of some system of symbolic logic. Special languages, such as PROLOG, have been developed with the primary aim of expressing and manipulating the symbols of logic, rather than arithmetic. PROLOG, for example, is effectively a version of clausal form logic, with a few extras thrown in to handle the necessities of programming.

The development of software for computer reasoning has become a significant activity in computer science. There are several major areas of application for such software, both theoretical and practical:

- **Intelligent knowledge bases.** Data processing can become a much more powerful commercial tool if reasoning capabilities can be added to the usual retrieval and sorting capabilities. To do this, the data needs to be represented in structures suitable for logical manipulation. Semantic nets provide one good way of doing this.

- **Expert systems.** An expert system is a software system that contains the knowledge of some human expert, for example, how to diagnose lung diseases from the symptoms, or how to control some complicated piece of machinery, or how to determine the structure of an organic molecule given its mass spectrogram. In all expert systems, this knowledge is the subject of reasoning by the software system to answer problems put to it by its users.

- **Reasoning about programs.** Logic is the best tool for describing and analysing the nature and behaviour of computer programs. A considerable part of software science now consists in the applications of symbolic logic to the verification of programs. Varieties of predicate calculus are the appropriate symbolic reasoning systems here, which are not only used as pencil-and-paper tools by computer scientists to analyse their software, but are themselves encoded in software as **theorem provers** to do the donkey-work of program analysis automatically. Not surprisingly, this line of research leads to the interesting problem of devising logic-based software which will synthesize programs from descriptions of their desired functions.

1.2.2   Logical systems

There are many systems of symbolic logic, each with their own uses and limitations. The two discussed in this book belong to the family of **deductive logics**, ones where the reasoning involved is *certain*. That is, no matter how complex a piece of deductive reasoning is, if you are sure of your initial data (the so-called **premisses** of your reasoning), you can be equally sure of any results your reasoning reaches – your **conclusions**. Any piece of reasoning you carry out in a deductive logic is called a **deduction** or **proof**. (P1) and Exercise 1.1 are examples of deductions.

Exercise 1.2   What are the premises and conclusions in the horse-race deduction?

By contrast to deduction, there is a family of **inductive** logics, where the reasoning is less than certain – reasoning of the sort that rules in natural science and daily life. These logics take seriously the common situation that, even if you are sure of your premises, the conclusions you reach are only more or less plausible. Inductive logics involve the assignment of probabilities to reasoning steps, and of confidence factors to conclusions. Inductive logics are important in computer reasoning too, for example, in managerial decision support systems and in expert systems dealing with uncertain reasoning, such as in medical diagnosis, where the best any doctor can do is to attach varying degrees of confidence to his or her diagnoses.

Inductive logics will not be tackled in this book. The main job of this book is to set out some rules and techniques for deductive symbolic reasoning, and to show how to use them. We must constantly bear in mind the methods of computer reasoning, because the overall motivation is to understand the principles of logic underlying computer reasoning systems. But actual computer reasoning systems will not be studied, either as software or in terms of their design. The main purpose of this book is to find the right symbolic structures and the right rules for manipulating them correctly.

1.2.3   Proof theory, syntax and semantics

The study of the manipulation rules of a system of symbolic logic and their behaviour is called **proof theory**. There are two important questions to ask about the proof theory for any system of logic:

- Can we tell if the proof theory is *sound*? That is, do we know that from true premises the rules will never let us deduce untrue conclusions?

- How *complete* is our proof theory? Are our manipulation rules strong enough to let us deduce *all* the conclusions that truly follow from given premises, or do some get left out?

To answer those questions about a system of symbolic logic, we will have to develop, in parallel with its proof theory, an account of the relation between the symbols of the logic and the information they encode and manipulate.

That is, we will develop an explanation of the *meaning* of symbols in the logic. Once we know their meaning, we can check that its proof theory will never let us deduce untruths from a basis of truths.

The study of meaning and truth in a symbol system is known as **semantics**. It is to be contrasted with **syntax**, the study of the symbols themselves, merely as symbols and without regard to their meaning. Syntax includes, for example, proof theory and also **grammar**, the study of how symbols may legitimately be strung together for the encoding of complex information. In arithmetic, for example, grammar tells you that:

$$3 + = 4\ 5$$

is not a formula of arithmetic, but that:

$$3 + 4 = 5$$

is a properly constructed formula. The semantics of arithmetic will tell you that the above formula is false, and the proof theory of arithmetic will give you manipulation rules that allow you to deduce the formula:

$$3 + 4 \neq 5.$$

Exercise 1.3   Which of these English expressions are grammatical, which are true, and which are false?

(a)   The yolk of an egg are white.
(b)   The yolk of an egg is white.
(c)   The yolk of an egg is yellow.

1.2.4 Manipulating symbols

In most systems of logic, deductions can be set out on a line-by-line format, as we did earlier for the butcher-baker example and the horse-race example. Each line contains a statement, numbered for convenience, and an explanation of how we obtained that statement.

Note incidentally, that logicians often talk of sentences, formulae and the like as **statements**, as we just did, to stress that they are interested in sentences that are true-or-false (have a **truth-value**), like 'Smith owed Brown $5.00,' rather than being questions ('Does Smith owe Brown $5.00?'), commands ('Smith! Pay Brown $5.00!') or some other mode of language use.

In a deductive symbolic logic, each statement in a deduction will be derived from earlier ones in the deduction – or else will be a premiss. Check that this holds in our two example deductions above, even though they are not deductions in a symbolic logic. In a symbolic logic, the difference is that there will be some rule for manipulating symbols that is used to derive a statement from earlier ones.

Here is a very simple example. We are told that everyone who is honest is poor, and that Socrates is honest. We are asked to deduce the obvious conclusion that Socrates is poor. Here is the way the logician would do it.

First, the two premisses must be written down in some standardized way. We will write them as we would in micro-PROLOG, a well-known micro-computer version of PROLOG. First we write the premiss that everyone who is honest is poor, as:

$$\text{X poor if X honest} \tag{1}$$

Note the use of the **variable X**, as in mathematics. We can read (1) as being true no matter what the value of X is. Next, we write 'Socrates is honest' as:

$$\text{Socrates honest} \tag{2}$$

And finally, what we have to deduce from these two premisses is:

Socrates poor

The logician then carries out some symbol manipulations to effect the proof.

(a)   Replace the variable X in (1) by the name Socrates, giving

$$\text{Socrates poor if Socrates honest} \tag{3}$$

Logicians call the rule used there, **Instantiation** (Inst). The idea behind it is simple: given that (1) is true for any object X, it is certainly true for Socrates. We say that statement (3) is an **instance** of the general statement (1). Note that Inst is a rule for manipulating symbols: replacing a variable by a name.

(b)   Next, note that the 'if' part of (3) is identical to the premiss (2). That is, (3) says that one statement is true if a second is, and (2) says that the second is indeed true. It follows then that the left side of (3) is true too. And that is what we want to deduce! Putting this insight in terms of manipulating symbols, the rule is that if we have a statement in a deduction of the form 'q if p,' and another which is identical to the p part of that statement, then we can deduce the q part. So we can now deduce:

$$\text{Socrates poor} \tag{4}$$

which is what we were trying to prove. This rule is called **Detachment** or **Modus Ponens** (MP) by logicians:

Given statements of the form 'q if p' and 'p',
deduce 'q'

The whole deduction can be set out like this:

Premiss	`X poor if X honest`	**(1)**
Premiss	`Socrates honest`	**(2)**
(1) Inst	`Socrates poor if Socrates honest`	**(3)**
(2), (3) MP	`Socrates poor`	**(4)**

If we had been using micro-PROLOG, the program could have deduced that conclusion for us. First, we would have entered those two premisses, exactly as written above, into micro-PROLOG's database. (Think of a database as a collection of premisses.) To have the program prove that Socrates is poor, we would then enter into micro-PROLOG this query:

`is (Socrates poor)`

Now PROLOG consists internally of program that carries out deductions using symbol-manipulation methods on its database. (For that reason, it is called a **logic programming language**.) Entering this query will trigger off that deduction program, and in a moment it will print out:

`yes`

to tell you that it has succeeded in deducing that Socrates is poor, as asked.

It is important to realize that although we have used the notation of micro-PROLOG here, we have not carried out the deduction in the way that micro-PROLOG would. There are many ways of carrying out deductions in symbolic systems, by different sorts of symbol manipulations. PROLOG uses a very different method of deduction, working backwards from the conclusion we want to prove, to the premisses that support it. Above, we worked forwards from premisses to conclusion. PROLOG's method is particularly suitable for machine computations, but not as obvious as the above deduction. We will look at PROLOG's method later in the book.

Exercise 1.4   What do you think this micro-PROLOG statement says?

`X higher-than Y if Y lower-than X`   (1)

Given (1) as a premiss, and a premiss stating that Stratus is lower than Cirrus, set out a deduction whose conclusion is that Cirrus is higher than Stratus.

1.3   The rest of this book

In the rest of this book we will be constructing, analysing and using the two symbolic logics mentioned above: semantic nets and clausal form logic. We will:

- Explain their grammars, so that it is quite clear what counts as expressions of the logic and what does not.
- Explain their proof theory, so that we can reason in the logics.
- Explain their semantics, so that we can understand what the symbols are saying, learn how to encode information in those symbols, and see why the proof theory works properly.

When that is done, we will have explored quite thoroughly the principles underlying the computer reasoning software that is increasingly used today; and which will be in wider use tomorrow when knowledge processing comes of age.

SUMMARY

- **Logic.** The study of how to reason correctly.
- **Symbolic logic.** Logical systems expressed in symbols, where reasoning is performed by manipulating the symbols.
- **Syntax.** The study of the symbols in a symbolic logic system, without regard to their meaning.
- **Grammar.** In a symbolic system, the study of how the symbols may legitimately be combined to make larger expressions. A part of syntax.
- **Proof theory.** In a symbolic logic system, the study of the manipulation rules. A part of syntax.
- **Semantics.** In a symbolic system, the study of the meaning of the symbols and expressions.
- **Statement.** A true-or-false expression, like 'It is raining' or '$2+3 = 4$'.
- **Truth-value.** Truth or falsity. Every statement has one of these values.
- **Premisses.** The data used in a piece of reasoning. These are statements.

- **Conclusions.** The results obtained in a piece of reasoning. These are statements.

- **Deduction.** A piece of reasoning that proceeds from premises to conclusions with complete certainty, that is, the semantics show that if the premises are true, then any conclusion must be true too. Also called a **proof**.

- **Deductive logic.** Any logical system whose reasoning is deductive.

- **Inductive logic.** Any logical system whose reasoning is not certain, but plausible.

- **Instantiation rule.** A manipulation rule that allows variables in a statement to be replaced by names – all occurrences of the same variable in the one statement, for example, X, must be replaced by the same name, for example, 5 or Adam.

- **Variable.** A symbol which may be replaced by a name using the Instantiation rule. Usually written using X, Y, Z, etc.

- **Detachment.** Also called **Modus Ponens**. A manipulation rule that says that if two statements of the form q if p, and p, occur in a deduction (where p and q are themselves statements), we may deduce q, that is, add it to the deduction.

- **Soundness.** A proof theory is sound if it will not permit the deduction of a false conclusion from true premises. Often called **consistency**.

- **Completeness.** A proof theory is complete if it permits the deduction of all the conclusions that truly follow from any given premises.

- **Principle of Inconsistency.** If a statement is inconsistent with a set of true statements, then it is false.

- **Non-principle of Consistency.** If a statement is consistent with a set of true statements, that does not mean it is true.

- **Data processing.** The storage, organization and retrieval of data in a computer.

- **Knowledge processing.** The representation of information in a computer in a structured symbolic form comparable to human knowledge, and the process of logical reasoning on that knowledge as performed by the computer.

- **Artificial intelligence.** The design and development of computer systems that exhibit intelligent behaviour.

Chapter 2
The atoms of logic

To begin the study of symbolic logic, we need to look at the makeup
of the simplest type of statement in logic, the **atomic statement**,
out of which all others are made. We will look at atomic statements
as they occur in English, to begin with, and learn:

- How to recognize them.

- Some of the ways in which they are compounded to make
  larger non-atomic statements.

- The two types of components that make up statements:
  terms and **predicates**.

Since the symbolism of English is not very suitable for carrying out symbolic logic, we will spend the second half of this chapter
developing a symbolism in which we can express atomic statements
and their components more suitably. This is the **semantic net** notation, a graphical network of arrows and boxes which makes the
structure and interrelationships of a set of atomic statements very
obvious visually.

2.1   The chemistry of logic

Logic has often been compared to chemistry in its structure. Chemists define *molecules* as the smallest units of any chemical substance, such as water, oxygen, or iron. When molecules are made or broken up in chemical reactions, the *atoms* are the bricks that are mortared together or split apart. *Atomos* means 'indivisible' in Greek, and in the laboratories of chemists, if not physicists, their atoms are just that.

2.1.1   Molecules of information

The **molecules** of logic are statements. Recall from Chapter 1 that statements are chunks of knowledge (or information, if you prefer) – expressions that are either true or false. Statements are expressed in English by declarative sentences, like 'Caesar conquered Gaul' or 'Caesar and Calpurnia lived in Rome'. Mathematics has its statements too, which are usually expressed in the form of equations or inequalities, such as '$x^2 - x - 6 = 0$' or '$5 \leq 4$'. Note that these four examples all say something true or false; that is, they make statements – they do not ask questions, issue instructions, express feelings, or anything else. The example of the equation is a bit more complex, since it is *true for* certain values of x ($x = 3$ and $x = -2$), and *false for* all the others.

As in chemistry, the molecules of logic can be often split apart into smaller units, which are still statements, until we reach the statements that cannot be fragmented any further without ceasing to be units of information. These are the **atomic statements**. The **molecular statement**:

Caesar and Calpurnia lived in Rome

for example, can be divided into two smaller units of information:

Caesar lived in Rome
Calpurnia lived in Rome

glued together by the idea of **and**. Those two statements are atomic; we cannot see them as compounded of yet simpler statements. A mathematical example is:

$5 \leq 4$

This is a shorthand for:

$5 < 4$ or $5 = 4$

Note that in this case the glue is **or**.

When we join statements together using 'and', we are saying that the statements glued together are all true. If we say 'Caesar is dead and a triumvirate rules Rome and Brutus is banished', we are asserting that all three component statements are true. Such a statement is called a **conjunction** and the statements glued together in this way are called **conjuncts**. When molecules are built out of simpler ones, you need to look closely at how the components are glued together, for that shows what information the molecule contains. Conjunctive glue, as we just saw, makes the molecule inform us that all its components (conjuncts) are true.

Another type of molecule-building glue is called **disjunction**, usually signalled in English by 'or'. We see this occurring in sentences like 'Octavius will become Emperor or the Republic will be restored for a time or the triumvirate will collapse'. The effect of this glue is to create a molecule out of component statements (its **disjuncts**) which carries the somewhat indefinite information that *some* of its component disjuncts are true. Maybe just one, maybe two, maybe all of them, but anyway at least one. 'Octavius will become Emperor or he will not' expresses a disjunctive statement.

You need to use your common sense to decide what sort of glue is indicated by English joining words. 'Or' sometimes signals conjunction, as in 'Pompey did not trust Caesar or Octavius'! And a comma can signal disjunction or conjunction. Compare 'Octavius, Mark Antony and Lepidus will rule Rome', with 'Octavius, Mark Antony or Lepidus will rule Rome'. The clue to finding the meaning of the glue often lies in thinking about how the truth or falsity of the whole statement molecule depends on the truth or falsity of its components. Conjunctive and disjunctive glue are both defined in just those terms.

Exercise 2.1 Which of the following make statements? Of those that do, which make atomic statements? If the statement made is non-atomic, what are the component statements, and how are they compounded together?

  (a)   Did Caesar conquer Gaul?
  (b) $2 + 3 = 9$.
  (c)   Caesar! Beware the Ides of March!
  (d)   Antony and Augustus were emperors.
  (e)   Calpurnia believed that Julius was in danger.
  (f)   The murderer of Caesar.
  (g) $4 \neq 6$.
  (h)   Let x = 9.
  (i)   If Caesar was an emperor, Calpurnia was an empress.
  (j)   Brutus and Caesar trusted each other.

We will not look further at molecular statements until the next chapter. Instead, we shall look at atoms and their structure, for in logic as in chemistry the internal structure of the atoms fixes the nature of the atoms and the molecules they make up.

2.1.2   Inside the atoms: terms and predicates

Here are three atomic statements, all of which are built in the same way:

Caesar conquered Gaul	**(1)**
Calpurnia was married to the noblest Roman of them all	**(2)**
Octavius is Augustus	**(3)**

In each case, a relation is being expressed that holds between two objects. In (1), the objects are Julius Caesar and the country of Gaul, the relation is that of conquering, the particular conqueror here is Caesar and the conquered is Gaul. In (2), the objects are Calpurnia and Caesar (who is the noblest Roman of them all). The relation is that of being married to someone. In (3), the relation is called **identity**, where one object is being said to be actually one and the same object as the other. The identity relation is familiar in mathematics as **equality**. '$+\sqrt{9} = 3$' says that the positive square root of nine is one and the same object as the number three.

The structure shared by all four of these examples of atomic statements is:

- There are two references to objects.

- A relation joining those two objects is described.

(Of course, the two references may be to the same object, in which case the relation relates the object to itself.) Relations that hold between two objects are called **binary** or **dyadic** or **two-place**. Atomic statements made up of a dyadic relation will contain, in addition, only the two references.

By contrast:

Caesar died	**(4)**

expresses an atomic statement of a different structure. Here, there is only one reference to an object, not two. The rest of the statement describes a feature of that object, namely that the object died. Features, unlike dyadic relations, attach to one object, so are said to be **one-place** or **unary** or **monadic**.

These examples of atomic statements show that the structure of such statements is very simple, containing parts of just two types:

(1)   There are references to objects – one, two, or indeed sometimes more than two references.

(2)   There is what is being described about those objects. What can be said about objects is called in logic a **property** of the objects.

Within an atomic statement, the expressions that do job (1) are called **terms**. In English, the common examples are names; in arithmetic, numerals.

Properties, we have seen, can be one-place (features) or two-place; indeed some are more than two-place. An example is the rather complex relation of *moving*: there is the thing moved, the agent moving it, the place from which the moving occurred, and the place to which the moving occurred. That makes it four-place. An example is:

Augustus moved Caesar from the Forum to the morgue   (**5**)

Expressions that describe properties are called **predicates** in logic. The predicates in (1), (2) and (3) above are 'conquered', 'was married to' and 'is' respectively. Roughly, in English you can find the predicate in an atomic statement by removing the terms and taking what is left over. That means the predicate in (5) is something like 'moved from to'. A better notation for predicates than the English one is desirable!

The fact that it can be hard or messy to specify the terms and predicates in an English sentence, as we saw with (5) above, is one reason for replacing English by a precise and controlled symbolic system in which to do logical reasoning. Another reason is that it can be quite arbitrary how we specify the structure of an English sentence. We could, for example, analyse (5), not as an atomic statement with a four-place predicate, but as a conjunction of two three-place statements:

Augustus moved Caesar from the Forum
Augustus moved Caesar to the morgue

Here is a similar difficulty about how to analyse the logical structure of English. Remember that an atomic statement contains just one predicate; indeed that is how we can tell it is atomic. But consider:

Brutus hated and despised Caesar   (**6**)

Do we have just one two-place predicate here: 'hated and despised'? Alternatively, we can break (6) up into a conjunction of two statements:

Brutus hated Caesar
Brutus despised Caesar

and now we have two atomic statements.

To sum up, we have two syntactic parts to atomic statements: their terms and their predicates. Semantically, these parts are related to objects and properties of objects, respectively. These correlations between the syntax and semantics of statements are set out in the following table. The **adicity** or **arity** referred to there is the number of places (one-place, two-place, etc.) of a property, and correspondingly of a predicate and of the whole atomic statement.

Syntactic part of atomic statement	Semantically related thing in the world
Term	Object
One-place predicate	Feature of object
Two-place predicate	Two-place relation between objects
Predicate (any arity)	Property (of same arity)

Remembering that an atomic statement is the basic chunk of information, what we are in fact saying is that the fundamental sorts of information are *either* that an object has some feature, *or* that two or more objects have a certain relation between them.

Exercise 2.2   Which of these express atomic statements? For those that do, what is their arity, what objects do they reference and what properties do they describe?

   (a)   I came, I saw, I conquered.
   (b)   Caesar is Julius.
   (c)   Caesar crowned himself.
   (d)   Caesar is dead.
   (e)   Caesar's wife distrusts everyone.
   (f)   Brutus stabbed Caesar.
   (g)   Nobody trusts Brutus.
   (h)   Antony carried Caesar from the Forum.

2.2   Pictures of atoms

For a while we are going to pretend that the only sort of atomic statement is the two-place one. The advantage of two-place statements is that they can be usefully represented in diagrams, which can be manipulated to carry out reasoning processes. The diagrams are called **semantic nets**, and with their manipulation we have our first reasoning machine.

2.2.1   Semantic nets

To draw a two-place atomic statement, such as 'Caesar loved Brutus', we put the two terms into boxes, then draw an arrow from one to the other and label that arrow with the predicate, like this:

$$\boxed{\text{CAESAR}}\underline{\quad\text{Loved}\quad}_{\rightarrow}\boxed{\text{BRUTUS}}$$

The two boxed terms are called **nodes**; the arrow joining them, which is labelled with the predicate, is a **link**. The whole, two nodes plus their link, we call a **relationship vector**. The node at the arrowhead end of a link is at the **head** of the vector, the other is at the **tail**. Which way do we draw the arrow? There is often an intuitively right way, as here, from the agent to the object. But the only thing that really matters is that once you use a labelled arrow one way, you must keep to that convention. For instance, if you decide to represent 'Caesar's wife is Calpurnia' by this vector:

$$\boxed{\text{CAESAR}}\underline{\quad\text{Wife}\quad}_{\rightarrow}\boxed{\text{CALPURNIA}}$$

you have in fact decided to put the husband at the tail of Wife links and the wife at the head. Then the vector:

$$\boxed{\text{JOSEPHINE}}\underline{\quad\text{Wife}\quad}_{\rightarrow}\boxed{\text{NAPOLEON}}$$

must mean that Napoleon is the wife of Josephine, and not the converse!

When we have a collection of information about a given matter (assuming it is all available as two-place statements), we can use a whole network of relationship vectors to represent the information. A semantic net is the resulting graph.

EXAMPLE 2.1_____

Suppose for example Sherlock Holmes has this information about a crime:

> Lee knew the victim.
> The victim knew Jay and Kit.
> The murderer knew the victim and conversely.
> Jay and Lee know each other.
> The victim is dead.
> The victim is male.

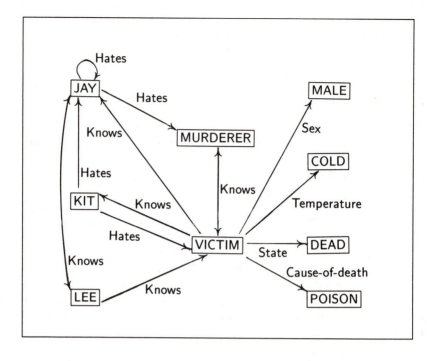

Figure 2.1 Murder mystery data as a semantic net.

The victim is cold.
The cause of the victim's death was poison.
Jay hates the murderer.
Jay hates herself.
Kit hates the victim and Jay.

If we represent the above information in relationship vectors, connected together so that we never have to write the same node twice, we obtain a semantic net. It is drawn up in Figure 2.1. (We choose to assimilate 'knows' and 'knew', since except for an irrelevant time reference they mean the same.)

Because there is a Knows link which goes both ways between MURDERER and VICTIM, we have economized by merging the two arrows into one double-headed one. You would not want to do that for two differently-labelled links, as between KIT and VICTIM!

Check that you can see how each statement has been represented in this net. Note that in some cases, we have replaced the rather colourless word 'is' by a predicate describing more unambiguously what we are talking about. Thus 'The victim is cold' was represented as:

| VICTIM | Temperature → | COLD |

There is a good reason for always doing this. When we look at the net we need to know what the relationship is between | VICTIM | and | COLD |. Is it the victim's personality, state of health (caught a cold) or what? An explicit, clear label on the link makes it obvious what is meant. A second advantage is this: if we are presented with a big semantic net and asked to find all the statements in it about the temperature of things, all we have to do is look for arrows labelled Temperature. Similarly, note how we expressed 'The victim is male' in the net. To find all we know about people's sex, all we have to do is look for Sex arrows.

2.2.2 How to build semantic nets

(1)   We always draw a frame around a semantic net, to indicate that the vectors shown belong together and define a little world of their own. A semantic net can be a diagram of somebody's beliefs, or of what is being said in a storybook, or of the knowledge base of a computer. In all cases, it is a diagrammatic representation of a collection of statements, and we call that collection a **world**. All the statements represented inside it we say are *true in that world*. The world in Figure 2.1 is the world of Holmes's beliefs about the crime; it is not all the facts about the crime – there is no Murdered link for example – and indeed some of Holmes's beliefs may be false. But that is just to say they disagree with the relationship vectors in another semantic net, the one labelled 'What really happened'. We have not drawn up that net.

(2)   Note the convention of putting TERMS in capitals, and Predicates with an initial capital. This helps remind you that they are different parts of a statement. You cannot use a term as a predicate, or conversely.

(3)   Of particular importance in Figure 2.1 was the method of representing those four one-place statements about the victim. We took a feature – for example, being dead – and turned it into a relationship! Here are some more examples:

The Sun is yellow: | SUN | Colour → | YELLOW |
3 is a prime number: | 3 | Member-of → | PRIME-NUMBERS |
Caesar stumbled: | CAESAR | Activity → | STUMBLING |

What we do in each case is to *objectify* the property, that is, turn it into an object, usually rather abstract. Then we find a way of expressing the relationship between the subject and this new object. And as mentioned earlier, do not fall into the easy habit of calling that relationship Is. We use an informative word to describe the relationship.

Exercise 2.3   Caesar is an emperor, and he is proud, curled up and asleep. Represent that little scenario in a semantic net.

---

(4)   Only atomic statements are represented in semantic nets. In the previous exercise we saw how to break up a conjunctive statement into its conjuncts, and work out how to represent them.

Exercise 2.4   Why can we not do that for disjunctions?

---

(5)   A fundamental rule in logic is that *different objects must be given different names.* If there are two people called Lee in the Holmes example above, we should use different names for them in the net, perhaps **LEE-1** and **LEE-2**. Think of what would happen to the net if we did not do that, but added the information that one Lee was male and the other female. This is a case of the **unambiguity rule** in logic, that is, ambiguous expressions are simply never allowed. On the other hand, there is no harm in representing one object by two or more terms. Sometimes, indeed, we must. Assuming that the murderer is one of Jay, Kit or Lee, that person is represented twice in the net of Figure 2.1, and has to be, if Holmes has not identified the murderer.

2.3   Properties of relations

This chapter is concluded by discussing some properties that two-place relations may have, and how those properties show up in a semantic net. So far, we have defined properties as holding of *objects,* and one type of property of objects is the two-place relation. Now we will be looking at properties of properties, which are called **higher-order properties**.

2.3.1   Symmetry of a relation

To say that a relation $\mathcal{R}$ is **symmetrical** in some world or other, is to say that, in that world, whenever one object x has the relation $\mathcal{R}$ to an object y, then y has the relation $\mathcal{R}$ to x too.

In terms of semantic nets, the visual test for symmetry of $\mathcal{R}$ is that every link in the net labelled $\mathcal{R}$ is double-headed: the arrow, in other words, goes both ways between its nodes.

There are no symmetrical relations in Figure 2.1. But suppose that Jay and Kit knew the victim, and the victim knew Lee. Then by adding those statements to the net in Figure 2.1, we would have a world in which Knows is symmetrical.

Some relations are symmetrical in every world, such as being married to, being in the same country as, and having a conversation with. Relations that are symmetrical in any possible world, such as these, are called **necessarily symmetrical**. This is contrasted to **contingently symmetrical** relations, which are symmetrical in some worlds but not in others.

The contrary of symmetry is **asymmetry**. To be *asymmetrical in a world* a relation $\mathcal{R}$ must *never* hold both ways between a pair of objects. That is, for $\mathcal{R}$ to be asymmetrical in a world, whenever $\mathcal{R}$ holds from an object x to an object y, it does not hold from y to x. Visually, in a semantic net a relation is asymmetrical if all links labelled by it are one-way. Knows is plainly not asymmetrical in Figure 2.1. Neither is Hates, because of the Hates loop on JAY . Remove that and we have a world in which it is asymmetrical. However Sex, Temperature, State, Cause-of-death are all asymmetrical in the world of Figure 2.1.

Exercise 2.5   Draw semantic nets of worlds in which the relation Brother-of is symmetrical, asymmetrical, and neither (one net per case). Put the brother at the tail of the link. It should be clear from your net why the relation is symmetrical (or whatever) in it, but make your worlds as simple as possible.

2.3.2   Reflexivity of a relation

A relation $\mathcal{R}$ is **reflexive** in a world when *every object* in that world has $\mathcal{R}$ to itself. That is, the statement '$x\mathcal{R}x$' is true for every object x in the world. So in a semantic net, every node will have an $\mathcal{R}$ link looped from itself to itself. This makes reflexivity a very obvious feature in a semantic net. If no object in the world has $\mathcal{R}$ to itself, then $\mathcal{R}$ is said to be **irreflexive** in that world. There are no reflexive relations in the world of Figure 2.1, and all except Hates are irreflexive. *Being aware of the existence of* is reflexive in worlds of awake and normally functioning humans (because 'x is aware of the existence of x'

will be true of all awake and normally functioning humans x); but the relation is no doubt irreflexive in slug worlds. *Being one's own grandfather*, that is, 'x is the grandfather of x' is necessarily irreflexive.

2.3.3 Transitivity of a relation

A relation $\mathcal{R}$ is **transitive** in a world if, wherever $\mathcal{R}$ holds from an object x in the world to an object y in the world, and also holds from y to an object z in the world, it also holds from x to z. That is, for transitive relations $\mathcal{R}$, for any objects x, y and z, if $x\mathcal{R}y$ and $y\mathcal{R}z$, then $x\mathcal{R}z$.

Suppose we know that Robert is taller than Ethel, who in turn is taller than William. (Draw a semantic net for that.) Then, since the relation of taller-than is necessarily transitive, we also know that Robert is taller than William. (Draw that link in, too.)

The above illustrates the appearance of a transitive relation in a net. Wherever we have a pair of $\mathcal{R}$ arrows linking three nodes to make a chain, and the links have the same sense (meet head to tail at the middle node), like this:

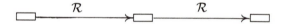

then an $\mathcal{R}$ link joins the two extreme nodes in the same sense:

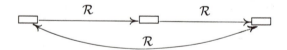

Exercise 2.6

> (a)   Draw the semantic net for a world of five people, A, B, C, D, E, where A hit B, B hit C, C hit D, and D hit E.
>
> (b)   Now you learn that the hitting relation is transitive in this world, so what other Hit links must you draw in?

(Avoid clutter – do not label your links; we know they are all Hit links anyway.)

$\mathcal{R}$ is **intransitive** in a world if, for any three objects x, y, z in the world such that x has $\mathcal{R}$ to y, and y has $\mathcal{R}$ to z; x does *not* have $\mathcal{R}$ to z. *Being married to* is intransitive in nearly all worlds (since people are married only in couples and a spouse is not married to him/herself); but you might dream up some world that allows bigamy and homosexual marriages, and show in your semantic net for it how marriage in this case is not intransitive, and maybe even transitive.

Check for yourself that both Knows and Hates in Figure 2.1 are neither transitive nor intransitive.

Exercise 2.7   A sociologist was studying friendship patterns in a group of seven subjects, anonymously called 'A' to 'G'. She discovered the following data:

A likes B	(1)	B likes A	(9)
C likes D	(2)	E likes B	(10)
B likes E	(3)	G likes B	(11)
E likes C	(4)	F asks A out	(12)
F likes C	(5)	D asks A out	(13)
B likes G	(6)	F asks G out	(14)
A likes C	(7)	C asks G out	(15)
A likes D	(8)	C asks A out	(16)

Draw a semantic net for this data, using Likes and Asks-out for the relations involved. Then answer the following questions. (We will call the world depicted in the semantic net, 'W'.)

(a)   Is Asks-out symmetrical or asymmetrical in W, or neither?

(b)   What is the smallest group of people we could remove from W to make Likes symmetrical in the resulting world?

(c)   In the world that results from (b), is Asks-out symmetrical?

(d)   What is the smallest group of Likes links we could add to W to make Likes symmetrical in the resulting world?

(e)   Having done (d), can you add just one further Likes link without destroying the symmetry of Likes in that world?

(f)   Remove just one person from W to make a world in which Likes is asymmetrical.

(g)   Is Likes reflexive or irreflexive in W, or neither?

(h)   Is Likes transitive in W?

(i)   Is Likes transitive in the world we get by removing B, E, F, and G from W?

(j)   Is Likes transitive in the world we get by removing just C from W?

(k)   What is the smallest group of Likes links we could add to W to make Likes transitive in the resulting world?

SUMMARY

- **Molecular statements.** Statements compounded out of simpler statements.

- **Atomic statements.** Statements that are not molecular.

- **Conjunction.** A type of molecular statement. A conjunction of statements is true only if each statement in the conjunction (each **conjunct**) is true, otherwise it is false. Approximately conveyed in English by *and.*

- **Disjunction.** A type of molecular statement. A disjunction of statements is true only if at least one statement in the disjunction (a **disjunct**) is true, otherwise it is false. Approximately conveyed in English by *or.*

- **Term.** Expression that refers to an object.

- **Property.** Anything that can be said about an object or objects.

- **Predicate.** Expression that expresses a property.

- **Arity or adicity.** Some properties belong to single objects (like their mass), others to pairs of objects (like being more massive than), others to triples (like being intermediate in mass between) or even more. The number of objects that any instance of the property must attach to is the arity of the property. The concept extends to predicates and atomic statements. Various names are given in the literature to properties of various aritities; here they are up to 4:

Arity	Name		
1	one-place	monadic	unary
2	two-place	dyadic	binary
3	three-place	triadic	ternary
4	four-place	tetradic	quaternary

- **Relation.** A property with an arity of two or more. Often **relation** just means a two-place relation.

- **One-place property.** A property that attaches to objects singly. Also called a **feature**.

- **Relationship vector.** A graphical representation of a two-place atomic statement, comprising two **nodes** representing the objects and joined by a directional **link** representing the relation. We draw the nodes as boxes containing the terms and the link as an arrow labelled with the predicate, from the **tail** node to the **head** node.

- **Semantic net.** A network or graph made of relationship vectors, and obeying certain restrictions (see text).

- **World.** A set of statements. (Imagine they are all true, then you are imagining that world.) A semantic net defines a world.

- **Changing features to two-place relations.** Objectify the feature, then relate the subject to it using a suitable two-place relation.

- **Unambiguity rule.** Distinct objects or properties must have distinct names.

- **Higher order property.** A property of a property, rather than a property of an object.

- **Necessary property.** A property of something which holds in all possible worlds. For example, '2 + 2 = 4' is *true* in all worlds, so is necessarily true.

- **Contingent property.** A property of something which holds in some possible worlds but not in others. For example, loving is a contingently symmetrical relation, and contingently asymmetrical.

Properties of a two-place relation R in a world W:

- **Reflexivity.** R is reflexive in W only if every object x in W has R to itself.

- **Irreflexivity.** R is irreflexive in W only if no object x in W has R to itself.

- **Symmetry.** R is symmetrical in W only if for every pair of objects x, y in W such that x has R to y, y has R to x too.

- **Asymmetry.** R is asymmetrical in W only if for every pair of objects x, y in W such that x has R to y, y does not have R to x.

- **Transitivity.** R is transitive in W only if for any three objects x, y, z in W such that x has R to y and y has R to z, x also has R to z.

- **Intransitivity.** R is intransitive in W only if for any three objects x, y, z in W such that x has R to y and y has R to z, x does not have R to z.

Chapter 3
If – the vehicle of reasoning

In this chapter we shall see how to use a particular type of non-atomic statement, called a *conditional statement*, in semantic nets. Conditional statements are if-then statements, such as 'If Brutus killed Caesar, then Brutus is a murderer.'

The importance of the conditional statements is that they permit us to carry out reasoning in the semantic nets, by specifying for us new vectors that may be added to the semantic net. If, for instance, the above conditional statement is represented in a semantic net, as well as a vector for 'Brutus killed Caesar', we shall see how these specify a new vector that can be added into the net, and the new vector will represent 'Brutus is a murderer'.

In this way we will have turned our semantic nets into a system for carrying out symbolic reasoning.

3.1   Reasoning with semantic nets

So far, the semantic nets we can construct contain just bare information: nothing more than two-place atomic statements. These are data we can reason about (see Exercise 3.1 below); but to reason about that data we need some rules about how to do so. What we need to add are some techniques for reasoning with the vectors in a net – some manipulation rules on them which give us a deductive logic.

We will begin with an exercise, which illustrates that when you deduce conclusions from statements in a semantic net, those conclusions are true in the world of the semantic net, so can be added into the net. Please refer to the Sherlock Holmes mystery of the previous chapter, and its semantic net, Figure 2.1 on p. 24.

Exercise 3.1   While he was pondering his murder case, Holmes suddenly realized that if one person hates a second then they must know the second one too. What new links can now be added to Figure 2.1?

When Holmes added links in this way, by deducing the new statements from facts already in the net, he did so by making use of a *rule* which struck him as right, that what you hate you know. (Maybe you do not think that rule is right, but Holmes did and Figure 2.1 is a map of Holmes's beliefs, not of reality.)

This is the way reasoning always works – we infer new statements (relationship vectors in a semantic net) from existing statements in the net using **rules**.

Holmes did some more thinking: he realized that everyone must know themselves too, so he drew in Knows loops on each of the five people nodes in Figure 2.1. Then, looking at his rather cluttered net, he realized two rather profound things about nets:

- His net contains only *specific* beliefs of his, and there seems to be no way they can contain the *rules* he believes.

The rules Holmes has considered so far are:

> If one person x hates another y, then x knows y.   (**Holmes 1**)
> If x is a person, then x knows x.   (**Holmes 2**)

- Given that Holmes does have rules permitting the deduction of new statements from existing ones, there seems to be no real reason to write all these consequences into the semantic net.

This idea, that you do not need to store in your memory everything you know, but instead you can derive or work out a lot of it when needed from a smaller knowledge base of premises, seems to be a fundamental principle about human memory. It is certainly a major consequence of the existence of reasoning processes. We need reasoning processes in the first place to deduce new information from available information, so we do not need to store those conclusions unless it is more convenient than to recompute them when needed. This leads us to the idea of **distributed storage of information**, and the beginning of an attempt to remove the two weaknesses Holmes noticed with semantic nets.

3.1.1 Distributed information

Once we start to reason with semantic nets, an important economy occurs: we can cut down heavily on the number of vectors shown in a semantic net, while still allowing that net to 'contain' all the information we need to encode in it. As long as we have suitable premises stored in the net, and have manipulation rules to deduce new statements, we have all that is needed to derive the new vectors when wanted. For example, because Holmes accepted the rule (Holmes 2) – a manipulation rule, as we shall see – he did not feel the need to write in a Knows loop on every person in Figure 2.1. He could add one on, using (Holmes 2) if it ever became important.

Here is a fuller example to illustrate this point. Figure 3.1 shows a semantic net containing certain data about some specific animals, and about kinds of animals. Look at the node for Hodge. The only links on HODGE are to tell us it is a cat and male. That information is specifically about Hodge. There is much more information we would like to have about Hodge, such as that its diet is meat and it has forward-pointing eyes. But that information is generic – true of all carnivores, or of all felines. So we store such information on the node, such as FELINE or CARNIVORE, to which it is appropriate.

Then, what we may wish to know about an individual animal in the net, such as Hodge, need not be recorded by a link on HODGE, if we have rules of reasoning that allow us to copy information attached to other nodes such as FELINE or CARNIVORE onto the HODGE node when we want it. Knowledge like this about some objects (such as Hodge) that is stored elsewhere on other objects (such as about felines) and becomes available through a process of reasoning, is called **distributed** or **implicit information**. In the semantic net in Figure 3.1, some links are labelled Ako, short for 'a kind of'. Ako links are used often in semantic net reasoning. The nodes they join represent **kinds** or **types** of objects, not individual objects. Ako links join a node representing a kind of thing, to another node representing a more general kind of thing. For example, in the vector:

CAT ___Ako___, FELINE

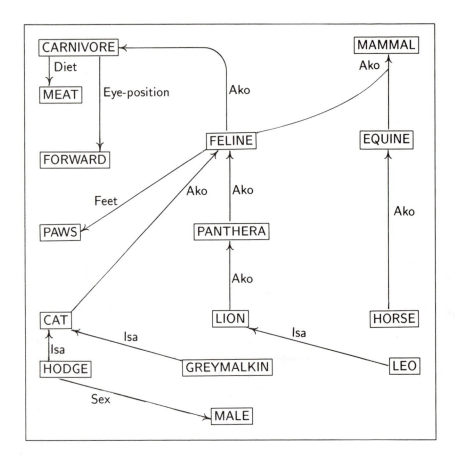

Figure 3.1   Distributed information about animals.

in Figure 3.1, we are saying that cats (which are a kind or type of thing) are a subkind or subtype of felines, which are another and more general kind of thing.

A kind or type is really rather an abstraction – it has all the properties which all objects *of* that kind have, and no others. For instance felines as a kind have fur, but no fur colour can be attributed to them – felines as a kind are not black, or ginger, or any other colour.

Readers familiar with set theory will see strong similarities between the Ako relation and the idea of subsets: the set of cats is a subset of the set of felines. Kinds or types can be treated set-theoretically as sets, and a statement x Ako y as $x \subseteq y$.

The Isa link is common too in semantic nets; being used to join an instance of a kind, to that kind. For instance, in the vector:

```
┌──────┐   Isa   ┌────┐
│HODGE │─────────▸│CAT │
└──────┘         └────┘
```

n Figure 3.1 we are saying that the *object* Hodge is an instance of the *kind*
·ats. This is like the idea of membership in set theory: x Isa y can be treated
n set theory as $x \in y$, where y is a set.

Note carefully the distinction between Isa and Ako links. When we say
: Ako y we are saying that every x-ish thing is also a y-ish thing (every cat is
 feline); that *things of* kind x are also of kind y. But when we say x Isa y, we
re saying that x itself is a y type of thing (Hodge is a cat); that *the thing* x
s of kind y. Confusing these two distinct concepts is a source of many logical
muddles, and occurs surprisingly often in the literature about semantic nets.

You will often find in semantic nets, chains of Ako links joining kinds
o more generic kinds, and these chains will have a cluster of Isa links at the
bottom, as we see in Figure 3.1. (A **chain** of links of a given type is just
 series of them joined head to tail, never head to head or tail to tail.) Isa
inks do not form chains. The usefulness of the Ako chains is that we can
·opy information that is stored at any node in an Ako chain, such as Diet or
Eye-position in Figure 3.1, backwards down a chain of Ako links, then down
n Isa link. In this way the net contains implicitly, in a distributed fashion,
he information that Hodge is a carnivore and that Hodge has paws. If Figure
3.1 represents what you know about animals, and if you have those reasoning
ules available to you, then you do not need to be told anything about Hodge,
·xcept that he is a cat, to infer that he is a carnivore. On the other hand, no
uch reasoning will reveal to you that he is male, for that is a fact specific to
iim.

Our task now is to find explicitly the rules for transferring this dis-
ributed information around a semantic net.

3.1.2   The transfer of distributed information

n the chemistry of genetics, RNA is a molecule whose job it is to transfer
information from the gene molecule, DNA, to another site where that infor-
nation is needed. It does that by impressing on itself the pattern of the DNA
molecule, like pressing putty onto a key, then it carries that pattern to its
lestination. The information is, of course, the program by which new cells
nd new organisms are built; the pattern in the DNA is the coding of that
information. In this way, the information needed to build a new cell is passed
rom the DNA to the cell-building mechanisms; robot tools that obey the
·rogram they are given.

This is an illuminating description of the way that reasoning goes on, as
ust described in the previous subsection. A world of statements – the relation-
hip vectors in a box – like the DNA, is the basic information we wish to use
n our reasoning. What we need are some 'transfer statements', like the RNA,
hat somehow pick up the pattern of that information and produce a result –

the conclusion we want from our reasoning. Those statement molecules will be the ones that literally carry the reasoning; maybe geneticists should call RNA the 'reasoning molecule'.

There is a transfer molecule in logic; it is known as an **if statement** or **conditional statement** or **implication statement**. How could we use such a transfer molecule in the world of Figure 3.1? From the information given in that world, we should obviously be able to infer the new information that Hodge's feet are paws. So we would like transfer molecules that would make a copy of this vector:

$$\boxed{\text{FELINE}}\underline{\quad\text{Feet}\quad}_{\rightarrow}\boxed{\text{PAWS}}$$

but on $\boxed{\text{HODGE}}$ instead of on $\boxed{\text{FELINE}}$. Then the copying will yield a new Feet link, with its head at the $\boxed{\text{PAWS}}$ node but with its tail at the $\boxed{\text{HODGE}}$ node:

$$\boxed{\text{HODGE}}\underline{\quad\text{Feet}\quad}_{\rightarrow}\boxed{\text{PAWS}}$$

We can design those transfer molecules easily. We begin by specifying precisely what we want them to do – writing their program, if you like:

> If a **Feet** link has its tail at the head of an **Ako** vector,
> and its head at some particular node n;
> then draw a new **Feet** link from the foot of the **Ako** vector
> to the node n. $\qquad$ (1)

The program for the next transfer molecule is similar except for the **Ako** link:

> If a **Feet** link has its tail at the head of an **Isa** vector,
> and its head at some particular node n;
> then draw a new **Feet** link from the foot of the **Isa** vector
> to the node n. $\qquad$ (2)

Exercise 3.2 Imagine two rules just like (1) and (2) above except that they refer to the **Eye-position** link, not the **Feet** link in Figure 3.1. Do these rules allow us to conclude that horses have forward-pointing eyes? Explain.

Exercise 3.3 In Figure 3.1, how many new links could we add altogether using rule (1)? How many could we add using just rule (2)? And how many could we add using rule (2) if we had exhaustively applied rule (1) first?

To encode rules (1) and (2) in semantic nets we will use *conditional statements*. So we will first spend a bit of time looking at the nature of this kind of statement.

3.2   Conditional statements

Conditional statements are ones that say that some statement *follows from* another statement or statements. We usually use 'if' or 'given' in English to express this idea. Here are some examples:

Calpurnia is Empress
if Caesar is Emperor and she is married to him.   **(3)**

If Caesar tries to become a dictator,
then Cassius will conspire with Brutus.   **(4)**

The car will move, given that the engine is running,
the gears are engaged and the brakes are off.   **(5)**

The use of conditional statements, like these, is to show what statement can be asserted if other ones are accepted. (Readers familiar with metatheory of logic may wonder if the conditional operator used here is object-linguistic like '⊃' or meta-linguistic like '⊢'. It is an object-linguistic operator. Putting a conditional statement into a semantic net is equivalent to asserting it, that is, prefixing the conditional statement with '⊢'.) In terms of semantic nets, they show what relationship vectors can be added to a net when other vectors are present in that net. In the example of the sentence (3) above, if a net contains the vectors:

$$\boxed{\text{CAESER}}\underline{\quad\text{Title}\quad}_{\rightarrow}\boxed{\text{EMPEROR}}\text{ and}$$
$$\boxed{\text{CALPURNIA}}\underline{\quad\text{Married-to}\quad}_{\rightarrow}\boxed{\text{CAESAR}}$$

then (1) says that we can add to that net:

$$\boxed{\text{CALPURNIA}}\underline{\quad\text{Title}\quad}_{\rightarrow}\boxed{\text{EMPRESS}}$$

Conditional statements are molecular and are built up from two groups of simpler statements, the **antecedent** group and the **consequent**.

The antecedents are associated with the 'if' or 'given' in the above examples – they are the statements which, on being true in a world (on being represented in a semantic net) allow us to conclude that the other statement, the consequent, is true in that world too (to add it to the net).

You can always think of an implication statement on the pattern of *if p then q* or equally *q if p*, where *p* is the antecedent and *q* is the consequent. Where there are several antecedents, use p_1 *and* $p_2 \ldots$ *and* p_n instead of *p*.

For technical reasons which will become clear later in the book, we will for now make this restriction on conditional statements:

- A conditional may have more than one antecedent, but only one consequent.

Exercise 3.4   Find the antecedents, and the consequent, in the sentences (4) and (5) above. Then represent them as vectors.

So that the conditionals can be represented in semantic nets, we will insist on this second restriction:

- The component statements of a conditional must be two-place atomic ones (or be capable of being forced into that mould).

Exercise 3.5   Which of the following are conditionals meeting both the bulleted restrictions? Explain why those that do not were disqualified. For those that do, write down the relationship vectors that represent their component statements.

(a)   Calpurnia believes that Caesar will die, since she had a dream about it.

(b)   If Caesar killed Pompey, then Caesar is evil and ambitious.

(c)   If the soothsayer and Calpurnia both warned Caesar, then he is in peril.

(d)   Caesar is in peril, and if he goes to the Capitol he will die.

3.3   Drawing conditionals in nets

Now, how do we draw these restricted conditionals into a semantic net? Well, we do not actually draw them *in* a semantic net, but in an **auxiliary net**, one per conditional. These look rather like ordinary semantic nets. We represent a conditional in its auxiliary net by using relationship vectors for its component two-place atoms, but with the antecedent ones drawn dotted. Figure 3.2 illustrates this.

Regard an auxiliary net as containing a pattern for adding vectors to the ordinary semantic net to which it is an auxiliary. We can define it as a manipulation rule thus:

Definition   Transfer rule

If all the dotted vectors of an auxiliary net occur (as solid) in the main net, then the solid vector in the auxiliary net may be added to the main net.

(Def. Xfer-Rule)

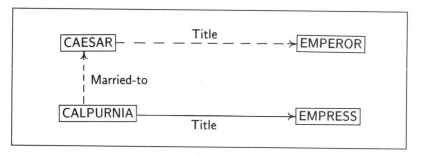

Figure 3.2   Auxiliary semantic net for the conditional (3): Calpurnia is Empress if Caesar is Emperor and she is married to him.

EXAMPLE 3.1

Given the auxiliary net in Figure 3.2 and this net:

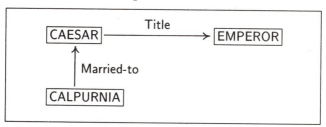

we can deduce that Calpurnia is an Empress. For both the dotted vectors of Figure 3.2 occur (solid, of course) in this main net, so by Xfer-Rule we may transfer the solid vector of Figure 3.2 to the main net, giving:

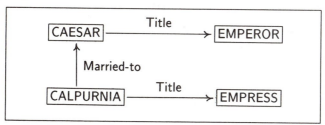

And this vector says that Calpurnia is an Empress.

You might like to think of auxiliary nets as drawn on transparent acetate sheets to be used as overlays on the main net. The acetate is very elastic, and you can distort it, rotate it and turn it over until the dotted vectors are exactly superimposed on the identical undotted vectors in the main net. (That is why they are dotted, so that you can see the solid version lined up beneath.) When that is achieved, the auxiliary net's solid consequent vector prints itself onto the main net beneath.

It should now be apparent that conditionals act as transfer molecules, along the lines we were sketching in Section 3.1.2. Look again at our attempt to conclude that Hodge's feet are paws.

EXAMPLE 3.2

Using the world of Figure 3.1, how can we deduce that Hodge's feet are paws?

We need the conditionals:

If the feet of felines are paws and cats are a kind of feline, then the feet of cats are paws.   **(6)**

If the feet of cats are paws and Hodge is a cat, then Hodge's feet are paws.   **(7)**

The auxiliary net for (6) is:

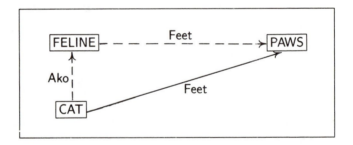

The dotted antecedents match vectors in the net of Figure 3.1, so its consequent, CAT Feet PAWS is added to the net in Figure 3.1. That is to say, we draw in a **Feet** link from CAT to PAWS .

The auxiliary net for (7) is:

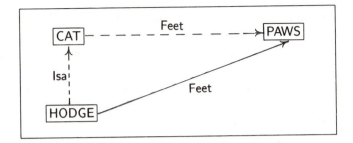

The antecedents in this auxiliary net both match vectors in the main net, thanks to the new vector we just put there. So now the conclusion vector, $\boxed{\text{HODGE}}\underline{\quad\text{Feet}\quad}_\rightarrow\boxed{\text{PAWS}}$, can be added to the main net.

Exercise 3.6 Devise conditionals that will allow us to infer that Greymalkin is a carnivore, draw up their auxiliary nets, and carry out the deduction.

3.3.1   Conclusion

Conditionals are the means of shifting distributed information around a semantic net. But it does seem, from the examples we have studied, that they are rigidly restricted in their use. We needed two conditionals, one per link, to span two links in Figure 3.1 and conclude that Hodge's feet are paws. To infer that Leo's feet are paws we need four conditionals, for the four links, and none of them are the same as the ones needed for Hodge.

In the next chapter, we will see how to generalize these conditionals so that they become very much more powerful and flexible information shifters, and even information changers. In fact, we will find two conditionals which suffice to prove that Hodge has paws, that Leo does, and any other conclusion based on shifting links down an Ako chain. With that, we will have marked out the essence of reasoning.

SUMMARY

- **Distributed information.** Information true of an object, which is stored not on the node for that object (or whatever represents it in a knowledge base) but elsewhere, and is made available for that object through a process of reasoning using the knowledge base.

- **Chain of links.** A series of links of the same type, joining nodes into a sequence, and the links having the same sense in the sequence, that is, joined head to tail.

- **Ako link.** A Kind Of. The relation that one kind of object bears to another more general kind that includes it.

- **Isa link.** Is A. The relation that an object bears to a kind of which it is an instance.

- **Conditional statement.** A statement that asserts that a particular statement (called the **consequent**) is true if other statements (the **antecedents**) are true. An English form is:

    If p_1 and $\cdots$ and p_n, then q.

    where the p_i are the antecedents and q is the consequent.

- **Auxiliary semantic net.** A semantic net used to represent a single conditional statement, which is done by drawing as dotted the links for all the antecedent vectors, and as solid the link to the conclusion.

- **Definition Transfer rule.** If all the dotted vectors of an auxiliary net occur (as solid) in the main net, then the solid vector in the auxiliary net may be added to the main net.

    (Def. Xfer-Rule)

Chapter 4
Universal conditionals

This chapter looks at a more powerful type of conditional statement, the *universal conditional*, that permits reasoning to occur in
a much more generalized way than the conditionals of the previous
chapter.

To understand universal conditionals, we first need to look
at the concept of a *variable*, a new type of term that can stand
in for any name at all. For instance 'If x killed Caesar then x is
a murderer' is a universal conditional containing the variable 'x',
and instances of it are 'If Brutus killed Caesar then Brutus is a
murderer' and 'If Cassius killed Caesar then Cassius is a murderer'.
It is this type of generality which we get by putting variables into
conditionals that gives us increased deductive power in semantic
net reasoning.

In this chapter we will:

- Look at the concept of a variable,
- Make vectors with variables in them.
- See how to treat vectors with variables as *patterns*,
- Use a concept of *matching patterns* to reason with variable
  vectors.

4.1 Variables

The machinery of conditionals developed in the previous chapter did not let us infer in Figure 3.1 that Greymalkin has paws. To do that, we would have had to add a conditional just like (7) of that chapter, except it is about Greymalkin, not Hodge. Such a duplication is hopeless, when you think of all the cats there are. What we really want is a conditional like (7), but which applies to *any* cat.

To overcome the problem, we adopt the RNA idea of making our transfer molecules take on the structure of the molecule to be matched, like putty. The conditionals in Chapter 3 could not do that – they were completely 'rigid'

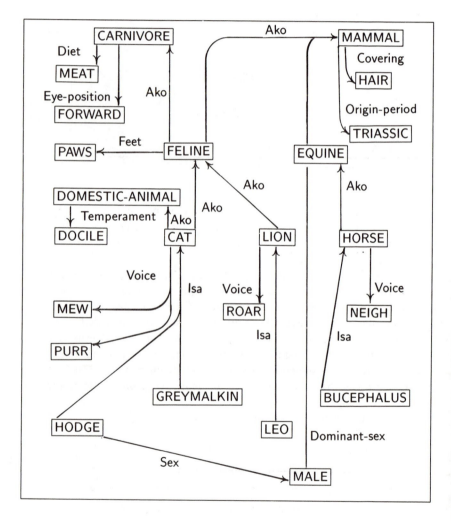

Figure 4.1 A more detailed animals net.

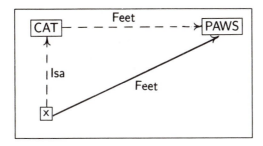

Figure 4.2   Auxiliary net for the universal conditional (1).

and the only thing an antecedent vector could match in the main net was an exact copy of itself. To see how to build in this idea of structural adaptation, we will develop the semantic net about animals a bit further. Figure 4.1 is the same as Figure 3.1 but with some further vectors added. We will replace the rigid (7) of Chapter 3 with a similar but more flexible conditional, which, as we shall see, will work both for Greymalkin and for Hodge. It is:

> If the feet of cats are paws and x is a cat,
> then x's feet are paws. **(1)**

The x here is called a **variable**, which acts rather like the RNA 'putty' which picks up the impression of the DNA structure. It is a new type of term, and should be distinguished from the type of term we have dealt with so far, such as PAWS, which we will now call a **constant.** We will mark the distinction syntactically by writing variables using lower-case letters, whereas constants are written in capitals. We will explain the semantics of variables soon.

The whole statement (1) is a conditional, so we represent it in an auxiliary net (see Figure 4.2). In it, we call nodes that contain variables **variable nodes** as opposed to **constant nodes** containing constants like PAWS. Similarly we have **variable relationship vectors** containing a variable node. They represent **variable statements**, so (1) and Figure 4.2 both represent a variable molecular statement.

Note that a given variable such as x will occur only once in its auxiliary net; though when we write a variable statement out in English, as in (1), it may have to occur more than once. The same is true of any term, of course, not just variables.

4.1.1   Manipulating variable vectors

The proper way to think of a variable vector, such as:

$$\boxed{x}\underline{\quad\text{Isa}\quad}_{\!\!,}\boxed{\text{CAT}}$$

in Figure 4.2, is as a **pattern** or **template** which can be superimposed on any vector in the main net that is labelled in the same way (except for the variable). So this variable vector may be matched onto any vector whose head is $\boxed{\text{CAT}}$ and whose link is Isa. What about the x? It is the putty. It should be read as the name in the box on which it is superimposed. So if we make that vector match the vector:

$$\boxed{\text{HODGE}}\underline{\quad\text{Isa}\quad}_{\!\!,}\boxed{\text{CAT}}$$

in Figure 4.1, we must read x as 'HODGE'. In that case the consequent vector in Figure 4.2 is to be understood as:

$$\boxed{\text{HODGE}}\underline{\quad\text{Feet}\quad}_{\!\!,}\boxed{\text{PAWS}}$$

which we may now insert into the world of Figure 4.1. Logicians say that the variable x in Figure 4.2 got **bound to** HODGE, and that HODGE is the **value** or **binding** of x. And, statements that are matched by a variable statement are called **instances** of it.

The proof theory of variables, then, is entirely a matter of pattern matching and binding. We can state these matters more formally and precisely thus:

Definition   Pattern matching

A vector V **matches** a vector W only if:

(a)   The links are labelled the same, and

(b)   If a node on V is labelled with a constant, the corresponding node on W is labelled with the same constant, and

(c)   If both nodes on V are labelled with the same variable, then both nodes on W must be labelled with the same term.

(Def. Match)

Note that this definition applies equally to the case where the pattern vector V is a constant vector. This definition will then cover the matching of constant conditionals as described in the previous chapter.

Binding is defined in terms of successful matching:

Definition   Variable binding

If a variable vector V matches a vector W, then for any variable v in V, the label of the node corresponding to it in W is the binding of v.

(Def. Binding)

Taking these two definitions together, it is plain that a variable in a vector has just one binding for any given match – even if that variable occurs twice in the vector. For example:

$$\boxed{x}\underline{\quad\text{Hates}\quad}_{\textstyle\rightarrow}\boxed{x}$$

cannot match:

$$\boxed{\text{BRUTUS}}\underline{\quad\text{Hates}\quad}_{\textstyle\rightarrow}\boxed{\text{CAESAR}}$$

or:

$$\boxed{x}\underline{\quad\text{Hates}\quad}_{\textstyle\rightarrow}\boxed{y}$$

Exercise 4.1   In Figure 4.1, what are the instances of:

$$\boxed{x}\underline{\quad\text{Voice}\quad}_{\textstyle\rightarrow}\boxed{y}$$

And, in each case, what are the bindings of x and y? (Use '$\mapsto$' to indicate the binding of a variable, for example, $x \mapsto$ CAT.)

4.1.2   Reasoning with variables

Using variables in place of constants in conditionals plainly gives us the power of economy: we can generalize an indefinitely large number of conditionals that have the same makeup except for their constants, by using just one conditional that has variables in place of those constants. (Any logical system that has this feature of using variables just for terms is called a **first-order logic**. A logical system that does not use variables at all, as in the previous chapter, is a **zero-order logic**.) The following problem illustrates the economy obtained for the purposes of reasoning.

EXAMPLE 4.1_____

Find two conditionals that allow you to infer, in Figure 4.1, that:

(1)   Hodge has paws,
(2)   Greymalkin has paws, and
(3)   all lions have paws.

They are:

(a)

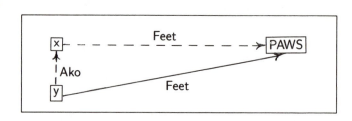

(b)

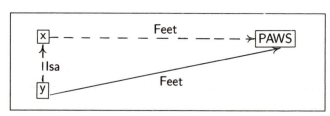

For case (1), we first match $\boxed{x}$___Feet___$\boxed{PAWS}$ and $\boxed{y}$___Ako___$\boxed{x}$ from (a) to the main net, with $x \mapsto$ FELINE and $y \mapsto$ CAT. We may then add the consequent of (a) with that binding for y, that is, $\boxed{CAT}$___Feet___$\boxed{PAWS}$ to the main net. With that added, we can match (b) to the main net, with $x \mapsto$ CAT and $y \mapsto$ HODGE. Now we can add the the consequent of (b), with that binding for y, that is, $\boxed{HODGE}$___Feet___$\boxed{PAWS}$ to the main net.

Cases (2) and (3) are left for the reader. For (3), only conditional (a) should be used.

The above problem illustrates three important features of the use of variables in conditionals for reasoning:

(1)   We must match *all* the antecedents of a conditional in such a way that each variable gets just *one* binding in a given match.

That is why we draw auxiliary nets so that each variable occurs only once: it makes it harder to give it two bindings by mistake. For example, in conditional (a) of the above problem, it would be wrong to match $\boxed{x}$___Feet___$\boxed{PAWS}$ to $\boxed{FELINE}$___Feet___$\boxed{PAWS}$ (with $x \mapsto$ FELINE), then match $\boxed{y}$___Ako___$\boxed{x}$ to $\boxed{LION}$___Ako___$\boxed{PANTHERA}$, for that would give a second binding to x, namely PANTHERA. Of course, when we match a given conditional a second time to a main net, the bindings can differ from the first match. This happens in the above problem in proving that lions have paws, in matching (a) successively to the two Ako links coming up from LION.

2)   The variable bindings set up in matching the antecedents determine how the consequent is added to the main net.

In the first match in (a) of the above problem, for instance, the binding given to y determined that the consequent was, for that particular matching, CAT⎵ Feet⟶ PAWS . This illustrates the third point also:

3)   In a successful pattern match, we are substituting the binding of a variable for the variable itself.

Put another way, the first match of (a) to the main net in the above problem transformed (a) to this instance of itself:

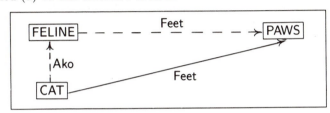

The added power of using variable conditionals is not, however, just the 'laziness factor' of economy in notation. For the advantage of the variable conditional of Figure 4.2 over constant ones such as (7) of Chapter 3 is that if we wish to add new cats to the net of Figure 4.1, then the information that they have paws is already available to us. A computer programmed with auxiliary nets containing variables, like Figure 4.2, needs no reprogramming when we add the names of new cats to its database; it can tell us straight away about those cats having paws.

The theoretically significant point here is that this is the way we, or any other reasoning machine, do think and must think. If we did not have generic information about cats stored in us, we would have to learn 'from the outside', all data about each new cat. If we were like that, we could not be said at all to 'understand what a cat is'.

The point applies significantly to computers too. A computer that merely stores data about things (company records, police files, etc.), is said to have a *database*. One that stores information using variable conditionals as well, and which can hence infer new information not explicitly stored, is said to have a *knowledge base*. Much of artificial intelligence is concerned with designing software to handle knowledge bases, for intelligence cannot exist without them.

Exercise 4.2 The Ako relation is transitive. State that in English using a variable conditional, then draw its auxiliary net. Using that net, prove in Figure 4.1 that lions are a kind of mammal.

4.1.3   Universal statements

To stress the generic nature of the information contained in variable conditionals (or any other variable statement, for that matter), they are also known
as **universal statements**.

Exercise 4.3   For each of the statements (a) and (b) below:

(i)   Write down, along the lines of (1), universal conditionals that will
        allow you to infer it from the world of Figure 4.1.
(ii)   Next, draw the semantic nets for those universal conditionals.
(iii)   Finally, explain how the required inferences are made.

The statements are:

(a)   All cats are docile.
(b)   Leo eats meat.

Universal statements contrast to those without variables, which are
called **ground** or **constant statements**. So the conditionals studied in the
last chapter were all **ground conditionals**. Not all instances of a universal
statement are ground statements, for one universal statement can certainly
match another. According to our definitions, for instance:

$\boxed{x}\underline{\quad Ako\quad}\_{\rightarrow}\boxed{y}$

will match all of these:

$\boxed{LION}\underline{\quad Ako\quad}\_{\rightarrow}\boxed{PANTHERA}$
$\boxed{y}\underline{\quad Ako\quad}\_{\rightarrow}\boxed{PANTHERA}$
$\boxed{LION}\underline{\quad Ako\quad}\_{\rightarrow}\boxed{y}$
$\boxed{y}\underline{\quad Ako\quad}\_{\rightarrow}\boxed{z}$
$\boxed{x}\underline{\quad Ako\quad}\_{\rightarrow}\boxed{y}$

In fact, we can generalize this idea of one vector (as pattern) matching another
(as instance). We can have two vectors, both as patterns, matching each other.
An example is:

$\boxed{A}\underline{\quad Rel\quad}\_{\rightarrow}\boxed{x}$
$\boxed{y}\underline{\quad Rel\quad}\_{\rightarrow}\boxed{B}$

where $x \mapsto B$ and $y \mapsto A$. The result is that both vectors have become, after
binding, $\boxed{A}\underline{\quad Rel\quad}\_{\rightarrow}\boxed{B}$. This process of matching two statements onto *each*

other to produce a single statement after binding, is called **unification**. It gives us the power to carry out far more powerful logical inferences than the methods of matching we have used so far. However, trying to use unification to manipulate vectors in auxiliary net pairs becomes rather clumsy, so we will leave those developments until we study the algebraic symbolism of clausal form logic in the next part of the book.

4.2 Collective properties

You have probably noticed something boringly repetitive about some of the universal conditionals we have been using for Figure 4.1. Many of them, for example, (1) and the one in answer to (i) in Exercise 4.3, are of the same pattern, which we might like to represent like this:

> If x has relation $\mathcal{R}$ to z, and y is a kind of x,
> then y has relation $\mathcal{R}$ to z. (2)

This is a cunning idea. We are now allowing ourselves to use variables that get bound to predicates, not just to terms. (Since predicates and terms are distinct types of linguistic object, we should use different types of variable to mark that – hence the use of '$\mathcal{R}$'.) A logic that has variables bindable to predicates is called **second-order**.

Certainly, this new conditional (2) will save us a lot of work. Together with the following:

> If x has relation $\mathcal{R}$ to z, and y is an x,
> then y has relation $\mathcal{R}$ to z (3)

it is all we need to carry out any of the inferences we have made on the net in Figure 4.1.

Exercise 4.4   Draw the auxiliary nets for (2) and (3), then show how they will allow us to infer in the net of Figure 4.1, that Bucephalus is covered in hair.

The trouble is that (2) and (3) are too powerful. Certain instances of them are quite false. Take this instance of (2), for example:

> If the origin period of mammals is Triassic
> and equines are a kind of mammal,
> then the origin period of equines is Triassic. (4)

In (4), both antecedents are true in the real world, but the consequent is false. Equines evolved only in the Eocene period, about a quarter as long ago. So (4) is not true in the real world.

Exercise 4.5   Draw up an auxiliary net for (4). What were the bindings of the variables in the auxiliary net for (2) (see the answer to the previous exercise) that yielded the auxiliary net for (4) as an instance?

Here is what has gone wrong. A property like *origin period of* is a property of a group of objects, it is not a property of the objects in that group. (It tells us when the group began, not when its members were born.) That sort of a property is called a **collective** one. On the other hand, a property like *type of covering* is not a property of a group as a unitary whole; it is a property of each object in the group. That is known as a **distributive** property. And the point is, that it is only distributive properties that we can let slide down an Ako or Isa link (be **inherited** by the node at the tail of the link). By definition, a collective property cannot obey the Isa rule (3), and it may or may not obey the Ako rule (2): it depends whether the collective property extends to subgroups or not. In Figure 4.1, Dominant-sex is a collective property (it fails to obey rule (3)), but unlike Origin-period it does obey rule (2). Rules (2) and (3) are called the **inheritance laws** for distributive properties $\mathcal{R}$.

Exercise 4.6   Find two other collective properties in Figure 4.1. Do they obey rule (2) or not?

SUMMARY

- **Variable.** Type of term. Typography: write using lower case letter(s). Proof theory: see **pattern matching** and **variable binding**, below.
- **Constant.** Type of term. Typography: write using capital letter(s). Semantics: refers to an object in a world (see Chapter 2). No constant is a variable.
- **Variable statement, vector, and node.** Variable statement. A statement, etc. containing a variable. Also called a **universal statement** etc. A statement, etc. that is not variable is a **constant statement** or **ground statement** etc.

- **Orders of logic.** A logic with no variables is a **zero-order logic**. One with variable terms is a **first-order logic**. One with variable predicates as well is a **second-order logic**.

- **Definition Pattern matching.** A vector V **matches** a vector W only if:

  (a)   The links are labelled the same, and

  (b)   If a node on V is labelled with a constant, the corresponding node on W is labelled with the same constant, and

  (c)   If both nodes on V are labelled with the same variable, then both nodes on W must be labelled with the same term.

  (Def. Match)

- **Instance.** The converse of matching. B is an instance of A if A matches B.

- **Definition Variable binding.** If a variable vector V matches a vector W, then for any variable v in V, the label of the node corresponding to it in W is the binding of v.

  (Def. Binding)

- **Matching variable conditionals.** When a conditional is matched to a main net, each antecedent in it must match a vector in the main net, and each variable in the antecedents must receive just one binding, no matter how many times it actually occurs in the antecedents. The consequent, with those bindings substituted for the variables in it, may then be added to the main net.

- **Distributive property of a group.** A property that is true of the members of a group. For example, 'The locusts are *hungry*.'

- **Collective property of a group.** A property that is true of the group itself, not its members. For example, 'The locusts are *deafening*.'

Chapter 5
Semantics

It is time now to turn from the proof theory of semantic nets to their semantics. We now treat semantic nets, for all their graphical appearance, as a meaningful language, and vectors as meaningful statements in that language.

For our purposes, questions about the meaning of a statement are treated as questions about its *truth-conditions*: that is, the conditions under which it will be true. Thus, this chapter concentrates on the notion of *truth*.

In this chapter we will:

- Explain the notion of a *world* more closely, and the allied notion of an *interpretation*.

- Define *truth in an interpretation* for ground vectors and conditionals.

- Define a concept of *satisfaction in an interpretation* that applies to variable statements.

- Use these notions of satisfaction and truth to demonstrate the soundness of our semantic net logic.

5.1   Worlds and interpretations

We have said that a semantic net represents a world – indeed it is easy (but very misleading) to think of it *as* a world. It is no more a world than a picture of a tiger, or a description of a tiger, is a tiger. What we will do now is:

(a)   Define what we mean by a world.

(b)   Define how a semantic net can represent a world – or fail to do so.

The aspects of reality that our semantic nets can describe are rather limited. The only ingredients of semantic nets are terms and two-place predicates. So the worlds that the nets can describe contain just objects and two-place relations between those objects. The objects could be anything at all: people, physical objects, numbers, ideas, sets, kinds of things..., and they need not be real, that is, in *our* world. Here are some examples of such worlds.

(W1)   World W1 consists of three people, Jay, Kit and Lee. Although there are many relationships between them and other people and things, we will build only two into the world we are considering: the relation of sending presents to someone, and the relation of liking someone. In this world, Jay has sent presents to Kit and Lee, Kit has sent a present to Lee, and that is all the presents that were sent. Everybody likes themselves and Kit, and that is all the likings that occur.

(W2)   In world W2, there are four numbers, 2, 4, 5, and 7, and just one relation, that of being less than.

These are very small worlds: we could consider worlds with any number of things in them at all, even an infinite number of things, such as the world of all integers, or of all real numbers. The smallest world we can consider has just one object in it. A world of no objects is not really something that can be described, so we do not consider it. The set of objects there are in a world is called the **domain of discourse** of that world.

5.1.1   Interpretations

Suppose we now take some semantic net, such as the one in Figure 5.1. We can relate that net quite easily to a world such as W1 or W2, or any other world we care to define. The rules for doing so are:

(1)   Let each constant in the net be the name of some object in the domain of discourse of the world. We usually say that the constant *denotes* the object.

(2)   Let each predicate in the net represent some relation that exists in the world. Again, we say that the predicate *denotes* the relation.

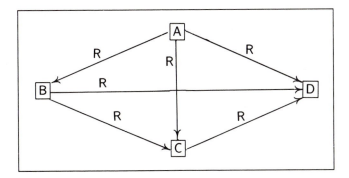

Figure 5.1   A simple semantic net. English words have not been used as node or
link labels, to reinforce that labels in a net have no meaning except that defined by
an interpretation.

When we have built a world according to (a) and (b), then related
the net to it as in (1) and (2), we call the result, world plus denotations, an
interpretation of the net.

EXAMPLE 5.1_____

How many interpretations are there of the net in Figure 5.1 in world
W1?

Each constant in the net can denote any of three objects in W1,
and there are four constants, giving $3 \times 4 = 12$ different denotation
patterns for the constants.

For each such denotation pattern for the constants, there are
two alternative denotations for the sole predicate R, either as giving
presents to or liking. Thus, there are $12 \times 2 = 24$ interpretations for
the net in world W1.

Note that there is no requirement that constants must denote *different*
objects in a world, nor that *all* the objects in a world must be denoted. The
same is true of predicates and the relations they denote.

5.1.2   Truth in an interpretation

Now that we have defined how semantic nets can be about a world, by defining
the notion of an interpretation, we would like to know whether the net *correctly*
or *truly* represents the world under the interpretation.

EXAMPLE 5.2

Consider just one of the 24 interpretations of Figure 5.1 in the world W1, where:

Label	Denotes
R	gives a present to
A	Jay
B	Kit
C	Lee
D	Jay

In this interpretation (call it $\mathcal{I}$), we say that the vector $\boxed{A} \underline{\quad R \quad}_{\rightarrow} \boxed{B}$ is *true*, since what A denotes (Jay) does indeed have the relation denoted by R (giving a present to) to what B denotes (Kit).

This example illustrates the idea of truth as a *correct picturing* by statements of a language, of the world they are about. In semantic net language, vectors are statements, so we talk of truth of vectors. How the vectors are *about* a world is fixed by the interpretation given to the constants and predicates in the net, which specifies how to link them to objects and relations in the world of the interpretation. (Since the interpretation fixes the denotation of a constant or predicate, the apparent English meaning of the constant or predicate is strictly irrelevant to its denotation in an interpretation. A predicate Loves could be made to denote *hates* in one interpretation, or *less than* in another. The reason for using English words is, of course, because we have a particular interpretation in mind, one in which, for example, Loves is to denote the relation of loving. Such a mnemonic use of English in terms and predicates is helpful in practical work with logic.) So truth is always defined relative to an *interpretation*, not just a *world*, as we did in the more simplified exposition of semantics in the earlier chapters.

How then, given an interpretation $\mathcal{I}$, can we define in terms of it the truth-conditions of all the statements that might occur in a semantic net and its auxiliary nets? The strategy is to define the truth-conditions for single ground vectors, then use that to help define the truth-conditions of a ground conditional – which is the only sort of molecule we have in the logic of semantic nets. Finally, we can use those definitions to help define the truth-conditions of universal conditionals.

5.1.3   Ground vectors

Definition   Truth-conditions of a ground vector

A ground vector $\boxed{a}\underset{\longrightarrow}{\quad R \quad}\boxed{b}$ is **true in** an interpretation $\mathcal{I}$ if the object denoted by a under $\mathcal{I}$ has the relation that R denotes under $\mathcal{I}$ to the object b denotes under $\mathcal{I}$. Otherwise it is **false in** $\mathcal{I}$.

(Def. Truth)

Exercise 5.1   Restricting your attention to the numbers world W2 and Figure 5.1:

- (a)   Find an interpretation, $\mathcal{I}$, for Figure 5.1 in W2 which makes every vector come out true in $\mathcal{I}$.
- (b)   Find another, $\mathcal{J}$, that makes them all come out false in $\mathcal{J}$.
- (c)   Find a third, $\mathcal{K}$, in which some but not all vectors are true in $\mathcal{K}$.

5.1.4   Ground conditionals

Now we need to extend the definition of truth in an interpretation beyond single ground vectors, since the conditional is another type of statement available in semantic nets, and as a statement it must have truth conditions.

The first step is to define the truth conditions of ground conditionals. The leading idea is, naturally, that for a true ground conditional, if all its antecedents are true then its consequent must be true too. We can express this more formally and precisely in this way:

Definition   Truth-conditions of a ground conditional

A ground conditional is *false in* an interpretation $\mathcal{I}$ if all its antecedents are true in $\mathcal{I}$ and its consequent is false in $\mathcal{I}$. Otherwise, the conditional is *true in* $\mathcal{I}$.

(Def. Truth)

The important thing to note about this definition is that it begins by noting the one case where we really insist that the conditional must be false – where true antecedents imply a falsehood. Then, since every statement must be true or false, we let all other cases work out true.

Exercise 5.2   Taking interpretation $\mathcal{I}$ for Figure 5.1 as given in the answer to (a) of the previous exercise, which of the following conditionals are true in $\mathcal{I}$, and which are false in $\mathcal{I}$?

(a)

(b)

(c)

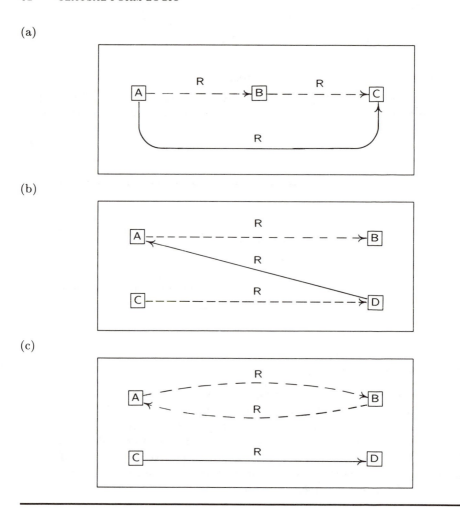

5.1.5   Soundness of the transfer rule

In Chapter 1, we noted that we use semantics to prove the *soundness* of a theory. For semantic nets, the proof theory consists of the two manipulation rules we have met: the transfer rule in Chapter 3, and the process of matching variable conditionals in Chapter 4. We can prove soundness for semantic net proof theory if we can show, for each of these manipulation rules, that if the vectors or conditionals they manipulate in a semantic net or its auxiliaries are all true in an interpretation $\mathcal{I}$, then so is the new vector they add to the main net. We can prove this now for the transfer rule.

Proposition 5.1   Soundness of transfer rule

If a ground conditional C in an auxiliary net is true in an interpretation $\mathcal{I}$, and if each antecedent of C occurs in the main net and is true in $\mathcal{I}$, then the consequent of C, which the transfer rule adds to the main net, is also true in $\mathcal{I}$.

Proof C is true in $\mathcal{I}$ and its antecedents are all true in $\mathcal{I}$. Hence, by Def. Truth for ground conditionals, its consequent is also true in $\mathcal{I}$.   □

5.2   Universal statements and satisfaction

The final type of statement for which we must define the semantics, is the universal statement. The only difference between this and types we have considered (atomic statements as vectors, and molecular statements as ground conditionals) is that the universal statements have variables in them. In a given interpretation $\mathcal{I}$, a variable in a vector can denote any object at all in the domain of discourse of $\mathcal{I}$. For example, take:

$$\boxed{x}\xrightarrow{\ R\ }\boxed{y} \tag{1}$$

and an interpretation $\mathcal{I}$ into the arithmetic world W2, where R denotes the less-than relation. x can denote any of the four objects in W2, and so can y. Any choice we make of objects for x and y to denote, is called a **valuation** for those variables, and what they denote is called their **value** under the valuation. Plainly, if the number of different variables occurring in the auxiliary nets of a semantic net is v, and the number of objects in the domain of discourse of the interpretation we have chosen for these nets is o, then there are vo different valuations for this set of variables in this interpretation.

In a given valuation of the variables in a vector, the variables effectively are behaving semantically just like constants, for their denotation is fixed; so we could now ask whether, in that valuation, the vector works out true in the interpretation. Suppose, in the example, we let x denote 4 and let y denote 7 in W2. Then since R denotes the less-than relation, and $4 < 7$, (1) is true in $\mathcal{I}$ *for that valuation*. In such a case we say that the valuation **satisfies** (1) in $\mathcal{I}$.

This definition can be extended to cover universal conditionals as well. We set this out in a formal definition, in which by 'statement' we mean either a vector or a conditional.

Definition Satisfaction of a universal statement

Let A be a statement, $\mathcal{I}$ an interpretation for the statement, and $\mathcal{V}$ a valuation in $\mathcal{I}$ of all the variables in A. Suppose that the variables in A are replaced by constants which denote in $\mathcal{I}$ the values of the variables they replace, and call this resulting statement A'. Then $\mathcal{V}$ **satisfies** A **in** $\mathcal{I}$ only if A' is true in $\mathcal{I}$.

(Def. Satisfaction)

Exercise 5.3 Referring to Figure 5.1 again, and to the interpretation $\mathcal{I}$ given in answer to part (a) of Exercise 5.1, find:

(a) a valuation that satisfies:

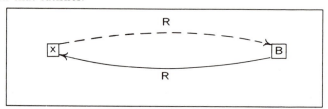

(b) a valuation that does not satisfy:

EXAMPLE 5.3

With $\mathcal{I}$ as in the exercise above, are there any valuations that do not satisfy:

A valuation that did not satisfy this conditional would, by the definition of truth-conditions for conditionals, make the antecedents both true, and the consequent false, under that valuation. Any valuation making the antecedents both true under it will have x denoting a number less than the number y denotes, which in turn will denote a number less than the one z denotes, for example, 2, 5 and 7 respectively. But in such a case x denotes a number less than the one that z does, so the consequent is true, not false, under such a valuation. That is, there is no valuation of the sort asked for.

In a case like this, where all valuations satisfy the conditional, we say it is **true** in the interpretation. This gives us the last part of our definition of truth:

Definition   Truth-conditions of universal conditionals

A universal conditional C is **true in** an interpretation $\mathcal{I}$ only if every valuation of the variables in C satisfies C in $\mathcal{I}$. Otherwise it is **false in** $\mathcal{I}$.

(Def. Truth)

Note that we have not defined the truth-conditions for universal vectors, only conditionals. This is because in our semantic net logic, we cannot assert them, so questions of their truth-value do not arise.

Exercise 5.4   Referring back to Exercise 5.3(b), is that conditional false in $\mathcal{I}$?

Now that we know the semantics for universal conditionals, it is not hard to see why the pattern-matching process of reasoning by matching variable conditionals – the process of matching antecedents of a conditional to vectors in a semantic net, binding the variables to constants in the process, then depositing the resulting consequent into the net – is sound (see Summary of Chapter 4). To show this, we first prove:

Proposition 5.2   Instantiation

If a universal conditional C is true in an interpretation $\mathcal{I}$, then every ground instance of that universal conditional is true in $\mathcal{I}$.

Proof   Consider any ground instance C' of C. The only difference between C and C' is that the variables in C are replaced by constants in C'. Those constants have denotations in the domain of discourse of $\mathcal{I}$. Consider now the valuation for the variables in C, in which its variables denote the objects in $\mathcal{I}$ that are denoted by their replacements in C'. Since C is true in $\mathcal{I}$, C is satisfied by that valuation, so by the definition of satisfaction of a universal statement, C' must be true in $\mathcal{I}$.   □

So now we know that all ground instances of a true universal conditional are true. We saw in the last chapter that a successful pattern match of a universal conditional into a semantic net amounted to transforming that conditional into an instance of itself – indeed a ground instance (unless the consequent contains variables not in the antecedent. We could generalize the present argument to cover that case, but we have not so far had anything to do with conditionals like that, so we will ignore them now.) This fact allows us to complete our soundness proof. (Soundness of a reasoning process, remember, amounts to saying that the process *preserves truth* – if the input statements are true, so is the output statement. For the process of matching variable conditionals, the output statement is the ground instance of the consequent of the conditional, which we add to the main net.)

Proposition 5.3   Soundness of reasoning by matching variable conditionals

If a conditional C is true in an interpretation $\mathcal{I}$, and there is a binding of the variables in C which makes the antecedents of C match vectors in the net, and all the matched vectors are true in $\mathcal{I}$, then the ground instance of the consequent of C which is obtained by replacing its variables by their bindings, is true in $\mathcal{I}$.

Proof The binding of the variables in C yields a new conditional C' just like C except that its variables are replaced by their bindings. By the previous proposition, C' is true in $\mathcal{I}$ since C is. Each antecedent vector in C' is true in $\mathcal{I}$, since it is one of the matched vectors in the net. So by the definition of truth-conditions for ground conditionals, the consequent of C' is true in $\mathcal{I}$ too.   □

Exercise 5.5   Find an interpretation $\mathcal{I}$ whose domain of discourse is the natural numbers (that is, $\{0, 1, \ldots\}$), and in which the statements made in both these nets are all true:

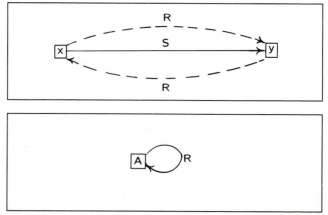

Show, using the method of reasoning using variable conditionals, how to infer ⬚A⬚ S → ⬚A⬚ in those nets. What does it mean in your interpretation? Show that it is true in $\mathcal{I}$.

5.3   The semantics of Ako and Isa

One small problem remains to be dealt with. If a predicate can be given any denotation at all, then the special meanings of Isa and Ako, upon which the performance of semantic nets hangs so heavily, need to be guaranteed to hold in every interpretation. How can we do that?

We can do it by including with every semantic net system we develop (that is, a main semantic net and its auxiliary nets), some auxiliary nets which assert the properties of Isa and Ako which we need. Then, any interpretation which makes all the auxiliary nets true in it, will give Ako and Isa the semantic properties we need.

The properties we need to assert are the inheritance properties of Ako and Isa (see Chapter 4):

If x has relation $\mathcal{R}$ to z, and y is a kind of x,
then y has relation $\mathcal{R}$ to z

and:

If x has relation $\mathcal{R}$ to z, and y is an x,
then y has relation $\mathcal{R}$ to z

where $\mathcal{R}$ is any predicate which is to be interpreted as a distributive property.

This does mean that we have to include in a semantic net system two such auxiliary nets for every single distributive predicate used in the system. For informal purposes, of course, we would not bother to draw all those nets: we would just understand, as a convention, that Ako and Isa must always behave that way.

SUMMARY

- **Interpretation.** An interpretation $\mathcal{I}$ of a semantic net and its auxiliary nets consists of a *world* $\mathcal{W}$ and a specification of the *denotations* in $\mathcal{W}$ of all the constants and predicates in the nets.

- **World.** A world consists of a non-empty set of objects, and one or more two-place relations defined over those objects.

- **Domain of discourse.** The domain of discourse of an interpretation $\mathcal{I}$ is the set of objects in the world of $\mathcal{I}$.

- **Denotation.** In any interpretation $\mathcal{I}$ of a semantic net and its auxiliary nets in a world $\mathcal{W}$, each constant in the nets is assigned an object in $\mathcal{W}$ as its denotation, and each predicate in the nets is assigned a relation in $\mathcal{W}$ as its denotation.

- **Definition Truth-conditions of a ground vector.** A ground vector

$\boxed{a}\!\underline{\quad R\quad}_{\!\!,}\boxed{b}$ is **true in** an interpretation $\mathcal{I}$ if the object denoted by a under $\mathcal{I}$ has the relation that R denotes under $\mathcal{I}$ to the object b denotes under $\mathcal{I}$. Otherwise it is **false in** $\mathcal{I}$.

(Def. Truth)

- **Definition Truth-conditions of a ground conditional.** A ground conditional is *false in* an interpretation $\mathcal{I}$ if all its antecedents are true in $\mathcal{I}$ and its consequent is false in $\mathcal{I}$. Otherwise, the conditional is *true in* $\mathcal{I}$.

(Def. Truth)

- **Valuation for variables.** In any interpretation $\mathcal{I}$ of a semantic net and its auxiliaries, a valuation of the variables occurring in the auxiliary nets is an assignment to each variable of an object in the domain of discourse of $\mathcal{I}$. The object so assigned to a variable is its **value** under the valuation.

- **Definition Satisfaction of a universal statement.** Let A be a statement, $\mathcal{I}$ an interpretation for the statement, and $\mathcal{V}$ a valuation in $\mathcal{I}$ of all the variables in A. Suppose that the variables in A are replaced by constants which denote in $\mathcal{I}$ the values of the variables they replace, and call this resulting statement A'. Then $\mathcal{V}$ **satisfies** A **in** $\mathcal{I}$ only if A' is true in $\mathcal{I}$.

(Def. Satisfaction)

- **Definition Truth-conditions of universal conditionals.** A universal conditional C is **true in** an interpretation $\mathcal{I}$ only if every valuation of the variables in C satisfies C in $\mathcal{I}$. Otherwise it is **false in** $\mathcal{I}$.

(Def. Truth)

- **Soundness of transfer rule.** If a ground conditional C in an auxiliary net is true in an interpretation $\mathcal{I}$, and if each antecedent of C occurs in the main net and is true in $\mathcal{I}$, then the consequent of C, which the Transfer Rule adds to the main net, is also true in $\mathcal{I}$.

- **Instantiation.** If a statement S is true in interpretation $\mathcal{I}$, then every ground instance of that statement is true in $\mathcal{I}$.

- **Soundness of reasoning by matching variable conditionals.** If a conditional C is true in an interpretation $\mathcal{I}$, and there is a binding of the variables in C which makes the antecedents of C match vectors in the net, and all the matched vectors are true in $\mathcal{I}$, then the ground instance of the consequent of C which is obtained by replacing its variables by their bindings, is true in $\mathcal{I}$.

Chapter 6
Denial and negation

So far we have studied only *positive* statements, those that assert that something is the case, for example, 'Caesar is dead'. We will now study *negative* statements, those that deny that something is the case, for example, 'Caesar is not dead'. Positive statements were represented in semantic nets by vectors; negative statements require a more complex representation.

In this chapter we shall:

- Show how negative statements can be represented by a special type of conditional.

- Represent these in semantic nets.

- Study the semantics of negative ground and universal statements.

- Learn a reasoning technique, *refutation*, for proving statements to be false.

6.1   Expressing falsehoods

Ground statements, as we have seen, are either true or false in an interpretation, and never both. When we draw a main semantic net to represent some world that we have in mind, we put in it only vectors representing statements which are true in that world. The vectors in a net are, in a word, **assertions**. Correspondingly, the conditionals in auxiliary nets are assertions, though the vectors in those conditionals are not.

But often we want to state what is false in a world. Take an example, the big semantic net in Figure 4.1 in Chapter 4 (see p. 46). Cats are not equines, but there is nothing in Figure 4.1 which says they are not. True, Figure 4.1 does not say they *are* equines. It is neutral on the subject. So the problem is, how could we add something to Figure 4.1 which denies that cats are equines?

6.2   Negation

The problem can be put this way. How, in the logic of semantic nets, can we represent the negation of an atomic statement. The **negation** of a statement S is the statement which expresses the falsity of S. In English, for example, the negation of 'Caesar is dead' is 'Caesar is not dead'. In semantic nets, the problem is to find a way of representing the 'not'. As a first try, we might simply cross out a link to negate a vector; but it is hard to devise manipulation rules for that device, to carry out the process of *reasoning* with negation. And there is a better way.

6.2.1   Semantics of negation

To deny some ground vector S, the trick is to use a conditional saying that if S is true, then a false consequent follows. (Compare 'If the moon is made of green cheese, then I shall eat my hat', – a good way of denying that the moon is made of green cheese.) The problem is, what falsehood shall we use as a consequent? What we really want is a **logical falsehood** – one that is false in *all* interpretations. Otherwise, in some interpretations, the denial will not be a denial at all.

Could we, for example, use $1 = 0$ for this logical falsehood? One certainly cannot imagine a world in which this is true. We could then deny that cats are a kind of equine by saying:

If cats are a kind of equine then $1 = 0$.

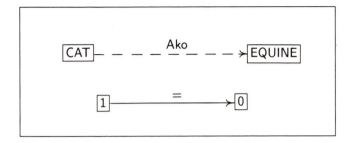

Figure 6.1 Attempt to deny that cats are a kind of equine.

The auxiliary net for this is shown in Figure 6.1.

Unfortunately this will not do. For while there is no way that the number 1 could equal the number 0, it is easy to find interpretations in which the *vector* $\boxed{1}\underline{\quad=\quad}\boxed{0}$ is true. We could let the constant 1 denote the planet Earth, let the constant 0 denote the planet Mars, and let the predicate = denote the relation of being bigger than. Then the vector $\boxed{1}\underline{\quad=\quad}\boxed{0}$ says that Earth is bigger than Mars, which is true, not false. And in this way, no matter what vector you choose, an interpretation can always be found that makes it true. There are *no* logically false vectors, or logically true ones either.

The way out is to invent a special statement, which we will call **falsum**, and will write like this: ⊗. It is not a vector: it has no nodes or link. But it is, like vectors, a statement, that is, every interpretation gives it a truth-value; only we will stipulate that falsum is *false* in every interpretation. Then we can properly deny that cats are a kind of equine by saying:

If cats are a kind of equine, then ⊗

This we can represent in an auxiliary net as in Figure 6.2.

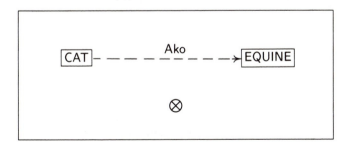

Figure 6.2 Auxiliary net denying that cats are a kind of equine. The symbol ⊗, which is logically false, is the consequent of the conditional.

How does this device of asserting 'if S then falsum' function as a denial of the ground vector S? Because that conditional must have the opposite truth-value to S itself, in any interpretation. This we can easily prove.

Proposition 6.1   Denials as conditionals

Let S be a ground vector. Then in any interpretation $\mathcal{I}$, the conditional with S as antecedent and falsum as consequent, has the opposite truth-value to S itself.

Proof   Suppose that the conditional is *true* in an interpretation $\mathcal{I}$. Then since its consequent is false in $\mathcal{I}$, its antecedent must, by Def. Truth for conditionals, be false in $\mathcal{I}$ too.

Conversely, suppose that the conditional is *false* in $\mathcal{I}$. Then since its consequent is false in $\mathcal{I}$, its antecedent S must be true in $\mathcal{I}$, by Def. Truth for ground conditionals.   □

Exercise 6.1   What is being denied in this conditional?

Exercise 6.2   The above proposition can be extended to cover satisfaction for universal statements S. Prove that for any valuation of the variables of S in an interpretation $\mathcal{I}$, the conditional whose antecedent is S and consequent is falsum, is satisfied only if S is not.

6.3   Refutation

So much for the semantics of negation and falsum. We will now look at how we reason with them in semantic nets. So far, our reasoning methods in semantic nets (the transfer rule and the matching of universal conditionals) are used to *prove* statements. Semantically, we know that this means that statements proved using these two rules are true in an interpretation $\mathcal{I}$, if the statements from which we proved them are true in $\mathcal{I}$ (the soundness of those rules). Now we will describe a reasoning method which is used to refute statements, not prove them. Semantically, a refuted statement is false in any interpretation

n which the statements used to refute it are true. (Avoid the recent jour-
nalistic habit of using *refute* to mean *deny*, as in 'The minister flatly refuted
the criticism', (when all he said was, 'It's nonsense.') To deny is to *claim*
something is false, to refute it is to *prove* it is false – and that distinction is
worth preserving, particularly in reporting politicians' pronouncements.)

EXAMPLE 6.1——————————————————————————

Given the semantic net of Figure 4.1 (see p. 46) and the denial in
Figure 6.2 (see p. 71), we can show that felines are not a kind of
equine in this way.

Step (1) Take the statement you wish to prove false, and add it to
the main net.
   In this example, we add to Figure 4.1 an Ako link from FELINE
to EQUINE, giving the new vector:

$$\boxed{\text{FELINE}}\underline{\quad\text{Ako}\quad}\boxed{\text{EQUINE}} \qquad\qquad (6)$$

This amounts to assuming *true* what we want to prove *false*, that
felines are a kind of equine.

Step (2) Use the manipulation rules for semantic nets (transfer rule
and matching variable conditionals) to add falsum to the main net.
If that succeeds, we have a **refutation** of the statement added in
Step (1).
   In this example, since Ako obeys the law of Ako inheritance
(see Exercise 4.6), we can use the auxiliary net:

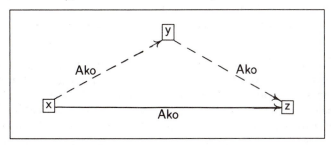

to add:

$$\boxed{\text{CAT}}\underline{\quad\text{Ako}\quad}\boxed{\text{EQUINE}}$$

to the main net as well. Once it is there, we use the auxiliary net in
Figure 6.2 to add $\otimes$ to the main net.

Steps (1) and (2) in the example define the **refutation technique**: to refute a statement, add it to the semantic net and thence prove falsum.

6.3.1   Semantics of refutation

To see what the refutation technique is doing, we state and prove this result:

Proposition 6.2   Soundness of refutation

Let S be the ground vector added to a semantic net in the refutation technique, and let the other statements in the net (including conditionals in auxiliary nets) used to deduce falsum, all be true in some interpretation $\mathcal{I}$. Then S is false in $\mathcal{I}$.

Proof   The deduction of falsum uses two procedures: the transfer rule and the matching of variable conditionals. By the soundness results for these procedures (see the previous chapter), if they are applied only to statements true in $\mathcal{I}$, then a statement deduced using them is also true in $\mathcal{I}$. But, we have used them to deduce falsum, which is not true in $\mathcal{I}$. So somewhere in the refutation, one of these procedures has been applied to a statement not true in $\mathcal{I}$. That can only be S, since all the other statements used were true in $\mathcal{I}$. □

Exercise 6.3   How would you state, using a universal conditional, that nothing can be male and female? Draw the auxiliary net for that statement, and use it to prove that Hodge in Figure 4.1 is not a female.

Conditionals whose consequent is falsum are called **negative statements**, for they are our means of saying that something is *not* true. When the antecedents are ground vectors, then what such a conditional asserts to be untrue, is the *conjunction* of all the antecedents, *not* each of them individually, as the answer to the last exercise reveals, and as Exercise 6.1 discussed explicitly.

But where we have a universal antecedent, the situation is a bit more complicated. Consider 'If x is happy then falsum'. In a semantic net, this is:

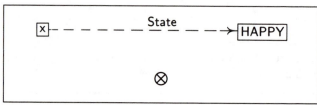

If $\boxed{\text{x}}\xrightarrow{\quad\text{State}\quad}\boxed{\text{HAPPY}}$ matches a vector in the main net, we can deposit falsum in the main net straight away. So the conditional must be denying that there is a single happy person. It says that nobody is happy. In that case it is denying that *somebody* is happy. In fact, what a negative universal statement says, is that its antecedent is not satisfied by any valuation. And if the conditional has more than one universal vector as antecedent, it asserts that no valuation satisfies *all* of them.

Exercise 6.4   Look again at the sociologist's knowledge base in Exercise 2.7 of Chapter 2 (see page 29). Consider this interpretation $\mathcal{I}$ for it, in which the domain of discourse is seven people, Alf, Bill, Charlie, Dean, Eve, Fiona, and Gail; each constant names the person with that initial; Likes denotes liking and Asks-out denotes asking out. To make things definite, we shall take it that the only Likes and Asks-out relationships between these people are the ones listed in the knowledge base.

Represent each of these conditionals in a semantic net. Which of these universal conditionals that you have drawn up are true in that interpretation, and which are false? Justify your answers.

(a)   If x likes y then x asks y out.
(b)   Gail likes everybody who likes Alf.
(c)   Nobody likes whom they ask out.
(d)   Nobody is liked by whom they ask out.
(e)   Everybody is liked by whom they ask out.

Exercise 6.5   Devise an auxiliary net that states that Ako is asymmetrical, and use it to prove, in the net in Figure 4.1, that an equine is not a kind of horse.

SUMMARY

- **Assertion of a statement.** A claim that the statement is true.

- **Denial of a statement.** A claim that the statement is false.

- **Negation of a statement.** The negation of a statement S is the statement that says S is false. To deny S, assert its negation.

- **Logically true (false) statement.** A statement that is true (false) in all interpretations. No vectors can be logically true or false.

- **Falsum.** An unstructured atomic statement, written $\otimes$, which by definition is logically false.

- **Negation as a conditional.** The negation of a vector S is the conditional with S as antecedent and falsum as consequent. It has the opposite truth-value and satisfaction-value to S.

- **Negative statement.** Any statement with falsum as its consequent. It negates the conjunction of its antecedents.

- **Refutation of a statement.** A disproof of the statement, that is, a method of proving its negation.

- **Refutation method in semantic nets.** To refute a vector S, add it to the main net and use the net manipulation rules to add $\otimes$ to the net.

Further reading for Part I

The rise of modern symbolic logic was pioneered by George Boole in England, in *The Laws of Thought,* 1854; Gottlob Frege in Germany in the *Begriffs-schrift,* 1879; and Charles Sanders Peirce in the USA. (c.1880). The pioneering work on machine reasoning was by A. Newell and H. A. Simon, 'The Logic Theory Machine', *IRE Transactions on Information Theory,* **2**, 61–79, 1956; followed by the more efficient system of H. Wang, 'Towards Mechanical Mathematics', *IBM Journal of Research and Development,* **4**, 2–22, 1960. These systems mechanized only the propositional calculus, a fragment of logic similar to Boolean Algebra and which lacks terms and predicates. The first satisfactory mechanization of the predicate calculus was by the philosopher J.A. Robinson, 'A Machine Oriented Logic Based on the Resolution Principle', *J. of the ACM,* **12**, 23–41, 1966. We will be looking much more closely at the Resolution approach pioneered by Robinson later in the book, as it is still the main method of mechanizing formal logic. Most of the classical papers in the mechanization of logic, up to 1970, are collected in J. Siekmann and G. Wrightson (eds) *Automation of Reasoning,* 2 vols. Berlin: Springer, 1983.

Semantic nets were developed originally as a means of representing knowledge and of modelling human memory, notably by M. R. Quillian, 'Semantic Memory' in M. Minsky (ed.) *Semantic Information Processing,* Cambridge, MA: MIT Press, 1968; and J. Anderson and G. Bower, *Human Associative Memory,* Washington, DC: Winston, 1973. G. Hendrix, 'Expanding the Utility of Semantic Networks through Partitioning', *Artificial Intelligence,* **7**, 21–49, 1976, developed a method of using semantic nets to carry out logical reasoning processes. His approach is rather different from ours. J. Sowa, *Conceptual Structures,* Reading, MA: Addison-Wesley, 1984, is a significant extension of the ideas of semantic nets, including their adaptation for reasoning processes. Sowa's work is based on the research of C.S. Peirce nearly a century earlier.

Introductory accounts of semantic nets are in A. Barr and E. Feigenbaum (eds) *The Handbook of Artificial Intelligence,* Vol.1, Los Altos, CA: Kaufmann, 1981; E. Rich, *Artificial Intelligence,* Singapore: McGraw-Hill, 1983; and P. Winston, *Artificial Intelligence,* 2nd edition, Reading, MA: Addison-Wesley, 1984. A recent collection of articles on semantic nets is N. Findler (ed.) *Associative Networks: the Representation and Use of Knowledge by Computers,* New York: Academic Press, 1979.

Part II
A LANGUAGE FOR REASONING

Chapter 7
From diagrams to symbols

In Part II, we make the shift from semantic nets to the symbolism of clausal form logic (CFL). Semantic nets had two uses:

- As a means of representing statements.
- As a means of performing deductive reasoning on the statements represented in the nets.

CFL is more powerful than semantic nets in both these uses; though, as this chapter shows, it is similar in many ways.

In this chapter we shall:

- Learn how to represent atomic statements in CFL.
- Look informally at the semantics of atoms in CFL.

7.1   Clausal form logic

Using diagrams is a very helpful way of coming to grips with an area of
thinking. But, in the end, it is limited to all the restrictions of the two-
dimensional medium of paper. In fact, to make semantic nets work at all well,
we have to use several sheets of paper (or acetate) and invent a pictorial fiction
of stretching them to fit the nets on each other. You may have realized at the
time that that was a white lie – you can easily draw a universal conditional
in an auxiliary net that matches data in the main net, yet no amount of
stretching or distorting, or even turning over, would make it superimpose on
the main net data. Figure 7.1 is an example.

There are other ways in which the constraints of diagrams inhibit our
study of logic. One is that we are limited to dyadic relations, but as we saw in
Chapter 2, there are also monadic predicates, such as 'dies', which we cannot
represent directly in semantic nets; and predicates of arity greater than 2,
such as 'between', which have not been given a semantic net representation
at all. (There is a useful way of reducing greater-than-two-place predicates
to two-place ones, which we will study later; but still, they have no *direct*
representation in semantic nets – as with one-place predicates, they must be
replaced by *other* predicates.) Also, the clumsiness of representing conditionals in auxiliary nets is compounded by the need to represent negation as a
conditional, requiring more auxiliary nets; even so, all we can negate is ground
vectors or conjunctions of them.

In fact, if we are to proceed much further with logic, we will need to
supplement semantic nets with a much more abstract way of representing
logical concepts. That will be a **symbolic system**, in effect a language in
which to talk logic. The language is known as **Clausal Form Logic** (CFL).
CFL may strike you as like learning maths, because it has precise rules for
manipulating it; or it may strike you as more like learning a foreign language,
since it is about words not numbers, and allows you to say the sorts of things
you say in English.

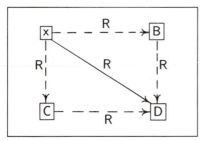
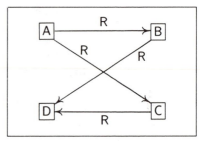

Figure 7.1   There is no way the auxiliary net on the left can be stretched, rotated
or flipped to match the main net on the right, yet plainly we should be able to infer
A   R   D .

7.2   Symbolic atoms and their parts

In Part I, we represented atomic statements using relationship vectors. The statement that *Caesar loves Calpurnia* was drawn as:

| CAESAR | Loves → | CALPURNIA |

Now, however, we will represent the statement in a style like that of **functional notation** in mathematics:

```
Loves(CAESAR, CALPURNIA)
```

This is an **atomic formula** or **atom**. The predicate in an atomic formula comes first, followed by the constants to which it applies, which we call its **arguments**, inside parentheses and separated by commas. (This idea of an **argument** is familiar in mathematics. In '$2 + 3 = 5$' the addition operator is applied to '2' and '3', so they are its arguments, while the equality predicate has '$2+3$' and '5' as its arguments. Do not confuse this meaning of 'argument' with its other meaning as 'reasoning'.) The above atomic formula is two-place, but unlike the case with semantic net representations, it is obvious that this notation will represent statements of any arity. Some examples are:

The Sun is yellow	`Yellow(SUN)`
3 is a prime number	`Prime(3)`
Caesar stumbled	`Stumbled(CAESAR)`
Brutus is the murderer	`Identical(BRUTUS, THE-MURDERER)`
Brutus is a murderer	`Murderer(BRUTUS)`
Antony carried Caesar from the Forum	`Carried(ANTONY, CAESAR, FORUM)`

Note that we are now using **typewriter font** for our logical language. This is to stress that CFL is a different logical system from semantic nets, where we used sans serif font. In this book, expressions of CFL will always be written in **typewriter font**; anything not in typewriter font is not an expression of CFL. So in the list above, the right-hand column contains examples of CFL, the left-hand column does not.

7.2.1   Typography of atoms

We will now lay down quite precisely the rules for writing expressions of CFL. We call these the **typographic rules**, since they specify the written appearance. Other authors, and various computer implementations of CFL such as the different PROLOG systems, will use other typographies. But the grammar underlying these typographies will be much the same – for instance there are atoms consisting of predicates with constants as arguments, however you write them.

Definition   Constant

A constant consists of either:

(a)   A capital letter, followed by zero or more capital letters, digits, o hyphens;

or:

(b)   A signed or unsigned integer, or decimal number.

(Def. Constant

We could specify fully the typography of the numerals in (b), but the poin' is clear enough for our purposes.

Definition   Predicate

A predicate consists of a capital letter, followed by zero or more lower-case letters, digits, or hyphens. Every predicate has a number $n \geq 1$ associated with it, called its **arity**, and the predicate is said to be **n-arity** or **n-ary**.

(Def. Predicate

The arity of a predicate specifies the number of arguments it must take in any atom in which it occurs.

Exercise 7.1   Which of the following are constants, which are predicates, and which are neither?

(a) dangerous	(f) 1000
(b) HELEN-OF-TROY	(g) SHIP-1000
(c) WoodenHorse	(h) Sea-god
(d) U	(i) -3.14159
(e) Conquers	(j) 4-legged

Now we know the fundamental particles, we can collect them into atoms.

Definition   Atom (a)

An atom consists of an n-ary predicate ($n \geq 1$) followed by a left parenthesis, followed by n terms separated by commas, followed by a right parenthesis. The terms are called the **arguments** of the predicate.

(Def. Atom(a)

In semantic nets, constants were one type of **term**, along with variables. But note that we have not defined a term here. For now, just remember that constants are terms. Later on, we will define terms fully, to include constants, variables and other things. Also, we have called this definition (a) for atoms, since we will have to modify it later, to account for some new types of atom about which we have not yet talked.

7.3 Informal semantics

When we come to investigate the semantics of CFL, we will observe a similarity to the semantics of semantic nets. In particular, the semantics of CFL is set up using an apparatus of interpretations, denotation, worlds, satisfaction and truth quite similar to the semantic net apparatus. Because of this, we can avoid for a while any careful formal statement of the semantics of CFL, and rely informally on the ideas we learned from semantic nets.

7.3.1 Intended interpretations and documentation

Atoms of CFL, like vectors in semantic nets, can be given an infinitely large number of interpretations. But usually, when we are setting up a logical system, for instance a knowledge base in a computer, we have one particular interpretation in mind for the system. It might be, for example, about the events in Shakespeare's *Julius Caesar*. In that case, we will choose predicates and constants with **mnemonic value,** to remind us of what we intended them to stand for. We might use CAESAR or J-C for Julius himself, and Emperor or Is-emperor or Emp to mean being an emperor.

However, even with mnemonic names like these, one can forget or become confused at a later time about what these names mean. Consequently, it is a good idea to document somewhere what the expressions in your logical system are intended to mean. Effectively, you should state the interpretation you intend for your symbols. Your **intended interpretation** should state:

(1)   What world your logical system is about – particularly, the domain of discourse.

(2)   What objects in that world your constants denote.

(3)   What properties or relations in that world your predicates denote.

Often, (1) and (2) will be quite obvious. But (3) can get tricky. For instance, should Mother-of(ANNE, BELINDA) be interpreted as saying that Anne is the mother of Belinda, or that the mother of Anne is Belinda? You need to make it clear.

In general, with polyadic predicates there is always a problem about being sure of how to interpret the role of the arguments. Should the first argument of `Mother-of` be the mother, or the child? You must specify.

Here is one useful way of doing it. We write down the predicate, then after it we put, in the places where the arguments go, a short description of the type of term that goes there; we put that description inside angle brackets ⟨···⟩, just to tell readers that what is there is a *description* of a type of expression, *not* an actual expression. (These angle-bracketed description devices are called **descriptors**.) For instance, if we want the first argument to `Mother-of` to name the mother, we would list `Mother-of` in our documentation this way:

Mother-of(⟨mother⟩,⟨child⟩)

Similarly, we can document the `Carried` predicate used above, like this:

Carried(⟨carrier⟩, ⟨thing carried⟩, ⟨start-place⟩)

Expressions containing descriptors are known as **schemata**. One advantage of using schemata in your documentation is that they show you the arity of the predicates you are documenting. You can have, for example, a two-place `Carried` predicate and a 4-place one, as well as the 3-place one. They will need their own separate documentation, for example:

Carried(⟨carrier⟩,⟨thing carried⟩)
Carried(⟨carrier⟩,⟨thing carried⟩,⟨start-place⟩)
Carried(⟨carrier⟩,⟨thing carried⟩,⟨start-place⟩,⟨finish-place⟩)

If the denotation of your predicate is not obvious, you can explain it using schemata, like this:

'C(⟨carrier⟩,⟨thing carried⟩,⟨start-place⟩,⟨finish-place⟩)

means that:

⟨carrier⟩ carried ⟨thing carried⟩ from ⟨start-place⟩ to ⟨finish-place⟩'

Or shorter:

'C(⟨a⟩,⟨b⟩,⟨c⟩,⟨d⟩) means that ⟨a⟩ carried ⟨b⟩ from ⟨c⟩ to ⟨d⟩'

Exercise 7.2 Translate each of the following sentences as atomic formulae of CFL. In each case state the denotations of your constants and use schemata to explain the interpretation of your predicates.

(a)   Ham is a son of Noah.
(b)   Cain is a son of Adam and Eve.
(c)   Noah built the Ark from gopher wood.
(d)   Jacob climbed a ladder from Earth to Heaven.
(e)   Moses led the Hebrews from Egypt to Israel, which took forty
       years.

Note that schemata are not expressions of the language CFL, because
the descriptors in them are not part of CFL. (That is why they are not written in `typewriter font`.) Rather, schemata are *descriptions* of expressions
in CFL.

Descriptors are devices that can be used anywhere, not just in argument places of predicates. We can use them, for example, to show the syntactic
structure of a monadic atomic formula:

$\langle$monadic-predicate$\rangle$($\langle$term$\rangle$)

Similarly the syntax of an n-ary atom ($n \geq 1$) can be described as:

$\langle n$-ary-predicate$\rangle$($\langle$term$\rangle$,...,$\langle$term$\rangle$)

where $\langle$term$\rangle$ is written n times.

7.3.2   Semantics of atoms

What we say here will parallel quite closely what we said about semantics for
ground vectors in Chapter 5. We will not, at this stage, define interpretations,
but will rely on the general understanding of the idea derived from Part I.

Predicates in CFL can have any arity, but whatever arity a predicate
has, it will denote a relation with that same arity (including the case of a
property as a monadic relation).In the intended interpretation, the relation
a predicate denotes is either quite obvious from the choice of predicate, or is
made clear in the documentation accompanying the logical system.

Saying that is enough to allow us to write down a rather informal definition of truth for an atom. The definition will be expanded later to take
account of types of term other than constants, and to fit in with other developments in the semantics of CFL. As a reminder that it will be improved
upon, we will call it definition (a) of truth for atoms.

Definition   Truth (a) for atoms

An atom $P(c_1,...,c_n)$ is **true in** an interpretation $\mathcal{I}$, where P is an n-ary
predicate and the c_is are constants, if the objects in the domain of discourse

of $\mathcal{I}$ that are denoted by the c_is are related by the n-ary relation in $\mathcal{I}$ that F denotes, and in the order defined for Ps denotation in $\mathcal{I}$. Otherwise the atom is **false in** $\mathcal{I}$.

(Def. Truth(a))

By saying 'the order defined for P's denotation in $\mathcal{I}$' we are insist-ing that the objects denoted by the arguments must be related in the right order, as set up in the interpretation of the predicate. Suppose we had a solar system interpretation for a small logical system, in which S(⟨body-1⟩, ⟨body-2⟩) is defined to mean that ⟨body-2⟩ is a satellite of ⟨body-1⟩. Then for an atom of this form to be true in the interpretation, we require that the body denoted by the constant that goes in the second argument place be a satellite of the body denoted by the constant that goes into the first argument place. So, with EARTH and MOON denoting the Earth and the Moon respectively, Def. (a) of truth for atoms makes S(EARTH, MOON) true in this interpretation and S(MOON, EARTH) false, since the Moon is a satellite of the Earth and not conversely. Similarly, suppose we use, in the same interpre-tation, B(⟨body-1⟩, ⟨body-2⟩, ⟨body-3⟩) to mean that ⟨body-2⟩ is between ⟨body-1⟩ and ⟨body-3⟩. Then since the Earth is between Venus and Mars, B(VENUS, EARTH, MARS) is true in this interpretation, as is B(MARS, EARTH, VENUS). But all other orderings of these constants, for example, B(EARTH, VENUS, MARS), are false in this interpretation. A full development of seman-tics for CFL will give a precise account of 'related in the right order', but the idea should be sufficiently clear now to be used without difficulty.

Exercise 7.3   A maths student defines G(⟨a⟩, ⟨b⟩, ⟨c⟩) to mean that ⟨b⟩ > ⟨a⟩ × ⟨c⟩ and ⟨c⟩ < ⟨a⟩. Write down the truth-values of the following atoms on this interpretation.

(a)	G(4, 30, 5)	(f)	G(1, 2, 3)
(b)	G(23, 3, 5)	(g)	G(3, 2, 1)
(c)	G(2, 1, 3)	(h)	G(1, 3, 2)
(d)	G(0, 3, 1)	(i)	G(3, 1, 2)
(e)	G(2, 5, 15)	(j)	G(2, 3, 1)

SUMMARY

- **Typography.** The written appearance of expressions of a logical sys-tem.

- **Definition Constant**. A constant consists of either:

  (a)   A capital letter, followed by zero or more capital letters, digits, or hyphens.

or:

(b)   A signed or unsigned integer, or decimal number.

(Def. Constant)

- **Definition Predicate.** A predicate consists of a capital letter, followed by zero or more lower-case letters, digits, or hyphens. Every predicate has a number $n \geq 1$ associated with it called its **adicity**, and the predicate is said to be n-**ary** or n-**place**.

(Def. Predicate)

- **Definition Atom (a).** An atom consists of an n-ary predicate ($n \geq 1$) followed by a left parenthesis, followed by n terms separated by commas, followed by a right parenthesis. The terms are called the **arguments** of the predicate.

(Def. Atom(a))

- **Term.** Comprises constants and other syntactic types in CFL, to be defined later.

- **Intended interpretation.** The interpretation of constants and predicates that the writer of a CFL system has in mind when he constructs it.

- **Documentation.** Intended interpretation should be documented by the author. Fully set out, this contains:

(a)   The world intended, especially the domain of discourse.

(b)   The denotation of each constant in the domain of discourse.

(c)   The denotation of each predicate.

- **Descriptor.** Description or label for some component part of CFL expressions; always written inside angle brackets, for example ⟨constant⟩.

- **Schema.** Expression containing descriptors, designed to show the reader the syntactic patterns or semantic structures of expressions of CFL. For example, the typographic structure of all dyadic atoms of CFL is exhibited by this schema:

⟨predicate⟩(⟨term⟩, ⟨term⟩)

- **Documentation of polyadic predicates.** Documentation explicitly recording the roles of the arguments is necessary, to remove ambiguities about which argument occurs where, in the relation denoted by the predicate. Example documentation: 'Loan(⟨lender⟩, ⟨borrower⟩, ⟨amount⟩) means that ⟨borrower⟩ was lent \$⟨amount⟩ by ⟨lender⟩.'

- **Definition Truth (a) for atoms.** An atom $P(c_1, \ldots, c_n)$ is **true in** an interpretation $\mathcal{I}$, where P is an n-ary predicate and the c_is are constants, if the objects in the domain of discourse of $\mathcal{I}$ that are denoted

by the c_is are related by the n-ary relation in $\mathcal{I}$ that P denotes, and i
the order defined for Ps denotation in $\mathcal{I}$. Otherwise the atom is **fals**
in $\mathcal{I}$.

(Def. Truth(a)

Chapter 8
Clauses

In the last chapter, we set out the typography and informal semantics of the atoms of CFL. These atoms congregate into molecules, which in CFL are called *clauses*. Clauses are conditional statements, similar to the conditionals of semantic net logic, which were always put into auxiliary nets.

In this chapter we shall learn:

• How to write clauses (their typography).

• How to understand the meaning of clauses (their semantics).

We shall see that clauses are much more general in their use than the conditionals of semantic nets. In addition to expressing conditionals as in semantic nets, clauses can be used to express:

• assertions,

• denials,

• more general conditionals that say if several antecedents are true, then one or more of several consequents are true.

8.1   Typography of clauses

When studying semantic nets, we saw how to draw diagrams that represented
conditional statements made out of atoms. Check your memory now by finding the atoms in the following three conditionals, representing those atoms as
vectors, and finally drawing up auxiliary nets to represent each conditional as
a whole. (This was actually Exercise 3.4 in Section 3.2.)

> Calpurnia is Empress,
> if Caesar is Emperor and she is married to him.   (1)

> If Caesar tries to become a dictator,
> then Cassius will conspire with Brutus.   (2)

> The car will move, given that the engine is running,
> the gears are engaged and the brakes are off.   (3)

In CFL too, we need to be able to represent conditionals such as these.
We already know how to represent the component atoms in CFL, so all we
have to do now is to represent the *if-then* connection between the atoms in
each conditional.

This is much easier than in semantic nets. In CFL, we write down
the antecedents (separated by commas for clarity), then an implication sign
'=>', then the consequent. For example, the sentences (1) to (3) above can be
written as:

```
Emperor(CAESAR), Married-to(CALPURNIA, CAESAR)
 => Empress(CALPURNIA)                                               (1')

Tries-to-become(CAESAR, DICTATOR)
 => Conspires-with(CASSIUS, BRUTUS)                                  (2')

State-of-engine(CAR-1, RUNNING),
State-of-gears(CAR-1, ENGAGED),
State-of-brakes(CAR-1, OFF)
 => Will-move(CAR-1)                                                 (3')
```

These three expressions of CFL are called **clauses**. Roughly speaking,
a clause is a conditional when it says, if its antecedent atoms are all true, then
so is its consequent atom. (People sometimes read the => sign as 'implies'.
Then, we could read (1') as 'Caesar is Emperor and Calpurnia is married to
Caesar, implies Calpurnia is Empress.' But using 'if-then' as in (1) and (2)
above is clearer, better English, and preferable for certain technical reasons
of logic.)

The semantic net conditionals we looked at in Part I, all had to have
one consequent and one or more antecedents. In CFL however, we can permit

any number of antecedents and any number of consequents, including zero. Why we should accept this, and what advantage there is in it, we shall see later in this chapter.

Definition   Clause

If $p_1, \ldots, p_m$ and $q_1, \ldots, q_n$ are atoms $(m, n \geq 0)$, then:

$$\{p_1, \ldots, p_m\} \Rightarrow \{q_1, \ldots, q_n\}$$

is a clause. The atoms $p_1, \ldots, p_m$ are known as the **antecedents** of the clause, and the set of those atoms, $p_1, \ldots, p_m$, is known as the **antecedent set** of the clause. Similarly, the atoms $q_1, \ldots, q_n$ are known as the **consequents** of the clause, and the set of them, $q_1, \ldots, q_n$ is known as the **consequent set** of the clause.

(Def. Clause)

Note that in this definition we have stipulated that the antecedents and consequents of a clause must be enclosed in braces: {...}. Normally, we will not worry very much about writing the braces if it is obvious where they would go, but in some cases, such as (5) to (8) below, putting them in might avoid some problems.

According to this definition, (1′), (2′) and (3′) above are clauses (forgetting about the braces), which we would expect; but so too are these five expressions (not forgetting the braces):

$$\{\text{Shines(HALLEY)}\} \Rightarrow \{\text{Star(HALLEY)}, \text{ Planet(HALLEY)}\} \qquad (4)$$
$$\{\} \Rightarrow \{\text{Rotates(EARTH)}, \text{ Rotates(SKY)}\} \qquad (5)$$
$$\{\text{Star(HALLEY)}\} \Rightarrow \{\} \qquad (6)$$
$$\{\text{Star(JUPITER)},$$
$$\text{Planet(JUPITER)}\} \Rightarrow \{\} \qquad (7)$$
$$\{\} \Rightarrow \{\} \qquad (8)$$

Plainly, we now have a job to determine what these clauses mean, that is, we must now set up the semantics of clauses. This we will do in the next section.

Exercise 8.1   Which of the following are clauses? If any are not, why not?

(a)   `Is-trojan(HECTOR)`
(b)   `{Stormy(AEGEAN-SEA) => Shipwrecked(ODYSSEUS)}`
(c)   `{} => {Built(GREEKS, WOODEN-HORSE)}`
(d)   `{Fight(GREEKS, TROJANS)} => {Will-Conquer(GREEKS, TROJANS)}`
(e)   `{} => {Killed(ACHILLES, HECTOR), Killed(HECTOR, ACHILLES)}`

8.2   Informal semantics

In logic, semantics amounts to truth-conditions. The definition of truth for clauses, that follows below, is meant to capture in an unambiguous way the obvious meaning of a conditional statement: that *if* the antecedent is true *then* so is the consequent. Where there are several antecedents, we read them conjunctively: if they are all true, so is the consequent. This is just the same as the way in which we read antecedents in semantic net conditionals.

But, where there are several consequents, we read them *disjunctively*: if the antecedent is true, then *one or more* of the consequents are true.

This may seem unreasonable: why not read the multiple consequents conjunctively too? The short answer is that this way, we can say more in CFL than otherwise. It makes CFL a more powerful language. As we will see in the next chapter, if we read multiple consequents conjunctively, then we cannot actually express in CFL any wider a class of statements than if we had just one consequent. But by reading multiple consequents disjunctively, we can represent statements in CFL that could not be represented otherwise.

What matters most with a conditional statement, is that it *must* be false if its antecedent is true and its consequent is false. Otherwise, it would be *truly* saying that from truth we can infer falsehood. After all, recall that we understand a conditional as saying that where its antecedent is true, so is its consequent. Where there are several antecedents, the conditional must be false if they all are true yet the consequent is false. And where there are several consequents, if the antecedent is true but they are all false, then the conditional must be false.

The definition below captures all these cases, and the limit cases where the antecedent set or consequent set is empty. This definition is not as formal and complete as it could be, mainly because we are relying on an informal understanding of an interpretation carried over from work on semantic nets. In time, we will replace this definition – not because it is wrong or misleading, but because we will want to state this matter in a different way. As with Def (a) of truth for atoms in the previous chapter, we will call this definition (a) too, as a reminder that it will be upgraded.

Definition   Truth (a) for clauses
If $p_1, \ldots, p_m$ and $q_1, \ldots, q_n$ are atoms $(m, n \geq 0)$, then the clause:

$$\{p_1, \ldots, p_m\} \Rightarrow \{q_1, \ldots, q_n\}$$

is **true** in an interpretation $\mathcal{I}$ unless both these conditions hold:
(a)   all its antecedents are true, and
(b)   all its consequents are false,
in which case it is **false** in $\mathcal{I}$.

(Def. Truth (a))

Note that condition (a) can equally be expressed as 'there are no false antecedents', and (b) can equally be expressed as 'there are no true consequents'. Reading (a) and (b) in this way shows how to evaluate the truth-conditions of clauses that lack antecedents or consequents.

Note also that Def. Truth (a) for clauses is stated in such a way as to guarantee that clauses obey two fundamental logical laws (two of the three **laws of thought**, known to Aristotle):

- **The law of non-contradiction**: No statement is both true and false.
- **The law of excluded middle**: Every statement is either true or false.

Satisfy yourself that atoms also obey these laws.

8.2.1   Reading clauses

Let us look at some concrete examples of clauses, to see how Def. Truth (a) for clauses works. In these examples, we will assume the obvious interpretation for the component atoms.

EXAMPLE 8.1

By truth (a) for clauses, the clause:

```
Round(MOON) => Made-of(MOON, CHEESE)
```

is false, since its antecedent is true and its consequent is false. It says 'If the Moon is round, then it is made of cheese.'

EXAMPLE 8.2

Because its very first antecedent is false, the clause:

```
Flat(EARTH), Finite(EARTH) => Has(EARTH, EDGE)
```

is true, by Def. Truth (a) for clauses. The truth-values of the other atoms are irrelevant. It says 'If the Earth is flat and finite, then it has an edge.'

EXAMPLE 8.3

The truth of the consequent in:

```
Made-of(MOON, ROCK) => Round(MOON)
```

ensures, by Def. Truth (a) for clauses, that this clause is true. The fact that the antecedent is true is irrelevant. The clause would be equally true if its antecedent were Made-of(MOON, CHEESE) – in that case it would say 'If the Moon is made of cheese, then it is round.'

EXAMPLE 8.4

The multiple-consequent clause (4) on p.93 has a true antecedent, so by Def. Truth(a) for clauses it will be true if it has a true consequent. Now in fact, Comet Halley is neither a star nor a planet, so both consequents are false, so the whole clause is false.

Exercise 8.2   Write these English sentences as clauses of CFL, with braces. Provide schemata to explain how to understand your predicates if you think the intention is unclear.

(a)   Pussy Galore is a traitor if she spies for SMERSH.
(b)   If baking powder is absent, the cake will be flat.
(c)   If Holland borders on Belgium, and if France does too, then Holland and France are in the same land mass.
(d)   The cricket match will be cancelled if the weather is rainy and the pitch is waterlogged.
(e)   If this creature is a chordate and has normal chromosomes, then it is either female or male.

8.2.2   Calculating truth-values

The type of logic we are looking at right now is known generically as **truth-functional logic**. That is, it is a system of logic whose atoms can be given truth-values, either true or false, and then the truth-value of any clause as a whole can be computed simply as a function of the truth-values given to its atomic components.

The examples above show us that we can use Def. Truth (a) for clauses to compute the truth-values of clauses, if we know the truth-values of the component atoms. Here is a convenient way of doing it. Take a clause of this form:

$$p_1, \ldots, p_m \implies q_1, \ldots, q_n$$

where the ps and qs are atomic formulae and $m, n > 0$. Now underneath each component atom write its truth-value if you know it. It is conventional to use '1' for true and '0' for false. Then, the three truth-condition definitions show that the only combination of truth-values of the atoms that yields a *false* clause is:

$$p_1, \ldots, p_n \; \Rightarrow \; q_1, \ldots, q_n$$
$$1 \qquad 1 \qquad 0 \qquad 0$$

So now, we can tell that the whole clause is *false*, which we show by writing '0' under the implication arrow:

$$p_1, \ldots, p_n \; \Rightarrow \; q_1, \ldots, q_n$$
$$1 \qquad 1 \; 0 \; 0 \qquad 0$$

Sometimes we can compute the truth-value of a clause via Def. Truth (a) for clauses even if we do not know the truth-values of all the component atoms. For example, if we are given only:

$$p_1, p_2 \; \Rightarrow \; q_1, q_2$$
$$1$$

or only:

$$p_1, p_2 \; \Rightarrow \; q_1, q_2$$
$$0$$

then we know in both cases from Def. Truth (a) for clauses, that the whole clause is true. Why?

8.3   T and F

Def. Clause allows for a clause to have no antecedents, and no consequents. How do we understand the semantics of such clauses?

8.3.1   Empty antecedent set

Suppose we have a clause with no antecedents and only one consequent:

$$\{\} \; \Rightarrow \; \{q\}$$

By Def. Truth (a) for clauses, this clause is true if q is true and is false if q is false. So this is the way of representing in CFL the **unconditional statement** that q is true. Representing these two cases in a table we have:

$$\{\} \; \Rightarrow \; q$$
$$1 \quad 1$$
$$0 \quad 0$$

Why not just represent this statement that q is true by the bare atom 'q', instead of the clause '$\{\}$ => $\{q\}$'? After all, they are equivalent in truth-value. The answer is simply that all computations in CFL are carried out using clauses, as we shall see, so we need to represent unconditional statements, as well as conditional ones, as clauses. (Some atoms, in chemistry too, are also molecules.)

At this point it is useful to introduce two **primitive atoms**, T and F. They have no internal structure, unlike other atoms. Treat T as an atom that is always true, and F as an atom that is always false. F is just like $\bigotimes$ in semantic nets. We should note a modification to Def. Atom from the previous chapter:

Definition   Atom

An **atom** is either:

(a)   T or F

or:

(b)   consists of an n-ary predicate ($n \geq 0$) followed by a left parenthesis, followed by n terms separated by commas, followed by a right parenthesis. The terms are called the **arguments** of the predicate.

(Def. Atom)

Where you have a clause with no antecedent, such as '$\{\}$ => $\{q\}$' above, Def. Truth (a) for clauses shows that you can always introduce T as an antecedent:

$$\{T\} \Rightarrow \{q\}$$

$\{T\}$	=>	$\{q\}$
1	1	1
1	0	0

The table here shows that the whole clause has the same truth-value as q, so adding T as an antecedent made no difference to the truth-value of the clause. That is, asserting q unconditionally is the same as asserting that it follows from the truth.

Exercise 8.3   Check that this table of truth-values is justified by Def. Truth (a) for clauses.

In a similar way, a clause with no antecedents but several consequents:

$$\{\} \Rightarrow \{q_1, \ldots, q_n\}$$

is the unconditional statement that one or more of $q_1, \ldots, q_n$ is true, that is, this is a disjunctive assertion of $q_1, \ldots, q_n$. Again, check these truth-conditions by reflecting on Def. Truth (a) for clauses.

EXAMPLE 8.5

What is the truth-value of clause (5)?

The earth rotates, so one consequent is true, so by Def. Truth (a) for clauses the whole clause is true. In tabular format:

```
{} => Rotates(EARTH), Rotates(SKY)
      1           1
```

8.3.2   Empty consequent set

How do we understand a clause with no consequents? That is:

$$\{p\} \Rightarrow \{\}$$

or in the general case:

$$\{p_1, \ldots, p_m\} \Rightarrow \{\}$$

Suppose one or more antecedents are false. Then by Def. Truth (a) for clauses the clause is *true*. On the other hand, suppose all antecedents are true. Then condition (a) of Def. Truth (a) for clauses holds. Next, since there are no true consequents, condition (b) of Def. Truth (a) for clauses holds. So by Def. Truth (a) for clauses, the clause is *false*. In other words, the clause can be read as saying 'Not all of $p_1, \ldots p_m$ are true.'

You might find it helps to understand a clause with an empty consequent set if you give it the consequent F. The clause:

$$p_1, \ldots, p_m \Rightarrow F$$

says that if $p_1, \ldots, p_m$ are all true, then falsehood follows. In other words, they are not all true. As with adding T as an antecedent, adding F as a consequent cannot make any difference to the truth-value of the clause.

Exercise 8.4   Prove that last claim.

EXAMPLE 8.6_____

What is the truth-value of clause (**6**):

$$\{\texttt{Star(HALLEY)}\} \Rightarrow \{\} \tag{6}$$

Halley's Comet is not a star, so `Star(HALLEY)` is false, so by Def. Truth (a) for clauses, the clause is true. In table form:

```
{Star(HALLEY)} => {}
  0              1
```

The clause says that Halley is not a star.

EXAMPLE 8.7_____

What does clause (7) say and what is its truth-value? Pretend that Jupiter is neither a star nor a planet; what is its truth-value then?

$$\{\texttt{Star(JUPITER), Planet(JUPITER)}\} \Rightarrow \{\} \tag{7}$$

It says that Jupiter is not both a star and a planet, or equivalently that if it is both a star and a planet, then falsehood follows. Jupiter is a planet, not a star, so the clause (7) is true, as shown:

```
{Star(JUPITER), Planet(JUPITER)} => {}
  0               1                  1
```

The first antecedent is false, so by Def. Truth (a) for clauses, the clause is true.

_____

Exercise 8.5   Work out the truth-value of the empty clause, '{} => {}', with no antecedents or consequents.

_____

The empty clause ('{} => {}'   above) probably strikes you as rather a logical fiction. It is not the sort of thing anyone could say or believe or claim. Indeed, it is a limit case of a clause, made possible only by the wording of the definition of clause. Excluding it, by modifying that definition, would be rather inelegant; anyway, as we shall see, it actually plays a very important role in logical inferences.

Exercise 8.6   Find a way of writing these in CFL:

(a)   Austria is in Europe.
(b)   Turkey is in Europe or Asia.
(c)   Austria is not in Asia.
(d)   Turkey is not in both Europe and Asia.
(e)   If Russia touches Turkey, Russia is in Europe or Asia.
(f)   If Russia is in Europe and Asia, it straddles the Ural Mountains or
         borders the Caspian Sea.

SUMMARY

- **Definition Clause.** If $p_1, \ldots, p_m$ and $q_1, \ldots, q_n$ are atoms $(m, n \geq 0)$,
  then:

$$\{p_1, \ldots, p_m\} => \{q_1, \ldots, q_n\}$$

  is a clause.

  (Def. Clause)

- **Implication sign.** The double shafted arrow: =>.

- **Antecedents.** In Def. Clause, the atoms $p_1, \ldots, p_m$ are the **antecedents** of the clause, and the set of those atoms, $p_1, \ldots, p_m$, is the
  antecedent set of the clause.

- **Consequents.** In Def. Clause, the atoms $q_1, \ldots, q_n$ are the **consequents** of the clause, and the set of them, $q_1, \ldots, q_n$, is the **consequent
  set** of the clause.

- **Definition Truth (a) for clauses.** If $p_1, \ldots, p_m$ and $q_1, \ldots, q_n$ are
  atoms $(m, n \geq 0)$, then the clause:

$$\{p_1, \ldots, p_m\} => \{q_1, \ldots, q_n\}$$

  is **true** in an interpretation $\mathcal{I}$, unless both these conditions hold:

  (a)   all its antecedents are true, and

  (b)   all its consequents are false,
  in which case it is **false** in $\mathcal{I}$.

  (Def. Truth(a))

- **Definition Atom.** An **atom** is either:

  (a)   T or F

  or:

(b)   consists of an n-ary predicate ($n \geq 0$) followed by a left parenthesis, followed by n terms separated by commas, followed by a
right parenthesis. The terms are called the **arguments** of the
predicate.

(Def. Atom)

- **Semantics of T and F.** T is true in every interpretation, and F is
false in every interpretation.

- **Law of non-contradiction.** No statement is both true and false.

- **Law of excluded middle.** Every statement is either true or false.

- **Tabular method of calculating truth-values.** In a clause, write
known truth-values for atoms under them, and for the clause under the
implication sign. Use Def. Truth for clauses to calculate other values
from those known, and write them in too.

- **Clauses with no antecedents.** Equivalent to having T as sole antecedent. Equivalent to asserting the (disjunction of) consequent(s).

- **Clauses with no consequents.** Equivalent to having F as sole consequent. Equivalent to denying the (conjunction of) antecedent(s).

- **The empty clause.** The clause {}=> {}. From the above, it is equivalent to the clause T => F, which is false in every interpretation.

Chapter 9
Representation

This is a chapter about representation rather than reasoning. The CFL clause is a surprisingly powerful way of representing in symbolic form a wide range of statements. It is more powerful than semantic net representation because of its disjunctive consequent set.

This chapter explores:

- How to use clauses to represent unconditional assertions and denials, as well as conditionals.

- How to make use of the disjunctive consequent set.

- How to extend semantic nets to give them the full representational power of CFL clauses.

9.1   Assertions and denials

The symbolic language of clausal form logic that we developed in Chapter 8, together with the semantical definition Def. Truth (a) for clauses, provides us with a language of considerable power. The limits of what CFL can express were certainly not reached in the examples of translation between English and CFL that we looked at in that chapter. In this chapter, we will look at some of the problems of representing a wider class of statements in CFL. We will also consider some of the implications this has for semantic nets.

It will help to explain how to represent statements in CFL if we define the notion of an **assertion**.

- An assertion is a statement which is being held to be true.

An assertion is not a *kind* of statement, it is what we call *any* statement when it is being considered as true, and not merely being thought of, or occurring, as part of a larger statement.

Some examples will help to clarify this. A statement counts as an assertion in cases like these:

- When someone believes it.
- When someone claims it to be true.
- When it is an item in a computer's knowledge base.

In CFL, we mark the difference between assertions and unasserted statements syntactically: assertions are always represented as clauses, and clauses are always assertions. For this reason it is *only* clauses that can be entered into a knowledge base, or used to represent someone's beliefs. In CFL, the difference between the unasserted statement that Caesar loves Calpurnia, and the assertion that Caesar loves Calpurnia, is made in this way:

- The statement that Caesar loves Calpurnia is represented by the dyadic atomic formula:

  Loves(CAESAR, CALPURNIA)

- The assertion that Caesar loves Calpurnia is represented by the clause:

  {} => Loves(CAESAR, CALPURNIA)

In general, an assertion is represented in CFL by one *or more* clause(s) containing the statements that were in the assertion. The next two sections of this chapter will explain in detail how this is done in many cases.

1.2   Negation

The first problem is how to represent negative statements in CFL. We have already seen how to represent assertions of negative atomic statements such as the claim that Halley is not a star. We saw (Example 8.6 in the previous chapter) that this assertion was represented as:

```
Star(HALLEY) => {}
```

In general, a negative atomic assertion 'not–p', where p is an atomic statement, is represented as 'p => {}'.

But what do we do if the statement 'not–p' is not an assertion, but part of a larger assertion? An example is the assertion that if Halley is gaseous but *not a star*, then it is cold. We can give this a partial translation into clausal form:

$$\text{Gaseous(HALLEY), not–Star(HALLEY) => Cold(HALLEY)} \qquad (1)$$

That is only a partial translation, however, because (1) is not a clause of CFL. It contains 'not–' in front of an atomic formula, but by Def. Clause, a clause can contain only atomic formulae and the implication sign. So the 'not–' is no part of a clause of CFL. The problem can be put this way: how do we get rid of the 'not'? The answer is, shift the negated atom to the other side of the '=>' and drop the 'not–'. So we end up with:

$$\text{Gaseous(HALLEY) => Star(HALLEY), Cold(HALLEY)} \qquad (2)$$

This says 'If Halley is gaseous, then it is either a star or cold.' That plainly says the same as the original 'If Halley is gaseous but not a star, then it is cold.' (2) unlike (1) is syntactically a perfectly correct clause, consisting only of atoms around an implication sign. The problem of trying to represent negation in clauses, which have no sign for negation, is solved: no sign for negation is needed.

The method we have used here for representing negative statements in clauses is the first of a series of **representation rules** that we will employ to help us translate from English to CFL, and conversely.

Representation of negative statements

If you want to add 'not–p' to one side of a clause, then add p to the other side instead.

We call this the rule of **negation by transfer**. It has two features worth commenting on. The first is its symmetry. In (1), the negation occurred in the antecedent, but we apply the same rule if the negation occurs in the consequent. To represent 'If Halley is a star, then it is not cold', we transfer the negated statement to the antecedent, to get:

```
Star(HALLEY), Cold(HALLEY) => {}
```

The second point is that our way of dealing with negative *atomic* assertions, ones of the form 'not–p' where p is an atom, obeys this representation rule. The plain way to represent such a statement in CFL is as the unconditional assertion ' => not–p', but we write 'p => {}' instead.

Exercise 9.1   Represent the following in CFL:

(a)   If Anne does not obey the law, she will be arrested.

(b)   If Bill is arrested, either he is not obeying the law or the policeman made a mistake.

(c)   If Cathie taps telephones, then either she is not obeying the law or she is not a civilian.

(d)   If Dick does not wear men's clothes and does not have any vices and compromises diplomats, then he is a woman or a spy.

(e)   If neither Ernie nor Fyodor are spies, then they are not both trying to expose each other.

9.3   Conjunction and disjunction

Representing a disjunctive assertion in CFL is straightforward: the disjuncts become consequents of a clause. The assertion that Halley is a star, planet or meteor becomes:

```
=> Star(HALLEY), Planet(HALLEY), Meteor(HALLEY)
```

A conjunctive assertion, for example 'Saturn is a planet and Titan is one of its satellites', amounts to just the assertion of its conjuncts, in this case that Saturn is a planet and that Titan is a satellite of Saturn. Each of these becomes a clause by itself:

```
=>  Planet(SATURN) ;
=>  Satellite(TITAN, SATURN)
```

So the representation rules for disjunctive and conjunctive assertions are:

Representation of disjunctive assertions

Represent a disjunctive assertion 'p_1 or p_2 or ...' as '{} => $p_1, p_2, \ldots$'.

Representation of conjunctive assertions

Represent a conjunctive assertion 'p_1 and p_2 and ...' by a separate clause for each conjunct.

EXAMPLE 9.1

Represent in CFL 'If Halley is a star it is hot and if it is a planet it is not hot'.

We represent 'If Halley is a star it is hot' and 'if Halley is a planet it is not hot' by separate clauses:

$$\texttt{Star(HALLEY) => Hot(HALLEY)}$$
$$\texttt{Planet(HALLEY), Hot(HALLEY) => \{\}}$$

Note the use of the rule of negation by transfer in the second clause.

A rather obvious extension of the representation rule for conjunctive assertions is the rule for representing a conditional with conjunctive consequents. To say:

If Halley is a comet, then it is cold, gaseous and unstable.

is just to say these three things:

If Halley is a comet, then it is cold.
If Halley is a comet, then it is gaseous.
If Halley is a comet, then it is unstable.

The representation rule we used there was:

Representation of a conditional with a conjunctive consequent

To represent:

If P then q_1 and q_2 and $\cdots$ and q_n,

(where P stands for the antecedent set); represent instead the separate conditionals:

If P then q_1
If P then q_2
$$\vdots$$
If P then q_n.

Note that the rule for representing a conjunctive assertion is just a special case of this, where there are no antecedents in P.

That leaves the question of representing a conditional with a disjunctive antecedent, for example:

If Halley is a planet, comet or meteor, then it is cold.

This says the same as three assertions:

If Halley is a planet, then it is cold.
If Halley is a comet, then it is cold.
If Halley is a meteor, then it is cold.

So the representation rule is:

Representation of a conditional with a disjunctive antecedent

To represent:

If p_1 or p_2 or $\cdots$ or p_m, then Q

(where Q stands for the consequent set); represent instead the separate conditionals:

If p_1 then Q
If p_2 then Q
$$\vdots$$
If p_m then Q.

Altogether these rules have a pleasing symmetry about them which makes them easy to remember, as is shown in Figure 9.1. Note that assertions and consequents are considered together, because an unconditional assertion is just an antecedent-less consequent.

Exercise 9.2   Represent the following assertions in CFL:

(a)   Anne was wearing jeans, a shirt, and shoes or boots.

(b)   Either Bobbie was in the room or she was not.
(c)   The number is odd or even or not a positive integer, and it is not
        real, it is positive, and it is less than or equal to 10.
(d)   If Carol fails maths, logic or computer science, she will leave uni-
        versity.
(e)   If Diane visits London or Paris, she will find culture and beauty.

	In Antecedent	In Consequent or as Assertion
Conjunction	Leave alone.	Split into separate clauses, one for each conjunct.
Disjunction	Split into separate clauses, one for each disjunct.	Leave alone.

Figure 9.1   Representation of conjunctions and disjunctions in clauses.

9.4   Atoms, clauses and semantic nets

For the rest of this chapter we will look at how the apparatus of clauses relates
to the semantic net method of representing statements.

9.4.1   Atoms

We already know how to represent two-place atoms in nets. Indeed, since
nets are made from relationship vectors, which are direct representations of
two-place atomic statements, the problem of representation for semantic nets
is mainly the problem of restructuring any type of statement as a two-place
atom. In Chapter 2, for example, we learned how to 'stretch' a one-place
atomic statement into a two-place one. This statement stretching can, of
course, be represented by atomic formulae. The one-place statement that
the Sun is yellow can be represented in CFL as Yellow(SUN); its two-place
equivalent, that the colour of the Sun is yellow, can be represented in CFL as
Colour(SUN, YELLOW).

What of 3-place statements and ones of greater arity? As an example,
take the three-place relation of giving: Gives(⟨donor⟩, ⟨recipient⟩, ⟨gift⟩).
We will represent this by a cluster of four vectors in a semantic net. To

represent the particular atomic statement that God gave Moses the first commandment, as an atom of CFL, we write:

```
Gives(GOD, MOSES, COMMANDMENT-1)
```

To represent this in a semantic net, we first decide on a name for this particular act of giving, G_1 say. We can say four things about G_1:

> G_1 is an act of giving.
> In G_1, God is the donor.
> In G_1, Moses is the recipient.
> In G_1, the gift was the first commandment.

Each of those is a two-place statement, so the representation as vectors is easy:

Exercise 9.3   Represent these four statements as two-place atomic formulae of CFL. Give a schema for each.

The process involved here is rather like the method of representing a one-place statement:

(1)   We invent a term (known as the **predicational term**) to replace the predicate. Here, GIVING replaced the predicate Gives. Treat it as meaning acts of giving.

(2)   Then, we invent a second new term (known as the **instance term**) to name the particular event that the statement is about. That was G-1 above, which named this particular act of God's giving the commandment to Moses. So it is connected by an Isa link to the predicational term.

(3)   What remains, is to say something about the objects involved in this event. Above, we had to say who the donor, recipient, and gift involved in G_1 were. To do that, we need a suitably labelled link from the instance term to each of the component terms of the original statement. That gave us the final three vectors, above.

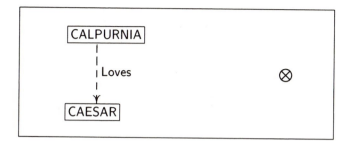

Figure 9.2   Representation of the denial that Calpurnia loves Caesar.

The final effect is that $n + 1$ vectors rooted in one instance term tell us everything about the event that the original n-ary statement did.

Exercise 9.4   Invent a four-place predicate in CFL to represent the concept of one person selling goods to another for a certain sum of money. Use it to represent these statements:

(a)   Con sold the Sydney Harbour Bridge to Hylas for $1000.
(b)   A trader bought Joseph from Joseph's oldest brother for 20 shekels.

Then, represent those two statements as relationship vectors, and as 4-ary and 2-ary atoms in CFL.

9.4.2   Assertions and denials

In semantic nets, we represent assertions by putting vectors, representing the component atomic statements in the assertion, into a semantic net in an appropriate way. We will now detail how to do this for a number of basic types of assertion. A good way to figure out how to represent an assertion in a semantic net, is to represent it first as clauses of CFL, then translate each clause into semantic net form.

Where the assertion is just an atomic statement, its vector (or vectors, if it was more than two-place) are put into the main net. In CFL, these end up as unconditional clauses, as we know.

Denials, that is, assertions that a statement is false, we know to represent as conditionals in an auxiliary net. The antecedent is the statement (possibly conjunctive) being denied, and the consequent is falsum: ⊗. For example, the statement that Calpurnia does not love Caesar, is represented as in Figure 9.2.

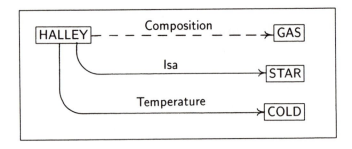

Figure 9.3   Auxiliary net for the assertion that if Halley is gaseous, it is a star or cold.

This semantic net method of representing a denial corresponds exactly in principle to the clausal way of doing it:

    Loves(CALPURNIA, CAESAR) =>

for that is the same as:

    Loves(CALPURNIA, CAESAR) => F

Exercise 9.5   With reference to the previous exercise, represent the assertion of (a), and the denial of (b), in a semantic net.

9.4.3   Conditional assertions

Where a conditional assertion has one consequent, representation in semantic nets proceeds as in Chapter 3 – assuming, of course, that we can represent the component atoms. Where it has no consequent, the assertion is a denial and we treat it as having falsum as consequent.

The difficult case is where it has more than one (disjunctive) consequent. We could, in fact, draw them all as solid-line relationship vectors in the auxiliary net for the conditional. For example,

    Gaseous(HALLEY) => Star(HALLEY), Cold(HALLEY)   (2

has the auxiliary net shown in Figure 9.3.

But we have to be careful when applying such an auxiliary net to a mai

World (a):

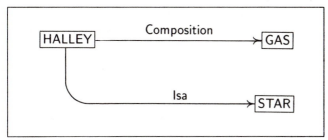

World (b):

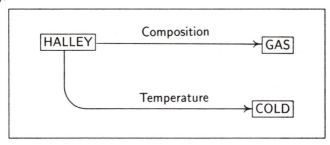

Figure 9.4 Possible astronomical worlds consistent with (2) and Halley being gaseous.

net. If we had a main net with HALLEY ___Composition___→ GAS in it, we could not, after matching the auxiliary to the main net, copy both consequents onto the main net. For then the main net would contain the assertions that Halley is a star and cold. But while those two statements are *consistent* with the data so far, neither of them *follow* from that data. So we cannot treat them as assertions, that is, we cannot write them into the main net. We can only write in there statements that *do* follow: if all the vectors in a main net are true in some world, and the conditional in the auxiliary net is true in that world too, then we want to be able to say that the conclusion we draw by matching the auxiliary net to the main one, must be true in that world too.

What we have to do is to *duplicate* the main net, and match the auxiliary first to one copy of it and deposit one consequent on it, then match the auxiliary in the same way to the other copy of the main net and deposit the other consequent on it. Now we have two different main nets, hence they represent two worlds. All we can say is that at least one of those worlds is to be taken as 'correct'. Hopefully, further pattern-matching in one of them will cause the illegal ⊗ to appear on it, so we know that that world can be rejected, leaving the other.

In the Halley example, we end up with two main nets, as in Figure 9. All we can say is that one of those nets (at least) represents the world we ar trying to describe. Which one it is, the data so far does not determine.

So the semantic net rule for reasoning with multiple-consequent auxi iary nets is:

Definition   Multiple consequent rule

If there are n consequent vectors in an auxiliary net which is being matche in a main net, then copy each consequent vector onto a separate copy of th main net, with the bindings for its variables as determined by the match.

(Def. Multiple consequen

Exercise 9.6   Suppose we also know that Halley is a comet, and that no comet are stars. Use semantic nets to deduce that Halley is cold.

SUMMARY

- **Assertion.** Statement that is being held as true.
- **Representation of assertions.** In CFL, clauses represent assertion:
- **Representation of negative statements.** If you want to add 'not–p to one side of a clause, then add p to the other side instead. (Negatio by transfer.)
- **Representation of disjunctive assertions.** Represent a disjunctiv assertion 'p_1 or p_2 or ...' as '{} => $p_1, p_2, \ldots$'
- **Representation of conjunctive assertions.** Represent a conjunc tive assertion 'p_1 and p_2 and ...' by a separate clause for each conjunc
- **Representation of a conditional with a conjunctive conse quent.** To represent:

    If P then q_1 and q_2 and $\cdots$ and q_n

(where P stands for the antecedent set); represent instead the separat conditionals:

    If P then q_1
    If P then q_2
    $\vdots$
    If P then q_n

- **Representation of a conditional with a disjunctive antecedent.**
  To represent:

    If p_1 or p_2 or $\cdots$ or p_m, then Q

  (where Q stands for the consequent set); represent instead the separate conditionals:

    If p_1 then Q
    If p_2 then Q
    $\vdots$
    If p_m then Q.

- **Representation of $>$2-adic predicates as two-place.** For a particular statement $P(c_1, \ldots, c_n)$ where $n > 2$ invent a **predicational term** p to replace the predicate, and an **instance term** i to name the particular event this statement is about. Invent n two-place predicates P_j (where $1 \le j \le n$) to denote the relations between this event and each of the n objects in it. Then the statement is represented by the $n + 1$ two-place statements $\texttt{Isa}(i, p)$ and $P_j(i, c_j)$ for $1 \le j \le n$. Similarly, we could use $n + 1$ vectors to obtain a semantic net representation.

- **Definition Multiple consequent rule.** If there are n consequent vectors in an auxiliary net which is being matched in a main net, then copy each consequent vector onto a separate copy of the main net, with the bindings for its variables as determined by the match.

  (Def. Multiple consequent)

- **Approximate semantics of multiple consequent rule.** Each copy of the net, with a vector added, represents a possible extension of the world described by the original net. If subsequent net manipulations (always done on each duplicate net separately) show all but one of these is impossible (by putting falsum into them) then the remaining net represents the true alternative.

Chapter 10
Variables

The clauses we have looked at so far are known as *ground clauses* because they contain no variables. We shall now introduce the variables of Chapter 4 into atomic formulae (atoms) and so into clauses. As with semantic nets, this will provide us with a universal conditional, which we call the *universal clause*. It is the most important type of expression in CFL.

In this chapter we shall:

- Define a typography for variables.

- Explain how to use and understand variables in clauses.

- Introduce the important idea of *instances* of a clause containing variables, and the rule of substitution for variables, which produces instances.

- Look informally at the semantic theory of interpretations for clauses with variables, which leads to the important concept of a *model*.

10.1   Using variables

The idea of a variable is familiar from our use of them in semantic nets. W
use them in a similar way in CFL, and we will adopt a similar way of writin
them too.

To write variables, we will use lower-case letters, hyphens and digit
but always with a lower-case letter first. Examples are:

```
x  u1  x5  murderer  victim-2
```

In this book, we will follow the usual style for variables in mathematic
and formal logic, and use one-letter variables from near the end of the alpha
bet, perhaps with index numbers following, such as x, y3, and z-10. Bu
many writers, particularly in computer science, like to use mnemonics for thei
variables as a reminder of what types of things the variables are intended t
have as values, as in murderer. If you like that style and it does not confus
you, it is perfectly proper for you to use it.

As with semantic nets, variables are a type of *term*, that is, they ca
be arguments of predicates. So we can write:

```
Loves(x, CALPURNIA)
```

or:

```
Loves(person-1,person-2)
```

but not:

```
x(CAESAR, CALPURNIA)
```

Exercise 10.1   Write a formal typographical definition for variables, as was
done for constants and predicates. Then write a typographical definition of a
term to include variables along with the expressions that have already been said
to be terms.

In the semantic net approach to logic, vectors containing variables wer
put into auxiliary nets, to signify that they were asserted as true. For example
a way of representing the assertion 'Everybody who stabbed Caesar, love
Rome', is to create the auxiliary net in Figure 10.1.

In CFL, we write that as:

```
Stabbed(x, CAESAR) => Loves(x, ROME)
```
(1

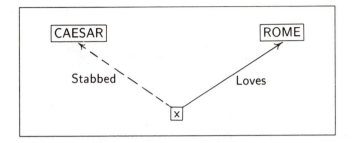

Figure 10.1   Auxiliary net representing the universal conditional assertion 'Everybody who stabbed Caesar, loves Rome'.

Any clause containing variables, as this one does, is known as a **universal clause**. This universal conditional clause behaves semantically in much the same way as the conditional in the semantic net in Figure 10.1. It is a pattern or template, in which the variable x can have as value any object in the universe of discourse. Semantically, being a pattern, if it is true, then each ground clause that it matches is true. (This will be familiar from the discussion of universal and ground conditionals in Chapter 4.)

So, a good way to read (1) is to say:

For any object x, if x stabbed Caesar, then x loves Rome.

Reading a clause in this literal way, though it does not really count as graceful English, can help the reader to check its meaning. We call this **quasi-English**.

0.1.1   Variables in clauses

Here are some more examples of universal clauses, their quasi-English reading, and their semantic net equivalents.

We begin with an unconditional universal clause:

```
=> Loves(x, ROME)
```

This can be read as 'For any object x, x loves Rome', that is, 'Everyone loves Rome'. ('Everyone' or 'everything'? We really need a word which covers both people and non-people, but English lacks it. Good English requires us to say 'everyone' here, even though it conveys information that was not in the CFL clause, that the domain of discourse is confined to humans.) To represent this using semantic nets, we must use an auxiliary net

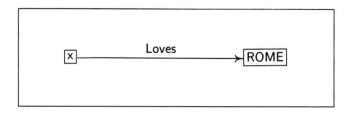

Figure 10.2   An unconditional statement in an auxiliary net. All universal state ments, whether conditional or not, must go into auxiliary nets since they are pat terns.

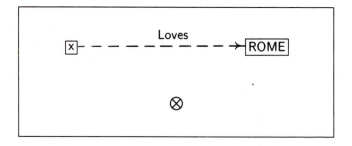

Figure 10.3   Nobody loves Rome. That is, if anybody x loves Rome, falsehoo follows.

containing no antecedents, as in Figure 10.2. This was not a device we dis cussed explicitly in Part I, but it follows from the treatment there of uni versal conditionals – which can have any number of antecedents includin₂ zero.

Why not put this vector into the main net, since it is not a conditional Well, the main net is reserved for ground assertions (non-variable vectors) whereas the auxiliary nets contain patterns for matching onto the main net Such matches result in adding further ground assertions to the main net. Th vector in Figure 10.2 matches the main net in as many ways as there are term in the main net. In that vector, $\boxed{x}$ will match any term in the net, since ther are no conditions in the auxiliary net constraining how it should match. Th result is that we can add the vector $\boxed{} \underline{\quad\text{Loves}\quad} \boxed{\text{ROME}}$ to each term in the main net. Everybody (everything) loves Rome.

How would we say that nobody loves Rome? As a semantic net, w know to represent that as in Figure 10.3.

A single match for the vector $\boxed{x} \underline{\quad\text{Loves}\quad} \boxed{\text{ROME}}$ will allow falsum t be inferred. Plainly, the corresponding clause is:

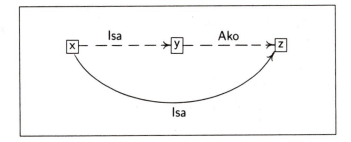

Figure 10.4 Inheritance of kinds. This universal conditional is exemplified by such assertions as 'If Leo is a lion and a lion is a kind of carnivore, then Leo is a carnivore.'

```
Loves(x, ROME) => F
```

Check by reading this in the literal way: 'For any object x, if x loves Rome, then falsehood follows.'

More generally, we can represent the statement that nobody loves anybody (anything?) as:

```
Loves(x, y) => F
```

The quasi-English reading is, 'For any objects x and y, if x loves y, then falsehood follows.' One single match of the antecedent atom here will allow falsehood to be inferred; that is, if anybody loves anybody (including himself or herself), falsehood follows. So nobody loves anybody.

In the next example, we look at a clause that needs several variables. It is one of the 'laws of inheritance of kinds':

- If an object is an instance of one kind of a thing, then it is also an instance of that thing.

Figure 10.4 shows this represented in an auxiliary net. The semantic net indicates how to write the clause, namely as:

```
Isa(x,y),Ako(y,z) => Isa(x,z)
```

Read literally, 'For any objects x, y, and z, if x is an instance of (kind) y, and y is a kind of z, then x is an instance of the kind z.'

In rather abstract cases like this one, the logic is much clearer than its reading in quasi-English, and certainly than in ordinary English: 'If an object is an instance of one kind of a thing, then it is also an instance of that thing.'

As with mathematics, a major justification for developing a symbolic notation for logic is to increase the clarity and precision with which abstract concepts can be expressed.

Exercise 10.2   Assuming a domain of people, and that the relation of one person listening to another talking is represented by Listens(⟨listener⟩, ⟨talker⟩), write the following in CFL:

> (a)   Socrates listens to Plato.
> (b)   Socrates listens to everybody.
> (c)   Plato listens to nobody.
> (d)   If Socrates listens to somebody, they listen to him.
> (e)   Anybody who listens to Socrates, listens to Plato.
> (f)   Socrates listens to everybody who listens to Plato.
> (g)   Nobody listens to Socrates or Plato.
> (h)   Everybody who listens to Socrates and Plato, is listened to by them.
> (i)   Aristotle listens to anybody who listens to Socrates or Plato.
> (j)   Anybody who listens to anybody, listens to Socrates.
> (k)   Everyone listens to everyone.
> (l)   Anyone who listens to Socrates or Plato is listened to by everyone.

10.2   Substitution for variables

In the next chapter, we will have a close look at the semantics of CFL. The significant part of that job will be to provide a tighter account of the semantics of variables than we did in Part I. To prepare for that, we will spend the rest of this chapter clarifying some syntactic aspects of variables (instances and substitution), and revisiting and extending the earlier informal theory of semantic interpretations.

First, we need to define an **instance** and a **ground instance** of a universal clause. We will state the definition now, then explain it. This definition serves to make precise the idea of ground instances that was introduced in Chapter 4.

Definition   Instance of a universal clause

An **instance** of a clause C is obtained by the uniform substitution of one or more variables in C by a term. If each variable is uniformly substituted by a constant term, the result is called a **ground instance**.

(Def. Instance)

Note, at present the only sort of **constant term** we have encountered
is the constant. We will meet others later.

The concept of **uniform substitution** is crucial to this definition. To
grasp it, we need to distinguish between a variable on the one hand (or any
symbol for that matter), and on the other, its **occurrences** in an expression.
For example, in the clause:

```
Capital(x,y),In(x,AUSTRALIA)
 => State(y),Territory(y),Eq(x,CANBERRA)
```

there are just two variables: x (which occurs three times) and y (which also
has three occurrences).

Exercise 10.3   What does that clause say? Give a reading in quasi-English and
idiomatic English, and draw the auxiliary net for it. The documentation for the
interpretation is:

```
Capital(⟨city⟩, ⟨area⟩)
In(⟨inside object⟩, ⟨surrounding object⟩)
Eq(⟨object⟩, ⟨object⟩)
```
– the two ⟨object⟩s are identical, that is, one and
the same.

The concept of identity here is the same as that conveyed by '=' in
mathematics, and from now on we will use Eq in this sense. Jupiter and the
biggest planet in the solar system are Eq objects, but two 'identical' twins are
not Eq, since they are different objects even though they look alike.

Definition   Uniform Substitution

Let E be any expression of CFL, let v be a variable, and let t be any term.
(Note that we talk about expressions of CFL here, not formulae or clauses.
An **expression** of CFL (or any language) is just a sequence of symbols of that
language. It need not be meaningful, or even syntactically correct.) Then the
uniform substitution of t for v in E – which we denote by $E\{t/v\}$ – is the
expression that results from E by replacing every occurrence of v in E by t.

(Def. Subst.)

For example:

```
Capital(x,y) => City(x){SYDNEY/x}
```

(read as 'Sydney for x') is the clause:

```
Capital(SYDNEY, y) => City(SYDNEY)
```

This notation for substitution allows us to describe **chains** of substitutions like this:

Capital(x,y) => City(x){y/x}{z/y}

(read as 'y for x, z for y') is the clause:

Capital(y,y) => City(y){z/y}

that is:

Capital(z,z) => City(z)

What we did was to apply {y/x} to the clause Capital(x,y) => City(x) *then* apply {z/y} to the result. The substitutions are done in sequence, not in a simultaneous fashion which would yield the clause Capital(y,z) => City(y).

Exercise 10.4   What CFL expressions are denoted by these substitution descriptions?

    (a)   P(x,y) => P(y,x){A/x}
    (b)   P(x,y) => P(y,x){x/y}
    (c)   P(x,y) => P(y,x){A/z}
    (d)   P(x,y) => P(y,x){A/x}{z/y}
    (e)   P(x,y) => P(y,x){x/y}{B/x}

EXAMPLE 10.1

In a particular application of CFL, the only two constants are S and P. Describe, using substitution notation, and list, all the ground instances of:

Taught(x,y) => Learned-from(y,x)

There are just four ground instances. If we call this clause C, then they are:

Description	Clause
C{S/x}{S/y}	Taught(S,S) => Learned-from(S,S)
C{S/x}{P/y}	Taught(S,P) => Learned-from(P,S)
C{P/x}{S/y}	Taught(P,S) => Learned-from(S,P)
C{P/x}{P/y}	Taught(P,P) => Learned-from(P,P)

Note that no matter how long the series of substitutions we perform on a clause C, the result is still an instance of C. To see this, observe that $C\{v'/v\}$ is an instance of C: every occurrence of v being replaced by v'. Then $C\{v'/v\}\{v''/v'\}$ is also an instance of C: every occurrence of v is now replaced by v''.

Exercise 10.5   Find substitutions that will transform $F(x,y,z)$ into $F(y,z,x)$.

10.3   Interpretations and models

Before going on to the formal account of the semantics of CFL in the next chapter, please check that you have a good grasp of the informal semantics with which we have been operating so far: particularly the idea of an interpretation and of the valuations of variables within an interpretation. The key to understanding semantics is the idea of an interpretation, and that a given set of clauses will, in general, have a very large number of interpretations in which they are all true. Many people suppose there is just one interpretation for a set of clauses (assertions) – the 'obvious' one that we have called the **intended interpretation** – and that all that matters is to show that the clauses are true in *that* interpretation.

Indeed, a particular set of assertions, or knowledge base, is set up by someone in order to record information about some subject matter – which we called an intended interpretation – such as the nature of the Solar System, Australian geography, or the events in Shakespeare's *Julius Caesar*. It helps to imagine a knowledge base as being information programmed into a computer, using CFL as the **knowledge base language**, that is, as the language in which the knowledge base is written. By typing in a set of CFL clauses, we add them to the computer's knowledge base; they become all the assertions that the computer 'knows'.

But just what the intended interpretation for a knowledge base is, may be far from precisely definable. Imagine a police knowledge base about an unsolved murder, containing the clause:

```
=> {The-murderer(SMITH),
    The-murderer(BROWN),
    The-murderer(JONES)}
```
(2)

The police plainly believe that one of these three suspects is the murderer, but do not know which. So, what is the intended interpretation for the knowledge base? We can imagine a world in which Smith is the murderer, another in which it is Brown and a third with Jones. But none of these is the *intended* interpretation, since the police have not identified which of the three did the crime. So, *no* world is the intended interpretation. But could we say the real, actual world is the intended interpretation? No, for perhaps the police are all wrong and McGurk was the murderer – so (2) is *false* in that interpretation.

For these reasons, and other deeper ones, logicians do not talk of intended interpretations when doing semantics. However helpful the idea might be to a user of CFL, such as the police, when setting up a knowledge base and translating between its clauses and English, it is far from being a clear enough notion to be useful in determining truth-conditions in a knowledge base.

Instead, it is necessary to do semantics in the manner in which we did for semantic nets:

- Define a world as a set of objects (domain of discourse) plus relations on those objects.

- Define an interpretation as giving denotations in that world to every constant and predicate in the knowledge base: objects to constants and n-ary relations to n-ary predicates (including properties as one-place relations).

We can expect that the police knowledge base will have all of its clauses true in very many interpretations. Then, any reasoning carried out in this knowledge base, which will use a number of those clauses as premises, will reach new conclusions in the form of new clauses. If our reasoning methods are consistent, those conclusions will be true in *every one* of the interpretations in which all the knowledge base clauses are true.

Any interpretation in which all the clauses in a knowledge base are true, is called a **model** of that knowledge base. Now, looking at our police knowledge base, we may not be able to tell if it has a model in which SMITH denotes an object with the property that The-murderer denotes, or a model in which BROWN does, or one in which JONES does. But to solve the crime, that is just what we want to know.

Suppose now, that by carrying out some reasoning on the knowledge base (the reasoning rules are the subject of the next few chapters), we are able to infer both these clauses:

```
The-murderer(BROWN) => {}                    (3)
The-murderer(JONES) => {}                     (4)
```

From what was said in the previous chapter, these clauses are *false* in any interpretation in which BROWN denotes an object having the property denoted by The-murderer, or in which JONES does. That is, the knowledge base has no model in which The-murderer(BROWN) is true, and no model in which

The-murderer(JONES) is true. Consequently, since (2) is a clause in the knowledge base, and is therefore true in every model of the knowledge base, it must follow that in *every model* of the knowledge base SMITH must denote an object having the property denoted by The-murderer. That is, in every model, The-murderer(SMITH) is true, and it does not matter what object SMITH denotes, or what property The-murderer denotes.

But, for all the vagueness of the police's intended interpretation, they did mean SMITH to denote Smith the suspect, and The-murderer to denote the property of being the murderer. So on any such interpretation, the police can conclude that Smith was the murderer.

Exercise 10.6   Given that (3) was deduced from the knowledge base by consistent manipulation rules, why does it follow that there is no model for that knowledge base in which The-murderer(BROWN) is true?

SUMMARY

- **Definition Variable**. A variable consists of a lower-case letter, followed by zero or more lower-case letters, digits, or hyphens.

  (Def. Variable)

- **Term.** Any constant or variable is a term.

- **Universal clause.** Any clause containing a variable.

- **Reading universal clauses.** Note the variables occurring in the clause, say $v_1, v_2, \ldots$. Then read as 'For any objects v_1 and v_2 and ..., if ⟨antecedent⟩ and ⟨antecedent⟩ and ..., then ⟨consequent⟩ or ⟨consequent⟩ or ...' Then rework that **quasi-English** into idiomatic English.

- **Unconditional universal assertion.** To assert the truth of a universal atom A for all values of its variables, write {} => A.

- **Unconditional universal denial.** To assert the falsity of a universal atom A for all values of its variables, write A => {}.

- **Definition Instance of a universal clause**. An **instance** of a clause C is obtained by the uniform substitution of one or more variables in C by a term. If each variable is uniformly substituted by a constant term, the result is called a **ground instance**.

  (Def. Instance)

- **Occurrences of expressions.** Distinguish between an expression (or any typographical entity) and its occurrences. There are just six different letters in 'occurrence', one of which occurs three times.

- **Definition Uniform substitution.** Let E be any expression of CFL, let v be a variable, and let t be any term. Then the **uniform substitution** of t for v in E – which we denote by $E\{t/v\}$ – is the expression that results from E by replacing every occurrence of v in E by t.

  (Def. Subst)

- **Substitution chaining.** An instance of an instance of an expression E is still an instance of E.

- **Knowledge base.** A set of statements, acting as assertions under some interpretation intended by their author. CFL is a knowledge base language.

- **Interpretation (revision).** Define a world as a set of objects (domain of discourse) plus relations on those objects, Define an interpretation as giving denotations in that world to every constant and predicate in the knowledge base: objects to constants and n-ary relations to n-ary predicates (including properties as one-place relations).

- **Model.** A model for a set of clauses is any interpretation in which they are all true.

Chapter 11
Interpretation and satisfaction

In this chapter and the next we shall formally define the semantics for CFL. Most of the ideas here will be familiar from our earlier and less formal exposition of them. The present aim is to make them tight and rigorous enough to explain the proof theory machinery that we shall shortly be introducing.

The job of explaining the semantic machinery for CFL falls naturally into three parts:

- Define the concept of an *interpretation* of CFL atoms and clauses; together with the associated notions of a *world*, *denotations*, and *valuations*.

- Define the concept of *satisfaction* of an atom in an interpretation, using the concepts, such as denotation, that have just been defined. We shall do both of these parts in this chapter.

- Use the concept of satisfaction to define the concepts of *truth* and *falsity*. We shall do that in the next chapter.

11.1   Interpretations

We begin with the idea of a **knowledge base**, K, which is simply any set of CFL clauses. The clauses in K are known as the **axioms** of K. Theoretically, there may be an infinity of axioms in a knowledge base, but for practical purposes, as in expert systems work, the number of clauses is hundreds, or at most thousands.

Each clause in a knowledge base consists of predicates and constants which, together with variables, are combined in stated ways using parentheses, braces, commas and '=>', to make up a clause. The approach taken in formal semantics is to say that the semantic significance of variables, parentheses, braces, commas and '=>' is quite fixed across all interpretations; consequently we call these the **logical symbols** in CFL. But the choice of constants and predicates, and the question of their meaning, is up to the user of the knowledge base. Consequently we call these the **non-logical symbols**. Once their meaning is fixed, the semantics of the non-logical symbols in an atom or clause can be employed to determine the semantics of the atom or clause as a whole.

An **interpretation** $\mathcal{I}$ consists of two things:

(1)   A **domain of discourse** $\mathcal{W}$, which is a non-empty set of objects; ($\mathcal{W}$ stands for *world*), and

(2)   A **denotation function** $\mathcal{D}$ from the non-logical symbols in K to objects in $\mathcal{W}$ and relations defined on objects in $\mathcal{W}$.

(Write this as: $\mathcal{I} = \langle \mathcal{W}, \mathcal{D} \rangle$.)

We need to specify $\mathcal{D}$ for constants and predicates:

- For every constant c occurring in K, $\mathcal{D}(c)$ is an object in $\mathcal{W}$. That is, every constant denotes an object in $\mathcal{W}$.

- For every n-ary predicate P occurring in K, $\mathcal{D}(P)$ is an n-ary relation in $\mathcal{W}$.

As will be recalled from high-school set theory, an n-ary relation in some set $\mathcal{W}$ of objects can be represented as a set of n-tuples of objects in $\mathcal{W}$. For example, in the set $\{1, 2, 3, 4, 5\}$, the relation of being one less than is the set of pairs:

$$\{\langle 1, 2 \rangle, \langle 2, 3 \rangle, \langle 3, 4 \rangle, \langle 4, 5 \rangle\}$$

A one-place relation, which is what a one-place predicate denotes, is simply some subset of $\mathcal{W}$.

Exercise 11.1   In the set $\{1, 2, 3, 4, 5\}$, write down:

(a)   The 1-ary relation of being an odd number.
(b)   The 2-ary relation of being the double of (with the number to be doubled coming first in each member of the relation).
(c)   The 3-ary relation of being the mean of (with the mean number coming second in each member of the relation).

EXAMPLE 11.1

In this example, we will set up a knowledge base and a particular interpretation for it. In the interpretation there are six objects: Rome, Caesar, Calpurnia, Brutus, Casca, and a slave. The information about this world, which we wish to represent in the knowledge base, is that Rome is a city and the rest are people, Brutus and Casca stabbed Caesar and the others did not, and the slave is the only person who does not love Rome, and Rome does not either. We are to put this information into a CFL knowledge base, and set up an interpretation I for it which represents this information only.

First, we set up the knowledge base K_R (R is for Rome):

$$
\begin{array}{lr}
\text{Stabbed(R,C)} \Rightarrow \{\} & \textbf{(1)} \\
\text{Stabbed(C,C)} \Rightarrow \{\} & \textbf{(2)} \\
\text{Stabbed(CL,C)} \Rightarrow \{\} & \textbf{(3)} \\
\{\} \Rightarrow \text{Stabbed(B,C)} & \textbf{(4)} \\
\{\} \Rightarrow \text{Stabbed(CS,C)} & \textbf{(5)} \\
\text{Stabbed(S1,C)} \Rightarrow \{\} & \textbf{(6)} \\
\{\} \Rightarrow \text{Loves(C,R)} & \textbf{(7)} \\
\{\} \Rightarrow \text{Loves(CL,R)} & \textbf{(8)} \\
\{\} \Rightarrow \text{Loves(B,R)} & \textbf{(9)} \\
\{\} \Rightarrow \text{Loves(CS,R)} & \textbf{(10)} \\
\text{Loves(S1,R)} \Rightarrow \{\} & \textbf{(11)} \\
\text{Loves(R,R)} \Rightarrow \{\} & \textbf{(12)} \\
\Rightarrow \text{City(R)} & \textbf{(13)} \\
\Rightarrow \text{Person(C)} & \textbf{(14)} \\
\Rightarrow \text{Person(CL)} & \textbf{(15)} \\
\Rightarrow \text{Person(B)} & \textbf{(16)} \\
\Rightarrow \text{Person(CS)} & \textbf{(17)} \\
\Rightarrow \text{Person(S1)} & \textbf{(18)}
\end{array}
$$

Secondly, we set up the interpretation. Note that no documentation has been given so far to explain the non-logical symbols in K_R; that is because the interpretation will do it instead.

Let $\mathcal{I}_R = \langle \mathcal{W}_R, \mathcal{D}_R \rangle$, where:

$$\mathcal{W}_R = \{\text{Rome, Caesar, Calpurnia, Brutus, Casca, the slave}$$
$$\mathcal{D}_R(\mathtt{R}) = \text{Rome}$$
$$\mathcal{D}_R(\mathtt{C}) = \text{Caesar}$$
$$\mathcal{D}_R(\mathtt{CL}) = \text{Calpurnia}$$
$$\mathcal{D}_R(\mathtt{B}) = \text{Brutus}$$
$$\mathcal{D}_R(\mathtt{CS}) = \text{Casca}$$
$$\mathcal{D}_R(\mathtt{S1}) = \text{the slave}$$
$$\mathcal{D}_R(\mathtt{City}) = \{\text{Rome}\}$$
$$\mathcal{D}_R(\mathtt{Person}) = \{\text{Caesar, Calpurnia, Brutus, Casca, the slave}\}$$
$$\mathcal{D}_R(\mathtt{Stabbed}) = \{\langle \text{Brutus, Caesar}\rangle, \langle \text{Casca, Caesar}\rangle\}$$
$$\mathcal{D}_R(\mathtt{Loves}) = \{\langle \text{Caesar, Rome}\rangle, \langle \text{Calpurnia, Rome}\rangle,$$
$$\langle \text{Brutus, Rome}\rangle, \langle \text{Casca, Rome}\rangle\}$$

11.1.1 Variables and valuations

To explain precisely the semantics of variables, our main job is to give a more rigorous account of an idea already familiar, **valuation**. We said in Chapter 5 that the value of a variable is any object in the domain of discourse. We adopt that now, and extend it to the non-logical symbols as well. This will allow a more rigorous definition of satisfaction. Note that a valuation is defined relative to an interpretation.

Definition Valuation

In any interpretation $\mathcal{I} = \langle \mathcal{W}, \mathcal{D} \rangle$ of a knowledge base K, a **valuation** $\mathcal{V}$ is a function such that:

(1)   For every constant c occurring in K, $\mathcal{V}(c) = \mathcal{D}(c)$.

(2)   For every predicate P occurring in K, $\mathcal{V}(P) = \mathcal{D}(P)$.

(3)   For every variable v, $\mathcal{V}(v)$ is an object in $\mathcal{D}$.

For any constant, predicate or variable E, $\mathcal{V}(E)$ is called the **value** of E in the valuation $\mathcal{V}$.

(Def. Valuation)

This means that in any interpretation, the valuation for constants and predicates is the same as their denotation. So, for constants and predicates, all valuations are the same. But for variables (and this explains their variability) different valuations will give a variable different values.

Note that we did not say in the definition, 'For every variable v in K.' This is because in CFL proof theory we often introduce new variables and a given valuation will need to include them too. This means that every valuation will, in theory, give values to an infinity of variables, since there is a (countable) infinity of them. Thus, there will always be an infinity of different valuations in any domain of discourse with more than one object in it. But fortunately, for practical purposes, a piece of reasoning will have only a finite set of variables in it, so the number of valuations that can be defined on them will be finite (provided the domain of discourse is finite). In this book, we will usually consider only the valuations definable on such a finite set of variables.

Exercise 11.2   Given K_R and $\mathcal{I}_R$ from the previous exercise, how many valuations are there if we must provide values for three variables, x, y and z? In general, if we are considering a number n_v of variables, and a (finite) domain of discourse containing n_w objects, how many different valuations are there of all the predicates, constants and variables in question?

11.2   Satisfaction

Our theory of interpretations, centering around the idea of words standing for objects and relations, is now complete. In terms of it, we can now define what it is for statements made out of those words to be true. As a slogan, our theory of truth is:

- A statement is true if the world is as the statement says it is.

For us, the world is a given interpretation, statements are clauses, and the denotation function in the interpretation fixes what the statement is talking about.

11.2.1   Satisfaction for an atom

Take any atom, $P(t_1, \ldots, t_n)$. Here, P is an n-ary predicate, and the t_is $(1 \leq i \leq n)$ are terms (variables or constants, at present). Now take an interpretation $\mathcal{I}$ which gives denotations to all the constants, and the predicate, in this atom. Not every interpretation will do this, for not every interpretation will contain definitions of the $\mathcal{D}$ function for the constants and predicate in an arbitrary atom, since an interpretation is always defined for a particular set of non-logical symbols (namely those found in some knowledge base), not for all non-logical terms. Where an interpretation does define the $\mathcal{D}$ function for the non-logical symbols of a CFL expression E, we will say that the interpretation is **applicable** to E. In discussing satisfaction, we deal only with **applicable interpretations**. And any valuation occurring within an applicable interpretation is called an **applicable valuation**.

In the present case, we are saying that $\mathcal{I}$ is applicable to the atom $P(t_1, \ldots, t_n)$. Consider now a valuation $\mathcal{V}$ for the terms and predicate of that atom in $\mathcal{I}$. In a valuation, every variable denotes some object in the domain $\mathcal{W}$ of $\mathcal{I}$, so behaves, in that valuation, just like a constant. So we can ask whether the objects denoted by those n terms are related in the right order by the relation which is the value of the predicate.

The objects denoted by the n terms in the atom are:

$$\mathcal{V}(t_1), \ldots, \mathcal{V}(t_n)$$

so what we now need to find out is whether the n-tuple of those objects:

$$\langle \mathcal{V}(t_1), \ldots, \mathcal{V}(t_n) \rangle$$

is in the relation which is the value of the predicate P, that is, whether it is a member of the set $\mathcal{V}(P)$. If it is, we say that the atom is *satisfied* by the valuation.

We distil all this discussion into the following definition:

Definition   Satisfaction of atom in valuation

Let $\mathcal{V}$ be a valuation in some interpretation $\mathcal{I} = \langle \mathcal{W}, \mathcal{D} \rangle$ that is applicable to the atom $P(t_1, \ldots, t_n)$, where P is an n-ary predicate and $t_1, \ldots, t_n$ are terms. Then $\mathcal{V}$ **satisfies** $P(t_1, \ldots, t_n)$ only if $\langle \mathcal{V}(t_1), \ldots, \mathcal{V}(t_n) \rangle$ is an element of the relation $\mathcal{V}(P)$ in $\mathcal{W}$.

(Def. Satisfaction)

To that account of satisfaction for *complex atoms* (ones with parts), we must not forget to add the satisfaction conditions of the *simple atoms* T and F. This is easy. T is always satisfied, and F is never satisfied.

Exercise 11.3   Again with K_R and $\mathcal{I}_R$, which valuations do not satisfy Loves(x, R)? (Take it that x is the only variable we need to consider in constructing valuations.)

11.2.2   Satisfaction for a clause

Atoms and clauses are the two types of expression in CFL that can be satisfied (or not satisfied) in a valuation. For this reason, it is useful to have one name for both of them. We will call atoms and clauses, **formulae**.

The definition of satisfaction for a clause *by* a valuation *in* an interpretation, follows closely the informal accounts given earlier. But note that in the definition below, as in the above Def. Satisfaction for atoms, the definition is given without appealing to a notion of truth. In previous chapters, we defined truth first, because it is easier to grasp and can be defined for formulae without variables (**ground formulae**). Then to account for variables, which were introduced later, we needed to define satisfaction; so we used truth, as defined for ground formulae, to help us. This time, we are starting out with variables, so we define satisfaction first using our extended notion of a valuation. Soon, we will define truth in terms of satisfaction. The result is much cleaner.

In the general case, we can describe a clause C as:

$$\{p_1, \ldots, p_m\} \Rightarrow \{q_1, \ldots, q_n\}$$

where $p_1, \ldots, p_m$ are the antecedent atoms, $q_1, \ldots, q_n$ are the consequent atoms, and $m, n \geq 0$. Now, take any interpretation $\mathcal{I}$ that is applicable to C. In that case, we know that each atom of C is either satisfied by a chosen valuation $\mathcal{V}$ in $\mathcal{I}$, or is not satisfied by it. Therefore we define the satisfaction of the whole clause in terms of the satisfaction of its component atoms, exactly as we did earlier for truth of ground conditionals in terms of truth of their component atoms or vectors. The valuation $\mathcal{V}$ in $\mathcal{I}$ is to satisfy C *unless* the forbidden case occurs, where all antecedents are satisfied and no consequents are satisfied. That is the case which would allow us to infer a non-satisfied atom or atoms from ones that are all satisfied (just like inferring falsehood from truth).

We state all that in the following definition, which is worded to account for cases where there are no antecedents or no consequents.

Definition   Satisfaction of clause in valuation

Let $\mathcal{V}$ be a valuation in some interpretation $\mathcal{I} = \langle \mathcal{W}, \mathcal{D} \rangle$ that is applicable to the clause $C = \{p_1, \ldots, p_m\} \Rightarrow \{q_1, \ldots, q_n\}$, where the p_is and the q_js ($0 \leq i \leq m$ and $0 \leq j \leq n$) are atoms. Then $\mathcal{V}$ **satisfies** C only if there is a q_j which $\mathcal{V}$ satisfies, or there is a p_i that $\mathcal{V}$ does not satisfy (or both).

(Def. Satisfaction)

The following facts follow immediately from this definition. Reflecting on them should help to grasp the point (and motivation) of the definition.

Proposition 11.1   Non-satisfaction for clauses

A clause C is not satisfied by a valuation $\mathcal{V}$ in an applicable interpretation only if:

(1) $\mathcal{V}$ satisfies every antecedent of C (or else there are no antecedents), and

(2) $\mathcal{V}$ satisfies no consequent of C (or else there are no consequents).   □

	$\{\} =>$ $q_1, \ldots, q_n$	$p_1, \ldots, p_m$ $=> \{\}$	$p_1, \ldots, p_m$ $=> q_1, \ldots, q_n$
$\mathcal{V}$ *satisfies* *clause*	$\mathcal{V}$ satisfies at least one q_j	$\mathcal{V}$ fails to satisfy at least one p_i	(Either condition to left holds)
$\mathcal{V}$ *does not* *satisfy clause*	$\mathcal{V}$ satisfies no q_j	$\mathcal{V}$ satisfies every p_i	(Both conditions to left hold)

Figure 11.1 Satisfaction conditions for atoms in clauses of various types, tabulated against the satisfaction conditions for the clauses. Table can be read from body to left guide column, or from left guide column to body. An applicable valuation $\mathcal{V}$ is assumed.

Proposition 11.2   Satisfaction of disjunctive consequents

A clause C with no antecedents is satisfied by a valuation $\mathcal{V}$ only if $\mathcal{V}$ satisfies at least one consequent of C.   □

Proposition 11.3   Non-satisfaction of disjunctive consequents

A clause C with no antecedents is *not* satisfied by a valuation $\mathcal{V}$ only if $\mathcal{V}$ satisfies no consequent of C, or C has no consequents.   □

Proposition 11.4   Satisfaction of conjunctive antecedents

A clause C with no consequents is satisfied by a valuation $\mathcal{V}$ only if there is an antecedent of C that $\mathcal{V}$ does not satisfy.   □

Proposition 11.5   Non-satisfaction of conjunctive antecedents

A clause C with no consequents is *not* satisfied by a valuation $\mathcal{V}$ only if $\mathcal{V}$ satisfies no antecedent of C, or C has no antecedents.   □

Proposition 11.6   Empty clause

A clause with no antecedents and no consequents is satisfied by no valuation in any interpretation.   □

We can set out all the above results in a table (see Figure 11.1). This table can be used in two ways. Choose one of the three types of clause.

a) Suppose you know which of the satisfaction conditions for its atoms, listed in the column below the clause type, hold for that clause. Then move across that row to the left side, and read off the satisfaction conditions for the whole clause.

b) Alternatively, suppose you know which of the satisfaction conditions for the whole clause, as listed down the left side, hold for that clause. Then move across that row to the cell in the column under the clause type you chose, and read off the satisfaction conditions for its atoms.

Exercise 11.4   Referring again to the Roman logic K_R and its interpretation $\mathcal{I}_R$, find in each case (if you can) a valuation that satisfies, and a valuation that does not satisfy, each of the following clauses:

(a)	Person(x)	=> Loves(x,R)
(b)		=> Stabbed(x,x)
(c)		=> Loves(x,y)
(d)	Stabbed(x,C)	=> {}
(e)		=> Loves(x,y), Loves(y,x)
(f)	Stabbed(x,y), Stabbed(y,x)	=> {}
(g)		=> Person(C), Person(CL)
(h)	Stabbed(x,C)	=> Loves(x,y)
(i)	Stabbed(x,y)	=> Loves(x,R)
(j)	Stabbed(x,y), Loves(y,z)	=> Loves(x,z)

SUMMARY

- **Knowledge base.** Any set of CFL clauses.

- **Axiom.** For any knowledge base K, any clause in K is called an axiom of K.

- **Logical symbols.** In our CFL typography, variables, parentheses, braces, commas, T, F and '=>'. Their semantic role is defined by the rules of CFL.

- **Non-logical symbols.** Predicates and constants. Their semantic role is defined by the user.

- **Definition Interpretation.** An interpretation $\mathcal{I}$ of a knowledge base K is an ordered pair $\langle \mathcal{W}, \mathcal{D} \rangle$, where:

  (1) $\mathcal{W}$ (the **domain of discourse**) is a nonempty set of objects, and

(2) $\mathcal{D}$ (the **denotation function**) is a function defined on all constants and predicates occurring in K such that:

    (a) $\mathcal{D}(c)$, for each constant c occurring in K, is an object in $\mathcal{W}$, and

    (b) $\mathcal{D}(P)$, for each n-ary predicate P occurring in K, is an n-ary relation in $\mathcal{W}$.

(Def. Interpretation)

- **Definition Valuation.** In any interpretation $\mathcal{I} = \langle \mathcal{W}, \mathcal{D} \rangle$ of a knowledge base K, a **valuation** $\mathcal{V}$ is a function such that:

(1)   For every constant c occurring in K, $\mathcal{V}(c) = \mathcal{D}(c)$.

(2)   For every predicate P occurring in K, $\mathcal{V}(P) = \mathcal{D}(P)$.

(3)   For every variable v, $\mathcal{V}(v)$ is an object in $\mathcal{D}$.

(Def. Valuation)

- **Value.** The object or relation assigned by a valuation to a term or predicate is commonly called its **value in** the valuation.

- **Applicability.** An interpretation $\mathcal{I} = \langle \mathcal{W}, \mathcal{D} \rangle$ is said to be applicable to an expression E of CFL just if $\mathcal{D}$ is defined for all predicates and constants in E. Where an interpretation $\mathcal{I}$ is applicable to E, every valuation occurring in $\mathcal{I}$ is also said to be applicable to E.

- **Definition Satisfaction of atom in valuation.** Let $\mathcal{V}$ be a valuation in some interpretation $\mathcal{I} = \langle \mathcal{W}, \mathcal{D} \rangle$ that is applicable to the atom $P(t_1, \ldots, t_n)$, where P is an n-ary predicate and $t_1, \ldots, t_n$ are terms. Then $\mathcal{V}$ **satisfies** $P(t_1, \ldots, t_n)$ only if $\langle \mathcal{V}(t_1), \ldots, \mathcal{V}(t_n) \rangle$ is an element of the relation $\mathcal{V}(P)$ in $\mathcal{W}$.

(Def. Satisfaction)

- **Definition Satisfaction of T and F.** Every valuation in every interpretation satisfies the atom T, and no valuation in any interpretation satisfies the atom F.

(Def. Satisfaction)

- **Formula.** Any atom or clause, that is, any expression that can be satisfied in a valuation.

- **Definition Satisfaction of clause in valuation.** Let $\mathcal{V}$ be a valuation in some interpretation $\mathcal{I} = \langle \mathcal{W}, \mathcal{D} \rangle$ that is applicable to the clause $C = \{p_1, \ldots, p_m\} \Rightarrow \{q_1, \ldots, q_n\}$, where the p_is and the q_js $(0 \leq i \leq m$ and $0 \leq j \leq n)$ are atoms. Then $\mathcal{V}$ **satisfies** C only if there is a q_j which $\mathcal{V}$ satisfies, or there is a p_i that $\mathcal{V}$ does not satisfy (or both).

(Def. Satisfaction)

- **Satisfaction of particular types of clause.** See propositions 1 to 6 on pp.135–6 above.

Chapter 12
Truth and satisfiability

This chapter completes the study of the semantics of CFL, which began in the last chapter. The primary task is to define truth and falsity for clauses of CFL, which we do in terms of the concept of satisfaction for clauses defined in the last chapter.

We shall explore some of the properties of truth and falsity as defined, and introduce the important related notions of unsatisfiability and logical truth.

12.1   Truth and falsity

The definitions of truth and falsity in terms of satisfaction should now be obvious. We define truth and falsity only for clauses, not atoms, since in CFL only clauses can be asserted (that is, occur in a knowledge base or, as we shall see, be derived by manipulation rules from a knowledge base) so there is no need to extend the concept of truth to an atom.

Definition   Truth of clause in interpretation

Let C be a clause and $\mathcal{I}$ an interpretation applicable to C. Then C is **true** in $\mathcal{I}$ only if every valuation in $\mathcal{I}$ satisfies C; and otherwise C is **false** in $\mathcal{I}$.

(Def. Truth)

When we previously and less rigorously defined truth and falsity just for ground clauses, we did so in such a way that if a clause was not true then it was false, and conversely. This may seem a bit puzzling, when the definition of truth for statements containing variables is compared to what happens in arithmetic, where statements containing variables may well be neither true nor false. In arithmetic, we take a formula like:

$$x + 3 = 5$$

and say it is satisfied by some values of x and not by others (in the standard arithmetical interpretation of this symbolism), but we do not say it is true or false. On the other hand, we do say that:

$$x + 3 = 3 + x$$

is true, because every value for x satisfies that formula; so the definition of *truth* in arithmetic is the same as ours. But in arithmetic we say that:

$$x + 3 = x + 1$$

is false, because *no* value for x satisfies that formula. It seems then, that in arithmetic we take a much narrower view of falsity: not *some* but *all* valuations must fail to satisfy.

The apparent difference can be explained. Suppose we treated our formulae in arithmetic as **identities**, that is, we read them as 'For all values of the variables, ...' Then $x + 3 = 5$ comes out *false*, since it is not true for all values of x. (The other two equations retain their truth-values when treated as identities.) In CFL, we are treating our clauses in the same way, as asserting that the conditional holds for all values of its variables. If we did not, we would end up in some very paradoxical situations indeed. The clause:

```
Person(x) => Loves(x,R)
```

which, as we saw in Exercise 11.4 on p.137, has a satisfying valuation and a non-satisfying one in the Roman logic and its interpretation, $\mathcal{I}_R$, would be neither true nor false. But it says in English that all persons love Rome. Now

hat surely (in the interpretation $\mathcal{I}_R$), is simply false, because the slave does
iot love Rome.

In the logical theory of arithmetic, we describe the difference between
he treatment of $x + 3 = 5$ as an identity and as an equation by saying that
is an identity, its variable is **implicitly universally quantified**, that is,
ve are tacitly treating the identity as an assertion that holds for *all* values
quantities) of the variable. By contrast, when we treat it as an equation,
ts variable is **implicitly existentially quantified**, that is, we are tacitly
reating the equation as an assertion that holds for *some* value (quantity) of
he variable.

In CFL, we always treat our clauses as implicitly universally quantified.

12.1.1 Properties of truth and falsity

3y combining the definition of truth for clauses with the definition of satis-
action for clauses in Chapter 11, we can derive a statement of the truth
:onditions and falsity conditions for clauses.

Proposition 12.1   Truth conditions of clause

A clause C is true in an applicable interpretation $\mathcal{I}$ only if, for each valuation
$\mathcal{V}$ in $\mathcal{I}$, either:

1)   There is an antecedent of C which $\mathcal{V}$ does not satisfy,

or

2)   There is a consequent of C which $\mathcal{V}$ does satisfy.

Proof Suppose this is not so. That is, suppose, contrary to this proposition,
:hat there is a valuation $\mathcal{V}$ in $\mathcal{I}$ which satisfies all antecedents of C (if it has
any), and satisfies no consequents of C (if it has any). Then by Proposition
11.1, $\mathcal{V}$ does not satisfy C. But in that case, by the definition of truth, C
s not true in $\mathcal{I}$. Therefore, our supposition here is incompatible with the
assumption that C is true in $\mathcal{I}$, so we reject it.   □

Proposition 12.2   Falsity conditions of clause

A clause C is false in an applicable interpretation $\mathcal{I}$ only if there exists a
valuation $\mathcal{V}$ in $\mathcal{I}$ which both:

1)   Satisfies every antecedent of C (or else there are no antecedents),

and

2)   Satisfies no consequent of C (or else there are no consequents).

Proof   Suppose this is not so. That is, suppose there is no such valuation as the one described here. In that case, for any valuation $\mathcal{V}$ in $\mathcal{I}$, one or other (or both) of these two conditions, (1) and (2), is false. But if condition (1) is false there is an antecedent of C not satisfied by $\mathcal{V}$, in which case $\mathcal{V}$ satisfies the clause. Similarly, if condition (2) is false, there is a consequent of C that $\mathcal{V}$ satisfies, in which case $\mathcal{V}$ satisfies the clause C.

Thus, under our supposition, every valuation $\mathcal{V}$ satisfies the clause C that is, by the definition of truth for clauses, C is true in $\mathcal{I}$. In that case by Def. Truth for clauses again, C is not false in $\mathcal{I}$, which contradicts our assumption that it *is* false in $\mathcal{I}$. So, where we have a clause C false in $\mathcal{I}$, we must reject our supposition above.   ☐

Now that the truth and falsity conditions of clauses are known, we can state a number of corollaries about special cases of clauses, which follow immediately from these two propositions.

Proposition 12.3   Truth of disjunctive consequents

A clause C with no antecedents is true in an interpretation $\mathcal{I}$, only if every valuation $\mathcal{V}$ satisfies at least one consequent of C. (Compare Proposition 11.2.)   ☐

Proposition 12.4   Falsity of disjunctive consequents

A clause C with no antecedents is false in an interpretation $\mathcal{I}$, only if every valuation $\mathcal{V}$ satisfies no consequent of C, or C has no consequents. (Compare Proposition 11.3.)   ☐

Proposition 12.5   Truth of conjunctive antecedents

A clause C with no consequents is true in an interpretation $\mathcal{I}$, only if for every valuation $\mathcal{V}$ there is an antecedent of C that $\mathcal{V}$ does not satisfy. (Compare Proposition 11.4.)   ☐

Proposition 12.6   Falsity of conjunctive antecedents

A clause C with no consequents is false in an interpretation $\mathcal{I}$, only if every valuation $\mathcal{V}$ satisfies no antecedent of C, or C has no antecedents. (Compare Proposition 11.5.)   ☐

Proposition 12.7   Falsity of empty clause

A clause with no antecedents and no consequents is false in every interpretation.   ☐

	{} => $q_1, \ldots, q_n$	$p_1, \ldots, p_m$ => {}	$p_1, \ldots, p_m$ => $q_1, \ldots, q_n$
clause *true*	Every $\mathcal{V}$ (a) satisfies at least one q_j	Every $\mathcal{V}$ (b) fails to satisfy at least one p_i	Every $\mathcal{V}$ (b) or (a)
clause *false*	some $\mathcal{V}$ (c) satisfies no q_j	some $\mathcal{V}$ (d) satisfies every p_i	some $\mathcal{V}$ (d) and (c)

Figure 12.1 Truth conditions for atoms in clauses of various types, tabulated against the truth conditions for the clauses. Table can be read from body to left guide column, or from left guide column to body. An applicable interpretation is assumed.

It is instructive to draw up a truth-conditions table for these results, to parallel the satisfaction-conditions table, Figure 11.1. See Figure 12.1.

Note that the cells in the *clause true* row are the same as in the *satisfies clause* row of Figure 11.1, except that the stated conditions now must hold for every $\mathcal{V}$ in the interpretation, that is, for a clause of a given type to be true, its satisfaction conditions must hold in all valuations.

In the *clause false* row, the conditions again are as in the *not satisfy clause* row, except they need hold only for some $\mathcal{V}$ or other in the interpretation. That is, for a clause of a given type to be false, its non-satisfaction conditions must hold in at least one valuation.

Exercise 12.1   Which clauses in Exercise 11.4 are true in the given interpretation $\mathcal{I}_R$, and which are false? Give English readings for them.

12.2   Unsatisfiability

In arithmetic, as we have seen, one wants to describe $x + 3 = x + 1$ as 're-ally' false – it seems 'falser' than $x + 3 = 5$, even on the implicit universal

quantification reading of the equations. In fact, we say that $x + 3 = x +$
is *unsatisfiable*, for no value of the variable satisfies it. This gives rise to
definition of a useful pair of concepts: *unsatisfiability* and *satisfiability*, whic
like truth and falsity, and unlike satisfaction and non-satisfaction, are define
by taking into account all possible valuations in an interpretation, not just i
terms of a particular valuation.

Definition   Satisfiability of a Clause

A clause C is **satisfiable** in an applicable interpretation $\mathcal{I}$, only if there is
valuation in $\mathcal{I}$ that satisfies C, otherwise the clause is **unsatisfiable** in $\mathcal{I}$.

(Def. Satisfiable

As we did for truth and falsity above, we can state and prove th
satisfiability and unsatisfiability conditions for clauses, by using the abov
definition in conjunction with Def. Satisfaction for clauses, from Chapter 1
Together, we call these four types of conditions **acceptance condition**
which show the manners in which a given clause can be accepted in an inter
pretation.

Proposition 12.8   Satisfiability conditions of clause

A clause C is satisfiable in an applicable interpretation $\mathcal{I}$, only if there exist
a valuation $\mathcal{V}$ in $\mathcal{I}$, such that there is an antecedent in C which $\mathcal{V}$ does no
satisfy, or a consequent that it does satisfy, or both.

Proof   The proof is immediate from Def. Satisfaction and Def. Satisfiabilit
for clauses.   [

Proposition 12.9   Unsatisfiability conditions of clause

A clause C is unsatisfiable in an applicable interpretation $\mathcal{I}$, only if for eac
valuation $\mathcal{V}$ in $\mathcal{I}$, both:

(1) $\mathcal{V}$ satisfies every antecedent of C (or else there are no antecedents), an
(2) $\mathcal{V}$ satisfies no consequent of C (or else there are no consequents)

Proof   The proof is immediate from Def. Satisfiability for clauses and Propo
sition 11.1.   [

Now we can write down, just as we did for truth and falsity, the coro
laries of these propositions for special cases of clauses. This will give us quite
welter of propositions, all with family resemblances, about satisfaction, truth
and satisfiability. It would be unwise to try to learn them by rote: they ar
here for reference purposes only, and all of them can be quickly and easily con
structed by anyone who grasps the underlying definitions of satisfaction/non

	$\{\} \Rightarrow$ $q_1, \ldots, q_n$	$p_1, \ldots, p_m$ $\Rightarrow \{\}$	$p_1, \ldots, p_m$ $\Rightarrow q_1, \ldots, q_n$
clause *satisfiable*	Some $\mathcal{V}$ (a) satisfies at least one q_j	Some $\mathcal{V}$ (b) fails to satisfy at least one p_i	Some $\mathcal{V}$ (b) or (a)
clause *unsatisfiable*	Every $\mathcal{V}$ (c) satisfies no q_j	Every $\mathcal{V}$ (d) satisfies every p_i	Every $\mathcal{V}$ (d) and (c)

Figure 12.2 Satisfiability conditions for atoms in clauses of various types, tabulated against the satisfiability conditions for the clauses. The table can be read from body to left guide column, or from left guide column to body. An applicable interpretation is assumed.

satisfaction, truth/falsity, and satisfiability/unsatisfiability. In fact, the test of your understanding of the semantics involved is simply to construct a given proposition when asked, for example 'What are the satisfiability conditions for a clause with no antecedents?' (For an answer, see the next proposition.) Figure 12.2 summarizes these results.

Proposition 12.10   Satisfiability of disjunctive consequents

A clause C with no antecedents is satisfiable in an interpretation $\mathcal{I}$, only if there exists a valuation that satisfies at least one consequent of C.   □

Proposition 12.11   Non-satisfiability of disjunctive consequents

A clause C with no antecedents is *not* satisfiable in an interpretation $\mathcal{I}$, only if, for every valuation $\mathcal{V}$ in $\mathcal{I}$, $\mathcal{V}$ satisfies no consequent of C, or C has no consequents.   □

Proposition 12.12   Satisfiability of conjunctive antecedents

A clause C with no consequents is satisfiable in an interpretation $\mathcal{I}$, only if there is a valuation $\mathcal{V}$ in $\mathcal{I}$ that does not satisfy some antecedent of C.   □

Proposition 12.13   Non-satisfiability of conjunctive antecedents

A clause C with no consequents is *not* satisfiable in an interpretation $\mathcal{I}$, only if every valuation $\mathcal{V}$ satisfies no antecedent of C, or C has no antecedents. ⸋

Note that this is the same as saying that no $\mathcal{V}$ satisfies any antecedent of C (which automatically includes the case of C having no antecedents).

Proposition 12.14   Unsatisfiability of empty clause

A clause with no antecedents and no consequents is unsatisfiable in every interpretation.   ⸋

The diagram we used to sum up these facts (Figure 12.2) is very similar to the two previous figures (Figures 11.1 and 12.1). The patterns that emerge in a study of these diagrams are what really matter for an understanding of semantics.

Exercise 12.2   Sum up the difference between truth and satisfiability, and between falsity and unsatisfiability.

Exercise 12.3   Repeat Exercise 12.1 for satisfiability and unsatisfiability.

12.2.1   Relations between acceptance conditions

We can draw a useful diagram of the acceptance conditions for a clause in an interpretation. See Figure 12.3.

This is how we use Figure 12.3 to study the pattern of acceptance conditions for clauses. For a given clause C, we look for a satisfying and a non-satisfying valuation. If there is a satisfying valuation, then write in C at $\boxed{\text{satisfaction}}$, and if there is a non-satisfying valuation, write in C at $\boxed{\text{non-satisfaction}}$.

Now, if C occurs at $\boxed{\text{satisfaction}}$, it is satisfiable, so we can immediately mark C in at $\boxed{\text{SATISFIABLE}}$ as well. If C is also satisfied by all valuations, mark C in at $\boxed{\text{TRUE}}$ as well. In this last case, C is marked in at both the left-hand acceptance values, as well as at $\boxed{\text{satisfaction}}$, but not at $\boxed{\text{non-satisfaction}}$, so we have completed our marking for C.

In the same way, if C occurs at $\boxed{\text{non-satisfaction}}$, mark it in at $\boxed{\text{FALSE}}$ as well, then check if this failure of satisfaction holds for all valuations. If so

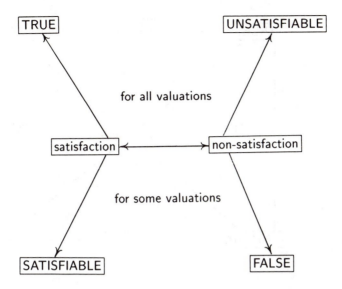

Figure 12.3   Relations between acceptance values and satisfaction for clauses.

mark C in at ⌞UNSATISFIABLE⌟ as well.

If we now look just at the four acceptance conditions, and forget the underlying satisfaction conditions, we get a square as in Figure 12.4 below, called a **square of opposition**. Where on this square could a given clause C be marked? The answers are all forthcoming from the discussion of Figure 12.3, above.

(1)   **Entailment**. For a start, if a clause is marked at a top corner of the square, it will also be marked at the corner below it. If a clause is true in an interpretation, it must also be satisfiable. Similarly, if unsatisfiable, it must also be false. Truth of a clause **entails** its satisfiability, and unsatisfiability entails falsity. If wherever something has one property A, it follows that it must have another property B, we say that property A **entails** property B.

(2)   **Exclusiveness**. If a clause occurs at one top corner, it cannot occur at the other. A particular clause might not be marked at either top corner, but certainly, no clause will be marked at both. This situation we describe by saying that truth and unsatisfiability are **mutually exclusive** properties of clauses. Another name for this is to say truth and unsatisfiability are **contrary** properties. In general, if two properties are such that no object can have both of them (though it could have

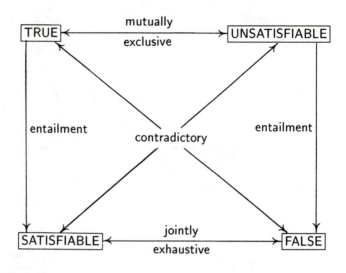

Figure 12.4   Square of opposition for acceptance values of clauses.

one or neither of them), we call those two properties **contraries** or **mutually exclusive**.

(3)   **Exhaustiveness.** If a clause does *not* occur at one bottom corner, it must occur at the other one. A particular clause might be marked at both bottom corners, but certainly, no clause will be marked at neither. This situation we describe by saying that satisfiability and falsity are **jointly exhaustive** properties. In general, if two properties are such that no object can lack both of them (though it could have one or other or both of them), we call those two properties **jointly exhaustive**. An old name for them is **sub-contraries**.

(4)   **Contradictoriness.** On any diagonal in this square, a clause will be marked at just one end of that diagonal, never both, never neither. So, truth and falsity are both mutually exclusive and jointly exhaustive, as are satisfiability and unsatisfiability. Wherever two properties are both mutually exclusive and jointly exhaustive, we say they are **contradictory** properties.

Squares of opposition were studied by classical and medieval logicians, though not in connection with CFL. They keep cropping up in all sorts of subject matter, just because the component relations of entailment, contrariety, etc. are so common. It is not hard to show that if four properties occur in two contradictory pairs, and *one* of the around-the-edge relations of a square of opposition holds between two of those four properties, then the four can be arranged into a square of opposition. For instance, if rich and poor are contradictories, and honest and dishonest are too, then on the view that wealth and honesty are mutually exclusive properties, we have a square of opposition. (But are those two pairs *really* contradictories, or just contraries?)

Exercise 12.4   In the sort of square of opposition we have looked at, we write *properties* into corners and then take a given *object* and mark it in at the two corners whose properties it has. Equally, we could write four objects in at the corners which have the opposition relations amongst themselves concerning a given property, which gets marked in at the two corners of whose objects it is a property. For example, we can take four sets of ground clauses:

(1) $\{\} => p; \quad \{\} => q$
(2) $\{\} => p, q$
(3) $p => \{\}; \quad q => \{\}$
(4) $p, q => \{\}$

and arrange them in a square of opposition according to having the property of being true in a given interpretation. Do so.

12.3   Logical truth

Logicians have traditionally been interested in statements that are true in every interpretation, for these are the **laws of logic** – statements that cannot be false no matter what. Examples in CFL are (where p, q are any atoms):

Id $p \quad => \quad p$
Weakening $p \quad => \quad p, q$
Weakening $p, q \quad => \quad p$

Exercise 12.5   Prove that Id is true in every interpretation.

Definition   Logically true clause

A clause C is **logically true** only if it is true in every applicable interpretation. It is also said to be a **logical law**.

(Def. Log. True)

Definition   Logically false clause

A clause C is **logically false** only if it is false in every applicable interpretation. It is also said to be a **logical contradiction**.

(Def. Log. False)

Exercise 12.6   Find a logically false clause.

Exercise 12.7   Could an atom be logically true?

SUMMARY

- **Acceptance conditions of clause.** The conditions under which, in a given interpretation, it is true, or false, or satisfiable, or unsatisfiable.

- **Acceptance values of a clause.** In any interpretation, the acceptance values of a clause are those two of its four acceptance conditions which hold.

- **Definition Truth of clause in interpretation.** Let C be a clause and I an interpretation applicable to C. Then C is **true** in I only if every valuation in I satisfies C; and otherwise C is **false** in I.

   (Def. Truth)

- **Truth conditions for clauses.** A clause C is **false** in an interpretation I only if, for some valuation V in I, there is no consequent of C it satisfies and no antecedent of C it does not satisfy. Otherwise C is **true** in I. (Note how this wording automatically allows for there being no antecedents or consequents.)

- **Satisfiability conditions for clauses.** A clause C is **satisfiable** in an interpretation I only if, for some valuation V in I, there is a consequent of C it satisfies or an antecedent of C it does not satisfy.

- **Acceptance conditions and satisfaction.** For valuations V in an interpretation I, a clause is satisfiable (true) in I only if its satisfaction condition holds for one or more (all) valuations V; and false (unsatisfiable) in I only if its non-satisfaction condition holds for one or more (all) valuations V.

- **Implicit universal quantification.** A universal formula is being asserted as implicitly universally quantified only if it is asserted as holding for all values of its variables.

- **Definition Satisfiability of a clause**. A clause C is satisfiable in an applicable interpretation $\mathcal{I}$ only if there is a valuation in $\mathcal{I}$ that satisfies C, otherwise the clause is **unsatisfiable** in $\mathcal{I}$.

  (Def. Satisfiable)

- **Mutually exclusive properties**. Two properties are mutually exclusive only if they cannot both hold of any object.

- **Jointly exhaustive properties**. Two properties are jointly exhaustive only if they cannot both fail to hold of any object.

- **Entailment between properties**. Property A entails property B only if anything with property A must also have property B.

- **Contradictory properties**. Mutually exclusive and jointly exhaustive pairs of properties.

- **Square of opposition**. Relationship set holding between four items occurring in contradictory pairs with two of them (one from each pair) being mutually exclusive, jointly exhaustive, or one entailing the other.

- **Definition Logically true clause**. A clause C is **logically true** only if it is true in every applicable interpretation. It is also said to be a **logical law**.

  (Def. Log. True)

- **Definition Logically false clause**. A clause C is **logically false** only if it is false in every applicable interpretation. It is also said to be a **logical contradiction**.

  (Def. Log. False)

Further reading for Part II

Clausal Form Logic arose out of the pioneering research of Gerhard Gentzen and Jacques Herbrand. See G. Gentzen, 'Investigations in Logical Deduction', (1936) in M. Szabo (ed.) *The Collected Papers of Gerhard Gentzen*, Amsterdam: North-Holland, 1969; and J. Herbrand, 'Researches in the Theory of Demonstration', (1930) in J. van Heijenoort (ed.) *From Frege to Gödel, a Source Book in Mathematical Logic*, Cambridge MA: Harvard University Press, 1967.

Important expositions of CFL and similar formalisms, especially in the context of their practical application in mechanical theorem proving, are found in J. Robinson, *Logic: Form and Function*, New York: North-Holland, 1979; D. Loveland, *Automated Theorem Proving*, Amsterdam: North-Holland, 1978; and R. Kowalski, *Logic for Problem Solving*, New York: North-Holland, 1979.

The semantical approach to symbolic logic, with its apparatus of interpretations, valuations and models, was developed in 1931 by Alfred Tarski in 'The Concept of Truth in Formalised Languages', in A. Tarski *Logic, Semantics and Metamathematics*, London: Oxford University Press, 1956. In the literature, that semantical theory is normally applied to first-order predicate calculus, not CFL. For a more readable exposition, see E. Mendelson, *Introduction to Mathematical Logic*, Princeton: Van Nostrand, 2nd edn. 1968.

Part III
PROOF THEORY FOR CFL

Chapter 13
Reasoning with clauses

In Part III we shall investigate the proof theory for CFL – the rules of symbol manipulation we may use to construct proofs in CFL. The material developed here is a more rigorous exposition of the proof-theoretical concepts introduced in Part I in connection with semantic nets.

In this chapter we shall:

- Introduce the main proof theory technique of CFL: *resolution*.

- Look at the two rules that make up resolution: *substitution* and *cut*.

- Set out the semantics for those two rules and demonstrate their soundness.

13.1   Proof theory

We now have sufficient grasp of the syntax and semantics of CFL to begin studying the third aspect of the language: its proof theory. The motivation for developing any system of logic is to use it as a vehicle in which to reason, and **proof theory** is the study of how to do that.

13.1.1   Proof theory and semantic nets

We developed a proof theory for the semantic net system of logic – the technique of pattern matching. It illustrates well the main ingredients involved in reasoning by using a system of logic, and we shall list them now.

(1)   We began with a knowledge base comprising all the vectors in the main net and all the conditional vectors in the auxiliary nets. Logicians refer to such a set of assertions, from which all reasoning must proceed, as an **axiom set**.

(2)   Any particular axiom set, such as the one about animals that we studied in Chapter 4, defines a particular application of the proof theory. An **applied logic** is not just an axiom set (knowledge base), but all the assertions that can be proved by applying the proof theory to that axiom set.

(3)   The activity of using a proof theory to prove assertions from the axioms, is called **deduction** or **proof**. The job of a proof theory is to define what counts as a deduction and what does not.

(4)   In a given deduction, only certain of the axioms might be used. For example, in the deduction, described in Section 4.1, of the statement that Hodge's feet are paws, only two axioms were used – the conditional in Figure 4.2, and the vector $\boxed{\text{HODGE}} \underline{\quad \text{Isa} \quad}_{\rightarrow} \boxed{\text{CAT}}$. The axioms used in a deduction are called its **premisses**.

(5)   A given deduction ends up by deducing one particular assertion, known as its **conclusion**. In the deduction referred to in item (4) above, the conclusion was $\boxed{\text{HODGE}} \underline{\quad \text{Feet} \quad}_{\rightarrow} \boxed{\text{PAWS}}$.

(6)   A deduction involves **symbol manipulation** – shifting marks on paper (or on acetate sheets!), pebbles in heaps, beads in an abacus, bits in a computer; and changing them, as if the whole business was a board game played with counters according to definite rules. In semantic nets, our board-game rules told us how to match vectors, how to attach or bind a variable (one sort of counter) to a constant term (another sort of counter), and when to write new vectors into the main net, thus reaching a conclusion.

We get our words 'calculus' and 'calculate' from this treatment of logic and mathematics as games of shifting counters. In Latin, 'calculus' means 'pebble', recalling the methods of adding and subtracting by pushing heaps of stones around.

13.1.2   Deduction as a board game

By proceeding entirely by symbol manipulation, a deduction makes no use at all of semantic concepts such as truth in a world, any more than the rules of chess require an understanding of the medieval cavalry battle. Euclid, Aristotle, and other ancient Greeks are credited with this idea of proving results by manipulating symbols, independently of the meaning we give them, by just obeying rules which describe their movements.

Though an ancient development, it is the leading idea behind the modern computer. Information is represented in program code and in database records, and ultimately as 'bits' – in fact, small electric charges on 'memory' chips. These are manipulated by the computer according to precise rules, and the resultant state of this game is decoded and printed out for us to see. The theory of computing, in fact, is a sophisticated branch of proof theory in logic.

However, you cannot make up just any set of rules for manipulating symbols and call the resulting game arithmetic or logic or whatever you please. You cannot, for instance, just push two heaps of pebbles together and call that multiplication, for counting the result will (usually) give you the wrong answer. For any symbol manipulation system, we need to be sure that the rules manipulate the symbols correctly according to the meaning we give them (even though the system makes no use of those meanings in what it does). Showing that it does so is called a **correctness proof** for the system.

Consider for example this pebble game for addition. We represent a number k by a heap of k pebbles. We represent addition of m to n by pushing together a heap of m pebbles and a heap of n pebbles. The sum is represented by the count of the resulting heap. The proof theory here is the rule that when told to add, you push the heaps together. The semantics is that the heaps represent numbers and the pushing together represents addition.

Does this game *correctly* represent addition? That question falls into two parts:

- Is every result of such a manipulation correct?

In other words, if you push together a heap of m pebbles and a heap of n pebbles, do you always get a heap of $m + n$ pebbles? This is known as the **soundness problem** or **consistency problem** for a proof theory – is the method sound with respect to its semantics? Well, you can see why we should not use rabbits or water droplets as counters in an addition game.

- Is the method capable of carrying out every operation the semantics can describe?

In our example, will the pebble method perform any and every addition of numbers for us? What if the numbers are enormous, or negative, or not integers? This is the **completeness problem** for a proof theory with respect to its semantics.

In Chapter 5, we studied the soundness of the semantic net method of doing logical reasoning. Later in this chapter we will do so for CFL proof theory.

The ideas of soundness and completeness apply specifically to a system of logic in this way: in a given system of logic, such as CFL or first-order predicate calculus, we are interested in being able to deduce a conclusion from premises, and so we particularly want to be sure that where the premises are all true, so is the conclusion. We express this requirement as follows:

Definition   Logical Validity

A conclusion C **logically follows** from premises $P_1, \ldots, P_n$ in a given system of logic only if C is true in every interpretation in which all of $P_1, \ldots, P_n$ are all true. We also say then that the inference from $P_1, \ldots, P_n$ to C is **logically valid**.

(Def. Logical Validity)

In that case, the **soundness** of a logical proof theory is the claim that *all* its deductions are logically valid; that is, you can never find an interpretation where the conclusion is false and all the premises are true. And **completeness** is the claim that a deduction exists for *every* logically valid inference.

We can put all this another way. A **model** of a set of formulae of a logical system (in our case, clauses) is an interpretation in which they are all true. A proof theory is **sound** if the conclusions it can deduce from a set of premises are true in every model of the premises. And a proof theory is **complete** if it can deduce all such conclusions. Finally, we say a conclusion **logically follows** from premises only if it is true in every model of the premises.

13.2   Proof theory for CFL

The proof theory for CFL is similar to that of semantic nets, and is called resolution. Resolution is quite a simple method of proof, as it involves the use of only two manipulation rules: the substitution rule and the cut rule.

13.2.1   The substitution rule

This is the simpler of the two rules we need, and the less powerful. It relies on the definition Subst given in Chapter 10.

Definition   Substitution rule

Any uniform substitution instance of a clause may be deduced from that clause.

(Def. Subst-Rule)

EXAMPLE 13.1

A knowledge base contains the clause:

$$P(x,y,z) \Rightarrow F(x,z), F(y,z) \qquad (1)$$

(Read this as 'If x and y are parents of z, then x or y is father of z.') It also contains the terms A, E and C (for Adam, Eve and Cain respectively). Deduce, using the substitution rule, that if Eve and Cain are Adam's parents, then Eve or Cain is Adam's father.

The deduction is:

Premiss	$P(x,y,z) \Rightarrow F(x,z),F(y,z)$	(1)
(1){E/x}	$P(E,y,z) \Rightarrow F(E,z),F(y,z)$	(2)
(2){C/y}	$P(E,C,z) \Rightarrow F(E,z),F(C,z)$	(3)
(3){A/z}	$P(E,C,A) \Rightarrow F(E,A),F(C,A)$	(4)

In the above example, we see a convenient and common way of setting out a deduction. In each line we write one formula, and give it a line number to its right. To its left we explain how we obtained it. In line (1) here, the clause we wrote down was a premiss. (It is hard to see what else a deduction could start with – premisses are the raw data for manipulation, and without them the manipulation rules would have nothing to handle.) The second clause was obtained from clause (1) by substituting E for x in it; then clause (3) by the substitution of C for y in (2). Clause (4) is the conclusion we were trying to prove, and we obtained it by substitution of A for z in clause (3).

When we use Subst-Rule in a deduction, we do not have to replace variables only by constants, for a check of the definition of Subst in Chapter 10 shows that we may use Subst-Rule to introduce variables as well, as the next example shows.

EXAMPLE 13.2_____

From clause (1) of Example 13.1 deduce $P(u,v,z) \Rightarrow F(u,z), F(v,z)$.

The deduction is:

Premiss	$P(x,y,z) \Rightarrow F(x,z), F(y,z)$	**(1)**
(1)$\{u/x\}$	$P(u,y,z) \Rightarrow F(u,z), F(y,z)$	**(2)**
(2)$\{v/y\}$	$P(u,v,z) \Rightarrow F(u,z), F(v,z)$	**(3)**

_____

The point of having variables is just to show substitution positions for using Subst; so if two expressions exhibit identical *patterns* of variables, as (1) and (3) of this example do, then they are **semantically equivalent** to each other, in that (1) will be satisfied by exactly the same valuations in the same interpretations as (3). In this example, they are **deductively equivalent** too, in that whatever can be deduced from (1) can be deduced from (3) and conversely. On the other hand, (1) and (1)$\{x/y\}$, which have different patterns of variables, are neither semantically nor deductively equivalent.

_____

Exercise 13.1   From clause (1) of Example 13.1 deduce $P(y,z,x) \Rightarrow F(y,x)$, $F(z,x)$.

_____

13.2.2   The cut rule

Definition   Cut rule

If the clauses:

$$P_1, p \Rightarrow Q_1 \quad \text{and}$$
$$P_2 \Rightarrow p, Q_2$$

are in a knowledge base or have been deduced from it, then we may deduce from them the clause:

$$P_1, \ P_2 \Rightarrow Q_1, \ Q_2$$

where P_1, P_2, Q_1, Q_2 are sets of atomic formulae (which may or may not be empty), and p is an atomic formula.

(Def. Cut-Rule)

That is, we may cut out an atom p occurring on opposite sides of two clauses, and merge the resultant clauses into a new one.

Here is a series of small illustrations, in which $p, q, r, \ldots$ are used for arbitrary atomic formulae.

EXAMPLE 13.3

From the clauses:

$$p \Rightarrow q \quad \text{and}$$
$$q \Rightarrow r$$

we may deduce:

$$p \Rightarrow r$$

Note that the order in which the premisses are taken does not matter.

EXAMPLE 13.4

From the clauses:

$$q, p \Rightarrow r \quad \text{and}$$
$$s \Rightarrow t, q$$

we may deduce:

$$p, s \Rightarrow r, t$$

Note that the order of atoms in the antecedent or consequent does not matter. (That is because antecedents and consequents of clauses are *sets* of atoms, and ordering is irrelevant to the membership of a set.)

Exercise 13.2   What can you deduce from these two clauses, using Cut-Rule?:

$$p, q \Rightarrow r \quad \text{and}$$
$$p \Rightarrow q, r \ ?$$

EXAMPLE 13.5

From the clauses:

$$\Rightarrow p \quad \text{and}$$
$$p \Rightarrow q$$

we may deduce:

$$=> \quad q$$

This is the logical law of **Modus Ponens** – what a true statement implies is itself true.

EXAMPLE 13.6

From the clauses:

$$q \; => \qquad \text{and}$$
$$p \; => \; q$$

we may deduce:

$$p \; =>$$

This is the law of **Modus Tollens** – whatever implies a false statement is itself false.

EXAMPLE 13.7

From the clauses:

$$p, q \; => \; r \qquad \text{and}$$
$$s \; => \; q, p$$

we may deduce both of these clauses:

$$p, s \; => \; p, r$$
$$q, s \; => \; q, r$$

but we may not deduce:

$$s \; => \; r$$

Note that Cut-Rule applies to only one atom at a time – you cannot cut two atoms out at one stroke. To do so can lead to deducing a false clause from two true ones, which violates the **truth preservation criterion** which any proof theory must obey (see below). To see this, suppose p and s are true, but q and r are false. Then the two premisses here are true, but the illegal conclusion is false.

EXAMPLE 13.8

From the clauses:

$$p \Rightarrow q, r \qquad \text{and}$$
$$q, s \Rightarrow p$$

we may deduce both of these clauses:

$$p, s \Rightarrow p, r$$
$$q, s \Rightarrow q, r$$

but we may not deduce:

$$s \Rightarrow r$$

The same remarks apply here as to the previous item.

Exercise 13.3   Find truth-values for the atoms in this last example, which make the premisses true and the illegal conclusion false.

13.3   Semantics for resolution

For the rest of this chapter we will look at the semantics for the proof theory we have just developed, with the aim of proving that the two rules we have studied are both *sound*.

The underlying idea which motivates the semantics for *any* system of logic, not just CFL, is this:

- Consistent (sound) principles of reasoning must guarantee that, if you reason from premisses that are all true in an interpretation, then the conclusions you reach will be true in that interpretation too.

This is called the **truth preservation criterion** for testing the soundness of a proof theory. In the case of CFL, we can give a precise statement of this criterion as follows.

Definition   Soundness of a rule

Let $\mathcal{I}$ be any interpretation for a knowledge base K; let P be any premisses (to which $\mathcal{I}$ is applicable) of any application of a CFL rule $\mathcal{R}$, and let C be the conclusion derived from those premisses by the application of $\mathcal{R}$. Let all the premisses P be true in $\mathcal{I}$. Then the rule $\mathcal{R}$ is **sound** only if the conclusion C is true in $\mathcal{I}$ too.

(Def. Soundness)

This definition allows us to formulate the **soundness theorem** for the resolution proof theory for CFL:

Proposition 13.1   Soundness theorem

For any interpretation $\mathcal{I}$, if all the premisses used in a deduction in CFL are true in $\mathcal{I}$, then so is the conclusion.

It is not hard to see why this soundness theorem holds. Since a deduction consists of a series of steps in which we apply a rule to one or else two clauses to derive another clause, all we have to do to prove the soundness theorem is to show that the rules are sound. There are only two rules to consider. We will show that each is sound, then prove this theorem.

Firstly, we can show the soundness of Subst-Rule, that is:

Proposition 13.2   Soundness of Subst-Rule

In any interpretation $\mathcal{I}$, if a clause C is true in $\mathcal{I}$, then so is every substitution instance of C.

Proof   Suppose that the proposition is wrong, that is, there is an interpretation $\mathcal{I}$ in which C is true but one of its substitution instances C' is not. We will show that this supposition is not tenable, by showing that in such a case C cannot be true in $\mathcal{I}$. By showing our supposition is impossible in this way we have proved the proposition.

C is true in $\mathcal{I}$. So by Def. Truth, every valuation in $\mathcal{I}$ satisfies C. But C', we are supposing, is not true in $\mathcal{I}$. Then by Def. Truth again some valuation $\mathcal{V}$ does not satisfy C'. Now the only difference between C and C' is that all occurrences of some variable v in C have been replaced by a term (variable or constant) t. (It will suit our argument if we can suppose that t does not already occur in C. Where it does, we simply do this: use a term t' not occurring in C instead, and give to it the value which was given to t. It should be reasonably obvious that *this* substitution instance will have exactly the same satisfaction conditions as the first one, so we have here too a substitution instance of C not satisfied by $\mathcal{V}$.)

Plainly, since C' is not satisfied by $\mathcal{V}$, $\mathcal{V}$ must give t a different value from that of v. Now, consider a valuation $\mathcal{V}'$ just like $\mathcal{V}$ except that it gives to v the value that $\mathcal{V}$ gives to t. Compare now what $\mathcal{V}$ does to C' with what $\mathcal{V}'$ does to C. We chose $\mathcal{V}'$ in such a way as to ensure that its satisfaction conditions for C are exactly those that $\mathcal{V}$ has for C'. Hence, $\mathcal{V}'$ does not satisfy C. So, by Def. Truth, C is not true in $\mathcal{I}$ after all. Since that contradicts the assumptions of our reasoning, we have shown the impossibility of the supposition we made, so the proposition is proved.   □

To understand abstract semantical arguments like this one, it helps to experiment' with small concrete examples as you go along. For instance, choose C as R(x) => S(x), and C' as R(A) => S(A); so that v is x. Next, find an interpretation that makes C true, such as five coins, with S denoting three of them, and R denoting two of those. Now work through the proof, selecting some value for x to fix the valuation $\mathcal{V}$, and of course some coin for A to denote. The machinery of the proof should then become clear. The example, of course, does not in any sense *prove* the proposition: you cannot prove a universal claim from the truth of one example of it. But it does *illustrate* how the proof works.

Secondly, we will show the soundness of the Cut-Rule:

Proposition 13.3   Soundness of Cut-Rule

If two clauses C and C' are true in an interpretation $\mathcal{I}$, then so is any clause D obtained from them by Cut-Rule.

Proof The argument for this is a bit easier. We can take C and C' to be as in the definition of Cut-Rule, that is:

$$P_1, p \Rightarrow Q_1 \quad \text{and}$$
$$P_2 \Rightarrow p, Q_2$$

and from them we deduce the conclusion, D:

$$P_1, P_2 \Rightarrow Q_1, Q_2$$

We will prove this by supposing the proposition is incorrect, and deriving an impossibility in it. That is, we suppose that there is an interpretation $\mathcal{I}$ in which C and C' are both true, but in which D is false. What we will then show is that in such a case C' is false; which shows the impossibility of our supposition.

If D is to be false in $\mathcal{I}$, then there is some valuation $\mathcal{V}$ in $\mathcal{I}$ that satisfies all atoms in P_1 and P_2, and satisfies no atoms in Q_1 or Q_2. That holds by Def. Truth for clauses. But since C and C' are true in $\mathcal{I}$, we know that $\mathcal{V}$ satisfies both of them. If so, in C, since $\mathcal{V}$ satisfies all atoms in P_1 but none in Q_1, it follows that $\mathcal{V}$ must fail to satisfy p. But in that case, $\mathcal{V}$ satisfies all atoms in the antecedent of C' and satisfies none of the atoms in the consequent of C'. In that case, C' is *not* true in $\mathcal{I}$ as assumed. So our supposition must be untenable, that is, the proposition is correct. □

Proof of Proposition 13.1 Those two soundness results for the rules of resolution show that if a chain of deduction starts with premises true in an interpretation, $\mathcal{I}$, then no matter how long the deduction, the final conclusion will be true in $\mathcal{I}$ too. That is, the resolution method is sound, and we have proved the soundness theorem.

Exercise 13.4   Suppose from a knowledge base K we can deduce {} => p and p => {}, where p is some atom. What does the soundness theorem show about K?

SUMMARY

- **Axiom set.** The set of all clauses in a knowledge base, that is, the logician's name for a knowledge base.

- **Applied logic.** An axiom set together with all the clauses that can be proved from that axiom set (that is, its **theorems**).

- **Proof theory.** The set of deduction rules for a particular system of logic; also the study of proof in logic and mathematics in general.

- **Premiss of a rule.** The clause(s) to which a proof-theory rule is applied.

- **Conclusion of a rule.** The clause produced by an application of a proof-theory rule.

- **Deduction.** Also a **proof**. The activity of deducing clauses from others using the manipulation rules of a logic. (To be defined tightly in the next chapter.)

- **Definition Logical validity.** A conclusion C **logically follows** from premises $P_1, \ldots, P_n$ in a given system of logic only if C is true in every interpretation in which all of $P_1, \ldots, P_n$ are all true. We also say then that the inference from $P_1, \ldots, P_n$ to C is **logically valid**.
  (Def. Logical Validity)

- **Soundness.** Also called **consistency**. A rule is sound (consistent) only if every application of it to premises true in an interpretation $\mathcal{I}$ always yields a conclusion that is true in $\mathcal{I}$ too. A logical system is sound (consistent) only if every rule in it is sound (consistent).

- **Completeness.** A logical system is complete if every clause in every interpretation in which a given set of axioms are true, is deducible using the rules of the logic.

- **Model.** A model of a set of formulae (clauses of CFL) is an interpretation in which they are all true. In a sound proof theory, a conclusion is true in every model of its premises.

- **Correctness.** A logic is correct only if it is sound and complete: for any model $\mathcal{I}$ of all the axioms for an applied logic, *soundness* says that *only* clauses true in $\mathcal{I}$ are deducible; *completeness* says that *all* clauses true in every such model are deducible.

- **Semantical equivalence.** Two clauses are **semantically equivalent** to each other only if they are satisfied by exactly the same valuations in the same interpretations as each other.

- **Deductive equivalence.** Two clauses are **deductively equivalent** to each other only if whatever can be deduced from one can be deduced from the other.

- **Definition Substitution rule**. Any uniform substitution instance of a clause may be deduced from that clause.

(Def. Subst-Rule)

- **Definition Cut rule.** If the clauses:

$$P_1, p \Rightarrow Q_1 \quad \text{and}$$
$$P_2 \Rightarrow p, Q_2$$

are in a knowledge base or have been deduced from it, then we may deduce from them the clause:

$$P_1, P_2 \Rightarrow \dot{Q}_1, Q_2$$

where P_1, P_2, Q_1, Q_2 are sets of atomic formulae (which may or may not be empty), and p is an atomic formula.

(Def. Cut-Rule)

- **Definition Soundness of a rule.** Let $\mathcal{I}$ be any interpretation for a knowledge base K; let P be any premisses (to which $\mathcal{I}$ is applicable) of any application of a CFL rule $\mathcal{R}$, and let C be the conclusion derived from those premisses by the application of $\mathcal{R}$. Let all the premisses P be true in $\mathcal{I}$. Then the rule $\mathcal{R}$ is **sound** only if the conclusion C is **true** in $\mathcal{I}$ too.

(Def. Soundness)

- **Soundness theorem.** For any interpretation $\mathcal{I}$, if all the premisses used in a deduction in CFL are true in $\mathcal{I}$, then so is the conclusion.

- **Soundness of Subst-Rule.** In any interpretation $\mathcal{I}$, if a clause C is true in $\mathcal{I}$, then so is every substitution instance of C.

- **Soundness of Cut-Rule.** If two clauses C and C' are true in an interpretation $\mathcal{I}$, then so is any clause D obtained from them by Cut-Rule.

Chapter 14
Unification

In the last chapter we introduced the two rules of deduction we need: Cut-Rule and Subst-Rule. In this chapter we shall study how to use both rules together to carry out non-trivial deductions.

- First, however, we shall bring together the remarks on deductions made in the last chapter, to form a proper definition of a deduction.

- We shall then look at another way of setting out deductions which is useful when one is trying to find deduction, rather than trying to present a finished deduction. This is the tree method. The tree method is not another set of logical rules for doing deductions, it is not another proof theory. It is the same proof theory with the same rules, but the deductions are displayed differently.

- Finally, we shall look at a particular way of using the Subst-Rule, called Unification. This is important since it is the way that most computer theorem proving systems use Subst-Rule.

14.1   Using the deduction rules

We begin with a more precise definition of deduction than we have used so
far.

Definition   Deduction

A sequence of clauses $C_1, C_2, \ldots, C_n$ is a **deduction** of its last member, C_n,
from a knowledge base $\mathcal{K}$, provided that each clause in the sequence is ei
ther:

(a)   An axiom of $\mathcal{K}$, or

(b)   Obtained from an earlier clause in the sequence by Subst-Rule, or

(c)   Obtained from two earlier clauses in the sequence by Cut-Rule.

A clause of type (a) is called a **premiss** of the deduction, and the
last clause C_n is called the **conclusion** of the deduction. A conclusion of a
deduction from $\mathcal{K}$ is called a **theorem** of $\mathcal{K}$.

(Def. Deduction

This chapter contains a series of problems involving deductions from a
knowledge base concerning the present British royal family – a conceptually
clear-cut topic whose facts are well-known. Some axioms in this knowledge
base, which we shall call BRF, are specific to that family, and so are some of
the theorems we shall prove. Others, however, make no mention of them, but
concern the structure of family relationships in the abstract. They would be
applicable to other families as well.

EXAMPLE 14.1──────────────────────────────────

Given a knowledge base containing the assertions:

(a)   Anybody who is somebody's father is male, and
(b)   Prince Philip is father of Prince Charles;
derive:

(c)   Prince Philip is male.

To prove this we choose this lexicon:

CFL	English
$F(\langle\text{p-1}\rangle, \langle\text{p-2}\rangle)$	$\langle\text{p-1}\rangle$ is father of $\langle\text{p-2}\rangle$
$M(\langle\text{p}\rangle)$	$\langle\text{p}\rangle$ is male
P	Philip
C	Charles

(For reference, we will number the axioms in the BRF system as A1, A2, etc. and the theorems we prove as T1, T2, etc.) Then (a) and (b) become the axioms:

$$F(x,y) \Rightarrow M(x) \qquad\qquad \textbf{A1}$$

and

$$\Rightarrow F(P,C) \qquad\qquad \textbf{A2}$$

while (c) becomes the conclusion:

$$\Rightarrow M(P) \qquad\qquad \textbf{T1}$$

Then the deduction of T1 is:

Premiss, A1	$F(x,y) \Rightarrow M(x)$	(1)
$(1)\{P/x\}\{C/y\}$	$F(P,C) \Rightarrow M(P)$	(2)
Premiss, A2	$\Rightarrow F(P,C)$	(3)
(2), (3) Cut-Rule	$\Rightarrow M(P)$	(4)

The example deduction involved primarily an application of Modus Ponens, and to apply it we needed first to derive an appropriate substitution instance of a universal clause. The next problem exhibits the same deduction technique in a more complex form.

EXAMPLE 14.2

Add to the knowledge base the rule that a parent of a parent of a person is their grandparent; add the fact that Philip is a parent of Charles, who in turn is a parent of Prince William; and deduce that Prince Philip is a grandparent of William.

To prove this we need to add to the existing lexicon:

CFL	English
$Par(\langle p\text{-}1\rangle,\langle p\text{-}2\rangle)$	$\langle p\text{-}1\rangle$ is a parent of $\langle p\text{-}2\rangle$
$Gpar(\langle p\text{-}1\rangle,\langle p\text{-}2\rangle)$	$\langle p\text{-}1\rangle$ is a grandparent of $\langle p\text{-}2\rangle$
W	William

Then the new axioms are:

$$Par(x,y),Par(y,z) \Rightarrow Gpar(x,z) \qquad \textbf{A3}$$
$$\Rightarrow Par(P,C) \qquad \textbf{A4}$$
$$\Rightarrow Par(C,W) \qquad \textbf{A5}$$

And we need to deduce:

$$\Rightarrow Gpar(P,W) \qquad \textbf{T2}$$

The deduction of T2 is:

Premiss, A3	$Par(x,y),Par(y,z) \Rightarrow Gpar(x,z)$	(1)
(1){P/x},{C/y}	$Par(P,C),Par(C,z) \Rightarrow Gpar(P,z)$	(2)
Premiss, A4	$\Rightarrow Par(P,C)$	(3)
(1),(2), Cut-Rule	$Par(C,z) \Rightarrow Gpar(P,z)$	(4)
(4){W/z}	$Par(C,W) \Rightarrow Gpar(P,W)$	(5)
Premiss, A5	$\Rightarrow Par(C,W)$	(6)
(5),(6) Cut-Rule	$\Rightarrow Gpar(P,W)$	(7)

The typical pattern of a deduction is becoming apparent in the above solution. The significant job in a deduction is the application of Cut-Rule, and we use Subst-Rule to prepare a couple of premisses or already deduced clauses for input to Cut-Rule. That preparation amounts to making an atom on one side of one clause identical to an atom on the other side of the second clause. Then Cut-Rule makes that atom disappear. In line (5) of the last problem, a substitution is performed on the previous clause to turn one of its antecedent atoms into Par(C,W), which is then the same as the Par(C,W) in the consequent of the axiom A5. We then invoke that axiom as a premiss, and use Cut-Rule to remove that atom and combine the remainder of the two clauses.

Exercise 14.1   Add to the knowledge base an axiom (numbered A6) that anyone who is someone's father is their parent, and show that A4 is no longer needed as an axiom.

Substitutions need not be confined to the introduction of constant terms. By introducing variables we can deduce new universals from old.

EXAMPLE 14.3_____

Prove that the father of the father of a person is their grandparent.

We need to prove T3: `F(x,y),F(y,z) => Gpar(x,z)`.

Premiss, A6	`F(x,y)`	`=> Par(x,y)`	**(1)**
Premiss, A3	`Par(x,y),Par(y,z)`	`=> Gpar(x,z)`	**(2)**
(1),(2) Cut-Rule	`F(x,y),Par(y,z)`	`=> Gpar(x,z)`	**(3)**
(1){z/y}{y/x}	`F(y,z)`	`=> Par(y,z)`	**(4)**
(3),(4) Cut-Rule	`F(x,y),F(y,z)`	`=> Gpar(x,z)`	**(5)**

Exercise 14.2   What is wrong with doing the substitutions in line (4) of the above example in the reverse order?

14.2   Displaying proofs as trees

The line-by-line layout of deductions, which we used in the three examples above, tends to hide from the eye the useful information about what clause was deduced from what. You might find it useful to adopt a **sideways tree** style of writing your deductions, like this:

In this approach to writing out a deduction, we write the premisses on the left, then move right to record the output of each deduction step. Horizontal lines indicate uses of Subst-Rule, and 'vees' indicate uses of Cut-Rule. The 'root' of the tree, on the right, is the conclusion of the deduction.

Various refinements of this sideways tree style can be helpful:

a)   Label each substitution line with the substitution(s) being made. Above, the top line would be labelled '{z/y}{y/x}.'

b)   In the pair of input clauses to an application of Cut-Rule (on the left prongs of a vee), underline the two atoms that are to be cut out. Those two atoms must be the same. In the tree above, the two premisses of the left-hand vee would get the atom `Par(x,y)` underlined.

(c)   Do not write down a given clause more than once if you can avoid it
even if the result looks more like a tree whose branches join up again

You are strongly advised to use the sideways tree method for all you
scratchpad work on deductions – though you may need to use fanfold pape
sideways! When you have your deduction worked out, you can then compres
it to the line-by-line format if you want to. You should also reconstruct eac
line-by-line deduction in this book, when you come to it, as a sideways tree

---

Exercise 14.3   Rewrite the deductions of theorems T1 and T2 as sideways
trees.

A last timesaving hint for sideways tree deductions:

(d)   Do not write clauses resulting from substitution moves into the tree
Rather, when recording a Cut-Rule step, write the required substitutio
instructions onto the arms of its vee.

If you do that for T3, the sideways tree shrinks to this:

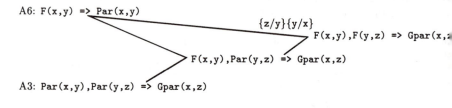

A6: F(x,y) => Par(x,y)

{z/y}{y/x}

F(x,y),F(y,z) => Gpar(x,z

F(x,y),Par(y,z) => Gpar(x,z)

A3: Par(x,y),Par(y,z) => Gpar(x,z)

Exercise 14.4   Do that for theorem T2.

14.3   Unification

The process of making substitutions into two clauses preparatory to usin
Cut-Rule on them, is known as **unification**.   It is so called because th
purpose of the substitutions is to make an atomic formula on one side o
one clause, and another on the other side of the second, become one and th
same. Then Cut-Rule will eliminate them. **Resolution** is the name given t
the combined process of unification followed by cutting, because two claus
get resolved into one simpler clause.

When we draw up a sideways tree according to (d) at the end of the ₁st section, each vee is one **resolution step** – unification followed by cutting. 'he clauses at the two left-hand tips of a vee are known as the **parents** or ₁**remisses** of the resolution step, and the clause at the point of the vee is its ₑsolvent or **conclusion**. Our proof of T2, for example, had two resolution ₜeps; in the first step (1) and (3) are the parents and (4) is the resolvent. It ₅ customary to measure the size of a deduction by the number of resolution ₜeps in it; one way of measuring the speed of a computer reasoning system ₅ by the number of resolution steps per second it performs.

The task of finding **unifiers**, that is, substitutions that will unify two ₜoms in a pair of clauses, is not always straightforward. In fact, in computa-ⁱonal logic the design of efficient procedures to find unifiers is an important ₒmponent of the design of deductive systems. The next problem illustrates ₑ more complex case of unification than any we have yet met.

EXAMPLE 14.4

Add to the BRF knowledge base a definition of the 'child-of' relation as the converse of the Par relation, and a rule saying anybody's female child is their daughter. Then deduce that if someone is a parent of a female, then the latter is their daughter.

(The *converse* of a relation R, which is usually denoted in logic as $\check{R}$, is the relation such that, for any objects x and y, $\check{R}(x, y)$ holds only if $R(y, x)$ holds. For example, the relations of 'older-than' and 'younger-than' are converses of each other.)

We define the 'child-of' relation as the converse of Par thus:

`Par(x,y) => Ch(y,x)`	**A7**
`Ch(x,y) => Par(y,x)`	**A8**

The required axiom for the 'daughter-of' relation is:

`Ch(x,y),F(x) => Dtr(x,y)`	**A9**

What has to be deduced is:

`Par(x,y),F(y) => Dtr(y,x)`	**T4**

The deduction is:

Premiss, A9	`Ch(x,y),F(x)`	`=> Dtr(x,y)`	(1)
Premiss, A7	`Par(x,y)`	`=> Ch(y,x)l`	(2)
(1){w/x}{x/y}	`Ch(w,x),F(w)`	`=> Dtr(w,x)`	(3)
(2){w/y}	`Par(x,w)`	`=> Ch(w,x)`	(4)

| (3),(4) Cut-Rule | Par(x,w),F(w) => Dtr(w,x) | (5) |
| (5){y/w} | Par(x,y),F(x) => Dtr(y,x) | (6) |

This deduction repays a closer look. We obviously need A9 as a premise since it is so similar to the conclusion. But we need to replace its unwanted C antecedent by Par; and A7 is just the clause to do the trick, by cutting. Thus we have our two premises. But unifying the Ch atoms in them is tricky 'obvious' substitutions yield Ch(y,y) or Ch(x,x). To avoid that we must introduce some new variable, and we choose w. Then substitutions introducing w into *both* premises permit unification. Cut-Rule is then applicable, and the resolvent is in line (5). While that resolvent says exactly what we want to prove, it unfortunately has a different variable from those in the formulation we gave to the conclusion, before commencing the deduction. (With foresight we could have formulated the CFL conclusion as clause (4), so shortening the deduction.) We fix the variable by a substitution in the last line.

Exercise 14.5   For this problem we introduce two new axioms:

| Par(x,y),M(x) => F(x,y) | A1 |
| => Ch(A,P) | A1 |

where the constant term A stands for Princess Anne.

(a)   What does A10 say?
(b)   Prove T5: Ch(x,y),M(y) => F(y,x). What does it say?

14.3.1   Standardizing apart

In computer-based resolution theorem proving systems, it is standard practice to handle unification in a more stylized way than we have done here. For one thing, the two clauses that are to be unified are inspected to see if they have any variables in common. If they do, the common variables in one clause are removed and replaced, using Subst-Rule, by variables not occurring in either clause. This process is called **standardizing apart**.

For example, in the deduction in Example 14.4, lines (1) and (2), which are the parents of a unification step, share the variables x and y. We can standardize these two clauses apart by the substitutions {u/x} and {v/y} in (2).

The point of doing this is to make it easy for the machine to find unifying substitutions for the parent clauses. Once they are standardized part, there is an efficient method, called the **unification algorithm**, for finding a set of substitutions that will unify the two clauses. All told, it is more efficient to standardize apart first, then apply the unification algorithm, than to try to unify directly two clauses that share variables.

It is not essential to see how the unification algorithm works; but we should note an important feature of its output – the substitution instructions.

14.3.2   Simultaneous substitution

The substitution instructions produced by the unification algorithm are intended to be carried out simultaneously with each other, not in sequence, as we have done so far. To see how this works and why it can be much simpler than the sequential substitution we have used so far, consider the problem of substituting in:

$$P(x,y,z) \Rightarrow F(x,z),F(y,z) \qquad\qquad (1)$$

to get:

$$P(y,z,x) \Rightarrow F(y,x),F(z,x) \qquad\qquad (2)$$

(This was Exercise 13.1 in the previous chapter.) No sequential substitution involving just x, y and z will work – variables will merge. For example, the sequence of substitutions $\{y/x\}$, $\{z/y\}$, $\{x/z\}$ will yield from (1) successively:

$$P(y,y,z) \Rightarrow F(y,z),F(y,z)$$
$$P(z,z,z) \Rightarrow F(z,z),F(z,z)$$
$$P(x,x,x) \Rightarrow F(x,x),F(x,x)$$

To avoid this collapse, we have to temporarily introduce new variables as extra substitutions. The sequence of substitutions used in Exercise 13.1 was, in fact, $\{x1/x\}$, $\{x/z\}$, $\{z/y\}$, $\{y/x1\}$. The introduction of $x1$ allowed the other variables to be rotated as required, keeping the substitute for x (meant to be y) distinct until the end when y is reintroduced.

By contrast, the simultaneous substitution method says, in effect, to do all the substitutions at the same time on the original clause, not on the output of some earlier substitution. The simultaneous substitution $\{y/x,z/y,x/z\}$ (note how we write it) replaces the x in (1) by y, the y in (1) by z, and the z in (1) by x, giving (2) as required.

It is not hard to prove that the effect of any given simultaneous substitution can be obtained by sequential substitutions, using temporary variables if necessary. Consequently, we may use simultaneous substitution from now on, as a sound rule. The definition, rule, and proposition we need are:

Definition   Simultaneous substitution

Let E be an expression of CFL, let $v_1, \ldots v_n$ be variables, and let $t_1, \ldots t_n$ be terms.   Then the **simultaneous substitution** of $t_1, \ldots t_n$ for $v_1, \ldots v_n$ respectively in E, denoted by $E\{t_1/v_1, \ldots t_n/v_n\}$, is the expression that results from replacing every occurrence of v_1 in E by $t_1, \ldots$ and every occurrence of v_n in E by t_n. It is known as a **simultaneous substitution instance** of E.

(Def. Sim-Subst)

Definition   Simultaneous substitution rule

Any simultaneous substitution instance of a clause is a clause, and may be deduced from that clause.

(Def. Sim-Subst-Rule)

Proposition 14.1   Soundness of Sim-Subst-Rule

In any applicable interpretation $\mathcal{I}$, if a clause C is true in $\mathcal{I}$, then so is every simultaneous substitution instance of C.   ⌐

Exercise 14.6   Axioms A2, A3, A7, and A9 are called *pure axioms* of family relationships, since they make no reference to any individuals. Use them to prove:

    Ch(x,y),Ch(y,z) => Gpar(z,x)

Use standardization apart and Sim-Subst-Rule.

14.4   Using theorems as premisses

In making deductions, it is legitimate, and almost always essential, to make use of theorems we have already proved, as premisses in the deduction.

By using as premisses some theorems we have already proved, we shorten the proofs greatly, make their structure more perspicuous, and avoid repeating deductions we have already made.   The next example illustrates this.

EXAMPLE 14.5_____

Prove that Philip is Anne's father.

The conclusion to prove is T6: `{} => F(P,A)`.

Premiss, T5	`Ch(x,y),M(y) => F(y,x)`	(**1**)
Premiss, T1	`=> M(P)`	(**2**)
(1){P/y}	`Ch(x,P),M(P) => F(P,x)`	(**3**)
(2),(3) Cut-Rule	`Ch(x,P)      => F(P,x)`	(**4**)
Premiss, A11	`=> Ch(A,P)`	(**5**)
(4){A/x}	`Ch(A,P)      => F(P,A)`	(**6**)
(5),(6) Cut-Rule	`=> F(P,A)`	(**7**)

In the above deduction we used the theorems T1 and T5 as premisses.
Why is that legal? The definition of a deduction, given at the beginning
of this chapter, does not permit anything other than an axiom to be a premiss.

Well, instead of using a theorem as a premiss, we could always insert
into the deduction instead the whole proof of that theorem. Then we would
end up with a deduction that does satisfy the definition. So introducing
theorems as premisses is a legitimate and convenient method of abbreviating
deductions, provided those theorems have already been deduced.

Exercise 14.7   Do the deduction of T6 once more, without using any theorems
as premisses.

SUMMARY

- **Definition Deduction.** A sequence of clauses $C_1, C_2, \ldots, C_n$ is a
  deduction of its last member, C_n, from a knowledge base $\mathcal{K}$, provided
  that each clause in the sequence is either:
  (a)   An axiom of $\mathcal{K}$, or
  (b)   Obtained from an earlier clause in the sequence by Subst-Rule,
        or
  (c)   Obtained from two earlier clauses by Cut-Rule.

  (Def. Deduction)

- **Premiss.** Any axiom used in a deduction is a **premiss** of that deduction.

- **Conclusion.** The clause at the last line of a deduction is the **conclusion** of that deduction.

- **Unification.** The process of making substitutions into two clauses so that they may be used in an application of Cut-Rule.

- **Unifiers.** Substitutions that will unify two clauses.

- **Resolution.** The process of unifying two clauses then applying Cut-Rule to them.

- **Parents of a resolution step.** The two clauses that are unified.

- **Resolvent of a resolution step.** The clause created by the application of Cut-Rule.

- **Definition Converse of a relation.** $\check{R}$ is the **converse** of R only for any x and y, $\check{R}(x, y)$ holds only if $R(x, y)$ holds.

  (Def. Converse)

- **Definition Simultaneous substitution.** Let E be an expression of CFL, let $v_1, \ldots v_n$ be variables, and let $t_1, \ldots t_n$ be terms. Then the **simultaneous substitution** of $t_1, \ldots t_n$ for $v_1, \ldots v_n$ respectively in E, denoted by $E\{t_1/v_1, \ldots t_n/v_n\}$, is the expression that results from replacing every occurrence of v_1 in E by $t_1, \ldots$ and every occurrence of v_n in E by t_n. It is known as a **simultaneous substitution instance** of E.

  (Def. Sim-Subst)

- **Definition Simultaneous substitution rule.** Any simultaneous substitution instance of a clause is a clause, and may be deduced from that clause.

  (Def. Sim-Subst-Rule)

- **Soundness of Sim-Subst-Rule.** In any applicable interpretation $\mathcal{I}$, if a clause C is true in $\mathcal{I}$, then so is every simultaneous substitution instance of C.

Chapter 15
Laws and rules

The proof theory for CFL is not yet complete in the sense of Chapter 13. A reasoning machine, armed only with cut and substitution rules, is unable to deduce from its knowledge base some things that it certainly should be able to. For example, if it has stored the fact that all kings are monarchs:

$$K(x) \implies Mon(x) \tag{1}$$

and it is asked to deduce whether all Scandinavian kings are monarchs, or whether all kings are monarchs or emperors:

$$Scan(x), K(x) \implies Mon(x) \tag{2}$$
$$K(x) \implies Mon(x), Emp(x) \tag{3}$$

it is unable to do so. At least, it cannot make the deduction just from (1) alone. (Try it!) But it should be able to, for it is easy to show that in any interpretation in which (1) is true, (2) and (3) will both be true too. Hence, the proof theory for CFL, as it stands, is too weak: it is incomplete.

In this chapter we will look at some additions to CFL proof theory which address this and other weaknesses.

15.1   Contraction

A **pleonasm** is the figure of speech in which a person repeats somethin;
at least twice or more, in a way which does not contribute to or add to th
meaning of the statement. Pleonasms occur in CFL too, when an antecede
or a consequent is repeated in a clause. In this line:

$$P(x), F(y,x), P(y), P(x) \Rightarrow G(x,x) \qquad (\cdot$$

$P(x)$ is written twice on the antecedent side; one of these does not need to l
there, and can be removed:

$$F(y,x), P(y), P(x) \Rightarrow G(x,x) \qquad (\mathfrak{t}$$

Equally, it is legitimate to remove a repeated consequent.

The rule we are discussing is known as **Contraction** and can be define
thus:

Definition   Contraction rule

If C is a clause containing two or more occurrences of an atom p in its a
tecedent set, or in its consequent set, and if C' is like C except that one
those repeated occurrences of p is removed, then C' may be deduced from C

(Def. Contrac

While Contract only allows us to delete one repetition in an antecede
or consequent set, we can plainly apply it over and over to delete as mar
repetitions as we like.

EXAMPLE 15.1

A computer expert system about the rules and titles of royalty, records
in its knowledge base that anyone married to a queen is male, and is
a monarch or a prince:

$Mar(x,y), Q(y) \Rightarrow Mon(x), Pr(x)$	**A1**
$Mar(x,y), Q(y) \Rightarrow M(x)$	**A2**

and that a male monarch is a king or a prince:

$$M(x), Mon(x) \Rightarrow K(x), Pr(x) \qquad \textbf{A3}$$

Can the expert system deduce that anyone married to a queen is a
king or a prince:

$$Mar(x,y), Q(y) \Rightarrow K(x), Pr(x)$$

The deduction is:

A2	Mar(x,y),Q(y) => M(x)	**(1)**
A3	M(x),Mon(x) => K(x),Pr(x)	**(2)**
(1),(2) Cut	Mar(x,y),	
	Q(y),Mon(x) => K(x),Pr(x)	**(3)**
A1	Mar(x,y),Q(y) => Mon(x),Pr(x)	**(4)**
(3),(4) Cut	{Mar(x,y),Q(y),	
	Mar(x,y),Q(y)} => Pr(x),K(x),Pr(x)	**(5)**
(5), Contract	Mar(x,y),Q(y) => K(x),Pr(x)	

Usually, applications of Contract to remove repetitions are quite obvious, and we will not bother to include them explicitly as steps in the deduction. At the end of the last deduction, we could have condensed the last two steps in this way:

$$(3),(4),\text{Cut} \quad \text{Mar(x,y),Q(y)} => K(x),Pr(x) \qquad (5)$$

Exercise 15.1   Given:

a)

F(x), G(x) => H(x,y)	**A1**
F(A), H(A,x) => I(x,y)	**A2**

Deduce:

    F(A), G(A) => I(x,y)

b)

F(x), G(x,y) => H(y)	**B1**
H(x) => F(x)	**B2**
G(x,y) => H(x), G(y,x)	**B3**

Deduce:

    F(y), G(x,y) => F(x)

15.1.1   Justification of the contraction rule

The justification of Contract is trivial. In any clause, antecedents are collected into a set, as are consequents. But sets do not permit their members to be repeated. If you *write* a set with an element repeated (as we did implicitly for the antecedent set of clause (4) above), then that is a pleonastic and wasteful way of writing the set. In that clause:

$$\{P(x),F(y,x),P(y),P(x)\} = \{P(x),F(y,x),P(y)\}$$

In other words, once you distinguish between the set (as an abstract object) and its written representation, the justification for removing repetitions of elements in the *written representation of* the set is trivial.

However, we bother to include Contract as a rule because proof theory does proceed by symbol manipulation. So deleting repetitions of a written atom is a rule we need, as Example 15.1 shows, if we are to deduce a clause *written down in a particular way.*

Those remarks apply yet more forcefully to a computer theorem prover which knows nothing about sets. If it is given the sequences of symbols A1 A2 and A3, and asked to prove the symbol sequence:

```
M(x),Mon(x) => K(x),Pr(x)
```

it must have Contract as a symbol manipulation rule to do so.

15.1.2   Reordering atoms in a clause

For similar reasons, if a computer is to be able to reorder atoms in an antecedent set or a consequent set, it needs a rule to allow it to do so. We call this rule, the **reordering rule**, and state it here for the sake of recording it. But in our deductions we will generally use it without mentioning it.

Definition   Reordering rule

If C is any clause, and C' is just like C except that the atoms in its antecedent set, or in its consequent set, have been reordered, then C' may be deduced from C.

(Def. Reorder)

Exercise 15.2   The deduction rule Contract applies only to repetitions of atoms in an antecedent or a consequent. Show that if an antecedent atom is repeated in the consequent set, it would not be sound to delete either atom. That is, it is unsound to deduce either (a) $P => p, Q$ or (b) $P, p => Q$ from $P, p => p, Q$, where P, Q are sets of atoms and p is an atom.

Exercise 15.3   A student thought that Contract allowed her to make this inference:

| Premiss | F(x), F(y) => G(x,y) | (1) |
| (1), Contract | F(x)   => G(x,y) | |

Show her why this reasoning is unsound.

5.2   Logical laws and 'Id'

Most clauses that one deduces will be true in some worlds, false in others. But there are clauses that will be true in any and every world. Clauses with that property we have called **logically true**, or **logical laws**. The simplest example is any clause of the form p => p, for example:

$$K(x) \Rightarrow K(x)$$
$$Mar(CHARLES, WILLIAM) \Rightarrow Mar(CHARLES, WILLIAM)$$

Any clause of that form is called an **Id law**. ('Id' stands for identity.)

Logical laws should be deducible from any knowledge base at all, but as our CFL proof theory stands at present, even Ids are not, in general, deducible. True, if a knowledge base had a couple of axioms of the form p => q and q => p, then we can deduce two Ids: p => p and q => q. But that would not allow us to deduce other Ids. So how are we to strengthen the proof theory to make Ids deducible?

We solve it in the simplest possible way: we require that Ids are to be axioms of any knowledge base at all. Put more precisely:

Definition   Id rule

In any knowledge base $\mathcal{K}$, any clause of the form p => p (where p is any atom) may be treated as an axiom of $\mathcal{K}$.

(Def. Id)

The effect of the rule *Id* on any given knowledge base is to add to that base an infinite number of axioms – an atom of the form p => p for every atom p which can be expressed in that base.

Exercise 15.4   Why an infinity of axioms?

If we are thinking of a knowledge base inside a computer or a brain, we do not really want to say literally that an infinity of clauses is stored there, for that is not possible. What we are saying is that the computer or brain can *generate* such axioms when needed as premises.

Since Id axioms are all logical laws, they are called **logical axioms**, and their form, p => p, is known as a **logical axiom form** or **logical axiom schema**. Similarly, any theorem that we can prove using just logical axioms as premises, is known as a **logical theorem**, since it too will express a logical law.

15.2.1   Soundness of the Id rule

The Id rule is not a manipulation rule at all: it transforms no clauses into other clauses. All it really does is enlarge the axiom set of any knowledge base. Our interest in proving consistency of rules was to ensure that the soundness theorem held for our logical system: that the conclusion of a deduction holds true in all interpretations in which the premisses do.

Adding the Id rule to our logic cannot change the validity of the soundness theorem, since the most Id can do is to add new premisses to a deduction. What does matter is that adding Ids as premisses in a deduction does not change the set of interpretations in which the premisses are true. In fact, more generally, adding Ids to any knowledge base does not change the set of models for that knowledge base at all, since they are logical laws.

More generally still, adding any logical laws to a knowledge base will not alter the models for that knowledge base. What logical laws are there, other than Ids? This has a simple answer:

Proposition 15.1   Logical laws

The logical laws are the following clauses:

(a)   Clauses with F as an antecedent.

(b)   Clauses with T as a consequent.

(c)   Clauses in which a particular atom p occurs both as an antecedent and as a consequent.

Proof   *Firstly* we show that all these clauses are logical laws:

(a)   In cases (a), no valuation in any interpretation can satisfy F, so no valuation satisfies all the antecedents of such clauses, so every valuation satisfies the clause as a whole, by Def. Satisfies for clauses.

(b)   Similarly in these cases, every valuation in every interpretation satisfies T, so satisfies a consequent, which guarantees that the whole clause is satisfied.

(c)   Each valuation in each interpretation either satisfies p or does not. If it does, then it satisfies a consequent, so the whole clause is satisfied. If it does not, then it does not satisfy an antecedent, which guarantees that the whole clause is satisfied.

Secondly, we show that a logical law must belong to one of these three types, by showing that for every clause C not of one of these three types has a valuation in an interpretation that does not satisfy it.

We do this by constructing an interpretation $\mathcal{I}$ in which there is a valuation $\mathcal{V}$ which does not satisfy C. Note first that there are no Fs in the antecedent, or Ts in the consequent, so the presence of constants in the clause will not prevent us doing this. Now, we start constructing the $\mathcal{I}$ and $\mathcal{V}$ by giving each term (constant or variable) some object as value, and make sure that each term gets a different object as value. We fix the interpretation for the predicates as follows. For each occurrence of a predicate in the antecedent:

(a)   If it is one-place put the object which is the value of its argument into the set of objects that the predicate is to denote. Put nothing else into that set.

(b)   If it is not monadic, but n-ary $(n > 1)$, put the n-tuple of objects that its arguments have as value, into the set of objects that the predicate is to denote. Put nothing else into that set.

Then we have fixed $\mathcal{I}$ and $\mathcal{V}$. Further, the way we have created it ensures that $\mathcal{V}$ satisfies every antecedent. Now consider any consequent atom. The value (or n-tuple of values) given to its argument (or arguments) by $\mathcal{V}$ will not be a member of the denotation of the predicate, since it is different from any antecedent atom. So, no atom in the consequent is satisfied by $\mathcal{V}$. Consequently, $\mathcal{V}$ does not satisfy the clause C.   □

Another way of stating this proposition is that every clause not of one of the three types above has a counterexample.

Exercise 15.5   Show that:

    F(A), G(x,y) => F(x), G(y,x)

is not a logical law.

It is plain from the above that there are logical laws, such as:

    F(x), G(x) => G(x)   and
        F(x) => T

that we are unable to deduce yet in our proof theory. These will become available as a result of rules added in the next two sections. Then all logical laws will be deducible in every applied logic.

15.3   A rule for T and F

T and F give rise to two Id axioms: T => T and F => F. The second of these is strange but correct: 'If The False is true, then it is true.' (After all, if *anything* is true, then it is true.) But there are two other but related logical laws about T and F that are more interesting:

The True is true:	{} => T	**(5)**
The False is false:	F => {}	**(6)**

These cannot be proved from Id axioms, or in any other way, so we must add a rule that allows us to deduce them.

Definition   Truth-value contraction
In any deduction, T may be removed from the antecedent set of a clause in the deduction, and F may be removed from the consequent set.

(Def. T/F Contract)

Exercise 15.6   Deduce (5) and (6) from any knowledge base at all.

Exercise 15.7   State and prove the soundness of the T/F Contract rule.

15.4   Weakening

Here we take up the problem raised at the beginning of this chapter. Suppose you are asked whether every Scandinavian king is a monarch. (See Clause (2) at the beginning of the chapter.) If you knew that every king, Scandinavian or not, was a monarch (see Clause (1)), then the answer to the question follows immediately. The rule of reasoning that you have just employed to get to the answer, is that extra antecedents can always be added to a clause in a deduction. This rule is known as **Weakening** or **Monotonicity**:

Premiss	K(x)	=> Mon(x)	**(1)**
(1), Weak	K(x),Scan(x)	=> Mon(x)	**(2)**

Extra consequents can also be added:

(1), Weak	K(x)	=> Mon(x),Emp(x)	**(3)**

The weakening rule can be stated thus:

Definition   Weakening rule

If P and Q are sets of atoms and p is an atom, then from the clause $P \Rightarrow Q$ may be deduced both $P, p \Rightarrow Q$ and $P \Rightarrow p, Q$.

(Def. Weak)

Exercise 15.8   Given:

$$p, q_1 \Rightarrow r_1 \qquad \textbf{A1}$$
$$q_2 \Rightarrow p, r_2 \qquad \textbf{A2}$$
$$q_3 \Rightarrow p, r_3 \qquad \textbf{A3}$$

deduce:

$$q_1, q_2, q_3 \Rightarrow r_1, r_2, r_3$$

Exercise 15.9   Show that $p, p \Rightarrow p, p$ is a logical theorem schema.

Exercise 15.10   Demonstrate the soundness of Weak.

Calling such a rule 'weakening' is appropriate. Consider the task of trying to show that a particular clause is true in some world. When we add an extra antecedent to a clause, that weakens the likelihood of having all antecedents true (increases the likelihood of having a false antecedent). And that increases the likelihood of the clause being true. We then say that the clause is *weaker* – the more likely that a statement is true, the weaker we say it is. Similarly, if a clause has an extra consequent, then that makes it more likely to have a true consequent, and so more likely for the whole clause to be true. That is, it is weaker.

Where the clause is a ground clause this is particularly easy to see. If such a clause has n_a antecedents, and n_c consequents, then there are $2^{n_a + n_c}$ different ways of assigning truth-values to those atoms. For only one such way, where all the antecedents are true and all the consequents are false, does the clause work out false. If we now add one further antecedent or consequent, we double the ways of assigning truth-values to the atoms of the clause, but still, only one such way falsifies the clause. The prior probability of the clause being false (that is, taking the probability of falsehood for each component atom to be $1/2$) has halved.

Weak statements, ones that are very likely to be true, say little, for they are true in most worlds and therefore do not sort out which world is being claimed to be actual. Someone who says 'It will rain today at some time, or at some time there will be some sunshine', is a weak forecaster, for such a prediction will work out true on most days. To say 'It will rain today at some time' is stronger – that will be falsified on more days. A really strong forecast will predict how much rain and just when, how much sun and just when, and other weather features to close tolerances. Such a forecast will be true on very few days – in few worlds – and therefore is strong. It gives us a clear and useful picture of the weather. A forecaster who makes strong predictions, and who is often right, is of much more value than one who makes weak predictions and is right only as often. Horoscopes and other superstitions thrive by making very weak predictions (especially if they sound strong), in that whatever world eventuates, one can usually 'interpret' the prediction as being true in that world.

The weakening rule, then, is one we could do without, in that whenever we deduce something using it, we could have deduced something stronger without it. On the other hand, if we are given something to prove, and it indeed follows from the knowledge base, then it is our job to prove it, and not to say it is unprovable on the grounds that something stronger is provable. Suppose the computer described at the beginning of this chapter failed to confirm the query whether all Scandinavian kings are monarchs, even though it knew that all kings are monarchs, because it did not have the weakening rule in it. Then it would appear to its users to be a rather defective reasoning machine. It would appear weaker as a reasoner than another computer that does not know that all kings are monarchs, only the weaker statement that all European kings are monarchs, and which knows that things Scandinavian are European. That could certainly deduce that all Scandinavian kings are monarchs.

15.4.1   The paradoxes of material implication

While Weak is needed to allow us to deduce quite legitimate weakened versions of deducible clauses, it can also be used to deduce some very paradoxical results indeed.

- A false statement implies anything:

  Given that p is false: p => {}   (1)
  (1), Weak p => q

- Anything implies a true statement:

  Given that p is true: {} => p (1)
  (1), Weak q => p

Numerous logicians regard these results as absurd. For instance, if in the royalty knowledge base we are able to deduce that Queen Elizabeth is a monarch:

```
=> Mon(ELIZ)
```

then we can also deduce that if Britain is a republic then she is a monarch:

```
Rep(GB) => Mon(ELIZ)
```

The absurdity in this example is that if indeed Great Britain were a republic, it is hard to see how Elizabeth could still be a monarch at all, and even harder to see how her being a monarch could *follow* from Britain's being a republic.

On the other hand, the paradoxicality of any such example does not extend to the deduction of unwelcome facts from it. For instance, suppose our royalty knowledge base allows us to deduce that Elizabeth is not a king:

```
K(ELIZ) =>
```

then by Weak we can deduce that if Elizabeth is a king, pigs fly:

```
K(ELIZ), Pig(x) => Flies(x)
```

However we cannot deduce from that, that pigs fly:

```
Pig(x) => Flies(x)
```

unless we can firstly deduce that Elizabeth *is* a king, for then we can use Cut appropriately. And we are unlikely to be able to deduce it:

```
=> K(ELIZ)
```

since we have already deduced its denial. (Unless, of course, our knowledge base is inconsistent.)

The two clauses:

```
K(ELIZ) =>    and
          => K(ELIZ)
```

are said to be **inconsistent**, or to form an **inconsistent set**, for there can be no interpretation in which they are both true. Similarly these two are an inconsistent set:

```
F(x) =>    and
       => F(x)
```

for there is no valuation in any interpretation which will satisfy them both. Hence there is no interpretation in which they will both be true.

We define consistency thus:

Definition   Consistency

A set S of clauses is **consistent** only if there is an interpretation in which they are all true, otherwise S is **inconsistent.**

(Def. Consistency,

How could inconsistency arise in a particular applied logic? We know that all our rules are sound in CFL, so the theorems we prove in an applied logic will be true in all the interpretations in which the axioms are all true. So if we find an inconsistent set of theorems in the applied logic, we know that the axioms are inconsistent too.

This illustrates the crucial importance of having a *sound* logical system. It will not guarantee consistency, but if we detect inconsistency in a sound system it shows that the assumptions (the axioms, the knowledge base) on which the system is built are inconsistent. So we know where to look to fix the problem.

In computational matters, most very large knowledge bases must be treated as not only containing falsehoods (because of the uncertainty of data collection and input methods) but even as inconsistent. Finding out how to detect, contain and remove such inconsistencies is a major area of AI research.

Exercise 15.11   The police computer recorded that Mr Smallfry had not paid his parking fine. When he did pay it, the computer recorded the fact, but due to poor program design, did not wipe the statement that he had not. Show how the computer concluded that the Prime Minister was a spy.

15.4.2   Paradoxes of material implication

Paradoxes like the one about Mr Smallfry are known as **paradoxes of material implication**, since they arise because our implication operation is defined **materially**, that is, purely in terms of truth and falsity of the atoms in the antecedent and consequent. But normally when we say one thing implies another, or if one thing then another, we are saying something stronger: that the antecedent *causes* or *brings about* the consequent. 'If it rains, then I will get wet', 'n^2 is odd implies n is odd'. Implications like that are called **relevant**.

One way to ensure that we treat our => operator as relevant, would be to ban the weakening rule, since only it can introduce non-relevant atoms into a clause (like the one about the Prime Minister). But that seems to be ιn exorbitant price to pay to prevent the deduction of irrelevant falsehoods from an inconsistent set of axioms – after all, we can still deduce relevant falsehoods from them. And we have seen that the weakening rule does have important uses.

The problems raised by the paradoxes, and the quest for relevance in reasoning, are lively and urgent research topics at present, because of the importance of computer reasoning. However, we can but touch on them in this book, and now must leave them.

SUMMARY

- **Definition Contraction rule**. If C is a clause containing two or more occurrences of an atom p in its antecedent set, or in its consequent set, and if C' is like C except that one of those repeated occurrences of p is removed, then C' may be deduced from C.

    (Def. Contract)

- **Definition Reordering rule**. If C is any clause, and C' is just like C except that the atoms in its antecedent set, or in its consequent set, have been reordered, then C' may be deduced from C.

    (Def. Reorder)

- **Definition Id rule**. In any knowledge base $\mathcal{K}$, any clause of the form $p \Rightarrow p$ (where p is any atom) may be treated as an axiom of $\mathcal{K}$.

    (Def. Id)

- **Logical law**. A clause that is true in every interpretation.

- **Logical axiom**. An axiom of a knowledge base that is true in every interpretation.

- **Logical laws**. The logical laws are the following clauses:

    (a)   Clauses with F as an antecedent.

    (b)   Clauses with T as a consequent.

    (c)   Clauses in which a particular atom p occurs both as an antecedent and as a consequent.

- **Finding counterexamples**. Let each term in a clause evaluate to a different object, and give each predicate as denotation only the (n-tuples of) objects to which the arguments of its occurrences in the antecedents evaluate.

- **Definition Truth-value contraction**. In any deduction, T may be removed from the antecedent set of a clause in the deduction, and F may be removed from the consequent set.

    (Def. T/F Contract)

- **Definition Weakening rule**. If P and Q are sets of atoms and p is an atom, then from the clause $P \Rightarrow Q$ both $P, p \Rightarrow Q$ and $P \Rightarrow p, Q$ may be deduced.

  (Def. Weak)

- **Weaker and stronger statements.** One statement is **weaker** than another if it has fewer ways of being false (false in fewer interpretations); that is, the **stronger** statement is false in all the interpretations the weaker one is, and more besides. A weaker statement should be deducible from the stronger one.

- **Material implication.** The type of account of implication or conditionals, such as in this book, that defines the concept purely in terms of satisfaction values or truth values, ignoring, for example, notions of causation.

- **Paradoxes of material implication.** Every statement implies any true statement, and any false statement implies any statement.

- **Relevant logics.** Systems of logic that try to improve the definition of implication by insisting that all antecedents must be relevant in some sense to determining the truth of the consequents.

urther reading for Part III

'he Resolution method of deduction described in this part is associated pri-
arily with the name of J.A. Robinson. The Cut Rule in Resolution was
udied initially by G. Gentzen ('Investigations in Logical Deduction' (1936),
G. Szabo (ed.) *The Collected Papers of Gerhard Gentzen*, Amsterdam:
orth-Holland, 1969). He used **sequents** as his notation for the statements
f logic. These were like our clauses, with conjunctive antecedents and dis-
nctive consequents; except that the antecedents and consequents could be
ny formula of first-order predicate calculus and not just atoms. Also, he
eated the implication arrow as meta-logical, as asserting that at least one
f the consequent formulae was provable from some or all of the antecedent
rmulae.

M. Davis, 'Eliminating the Irrelevant from Mechanical Proofs,' *Pro-
eedings, AMS Symposia of Applied Mathematics*, **15**, 15–30, 1963, used the
ut Rule with formulae in Conjunctive Normal Form (effectively our clauses),
ut did not have clearly developed substitution rules to go with it. Substi-
ttion, and indeed Unification, had been first set out by J. Herbrand in 1930
Researches in the Theory of Demonstration', in J. van Heijenoort (ed.) *From
rege to Gödel, a Source Book in Mathematical Logic*, Cambridge, MA: Har-
ard, 1967). Robinson combined the ideas of Unification and Cut to invent
he Resolution method in 1963 ('Theorem-Proving on the Computer', *Journal
f the Association of Computing Machinery*, **10**:2, 163–74) and in his most
nportant 1965 paper: 'A Machine-Oriented Logic based on the Resolution
rinciple', *Journal of the Association of Computing Machinery*, **12**:1, 23–41.

There is, however, one big difference between the proof methods we
ave used, and those used by Robinson and by Davis. We use Cut and
ubstitution to reason 'forward' from premises to conclusion. They use them
） reason backwards from the desired conclusion to find premises from which
hat conclusion follows deductively. We will study that *backward chaining*
pproach later in the book.

Important textbooks on the Resolution method in CFL and similar
rmalisms, especially in the context of mechanical theorem proving, are
. Kowalski, *Logic for Problem Solving*, New York: North-Holland, 1979;
). Loveland, *Automated Theorem Proving*, Amsterdam: North-Holland, 1978;
. Nilsson, *Principles of Artificial Intelligence*, Palo Alto, CA: Tioga, 1980;
nd J.A. Robinson, *Logic: Form and Function*, New York: North-Holland,
979.

Part IV
EXTENSIONS TO CFL

Chapter 16
Functions

In this last part of the book, we look at ways of extending the expressive powers and deductive techniques:

- In Chapters 16 to 18 we introduce three related notational devices into CFL: functions, identity, and existence.

- In Chapters 19 to 21 we introduce the refutation method for performing deductions in the extended logic with functions, identity and existence.

- Finally, in Chapter 22 we look at the logic programming language PROLOG, which we introduced in Chapter 1, and compare it with all we have learned about CFL.

  In this chapter, we discuss functions, which are a device that allows us to express complex terms such as 'the mother of Charles' and 'the sum of 2 and 3'. We shall consider:

- The basic idea of functions as terms that say 'the (unique) so-and-so'.

- The syntax of functional terms, showing how they are constructed out of simpler terms.

- The semantics of functional terms, which involves extending our familiar valuation theory to cover them.

16.1   Uniqueness

Suppose we want to set up a knowledge base K about people's personal lives. To begin, we can record that people are married:

=> Mar(JOHN)	**A1**
=> Mar(ANNE)	**A2**
=> Mar(PIERRE)	**A3**
=> Mar(MARIE)	**A4**
=> Mar(IGOR)	**A5**
=> Mar(OLGA)	**A6**

Suppose we want to record to whom they are married. One way to do it is to create a dyadic predicate, Mar-to say; then we can write, for example:

    => Mar-to(IGOR,OLGA)

We should then add the axiom that Mar-to is symmetrical:

    Mar-to(x,y) => Mar-to(y,x)   **A7**

(Of course, there are other ways of recording who is married to whom, such as writing Husband(PIERRE,MARIE) and having an axiom: Husband(x,y) => Wife(y,x). But we will remain with the Mar-to approach for now.)

Suppose next we want to refer to somebody's spouse, for example, to say that Pierre's spouse is at her home. We could do it this way:

    Mar-to(PIERRE,x), Home(x,y) => At(x,y)   (1)

This can be read as 'For any objects x and y, if Pierre is married to x, and if y is a home of x, then x is at y.' Note that the computer has not been told that a person is married to only one spouse and has only one home. Even if it did have such information in its knowledge base, (1) would still say that all of Pierre's spouses are at all of their homes. And that is not quite what we were trying to say.

Exercise 16.1   Jill Tar is a sailor, and her men friends follow her to whatever port she is in. How would you express that Jill meets all her men at every port she is in?

Since however, people have only one spouse (at least, we will take it that the people in our knowledge base do), it would be better if we could talk in CFL about *the* spouse of a person and similarly, since these people have only one home, *the* home of a person. There is a common device in logic for doing that, the **function**.

Functions are familiar enough in English. We express them with locutions like 'the home of Pierre', 'Olga's spouse', and 'the minister who married Marie to Pierre'. These are expressions whose job it is to refer to just one object, and typically we use 'the' or the possessive to construct them. Structurally, they consist of **function names**, such as 'the home of ...' and '...'s spouse' and 'the minister who married ... to ...'. When those expressions are given arguments, as in 'the home of Pierre', 'Olga's spouse' and 'the minister who married Marie to Pierre', the result is a **term**, an expression that denotes an object. In this respect, they are just like proper names such as 'Pierre'.

16.2   Syntax of functors

In logic, function names are usually called **functors**. Compare relation or property names, which we call **predicates**. In CFL, we will write functors just like predicates, except that the first letter must be lower-case. So we can define their typography thus:

Definition   Functor

A functor consists of a lower-case letter, followed by zero or more lower-case letters, digits, or hyphens.

(Def. Functor)

Now we can give a definition of terms which extends our earlier definition to include functors and their arguments.

Definition   Term

A term is either:

(a)   A variable, or

(b)   A constant, or

(c)   An *n*-ary functor ($n > 0$), followed by a left parenthesis, followed by n terms separated by commas, followed by a right parenthesis.

(Def. Term)

Figure 16.1 shows some examples of functors, and terms constructed by putting terms in their argument places.

Note carefully that terms built up using functors, such as spouse(OLGA) (Olga's spouse), are very different syntactically and in meaning from atoms built up in a similar fashion using predicates, such as Mar(OLGA) (Olga is married). An atom can appear as an antecedent or a consequent in a clause. But a term built up using a functor cannot, since after all it is a term. Instead, it appears as an argument to a predicate, as in Mar(spouse(OLGA)) (Olga's

English	CFL	Example
the spouse of ...	spouse(...)	spouse(OLGA)
the home of ...	home(...)	home(spouse(OLGA))
the minister who married		
... to ...	m-w-m(...,...)	m-w-m(MARIE, PIERRE)

Figure 16.1 English examples of expressions for functions, with corresponding CFL functors and completed terms.

spouse is married), and in `Mar-to(spouse(OLGA), OLGA)` (Olga's spouse is married to Olga.)

Because predicates and functors are syntactically quite different, we make them typographically different too, by giving them an initial lower-case letter instead of an initial capital, to help make the distinction visually obvious.

Semantically, a predicate with its arguments makes a statement, that is, like a statement in conversational English it says something true or false. More precisely, it is satisfied or not by valuations in interpretations. But a functor with its arguments does not make a statement, it denotes an object, just like a proper name does. (Or, if it contains variables, we should say it has as value an object in the domain of an interpretation. We will look at its semantics later in the chapter.)

Figure 16.2 tabulates the differences between functors and predicates.

	Functor and args	Predicate and args
Typographic difference	lower case initial	capital initial
Example	spouse(x)	Mar(x)
Syntactic type	term	atom
Syntactic role	argument of predicate	antecedent or consequent of clause
Semantic type	name	statement
Semantic role	denotes an object	satisfaction in valuation

Figure 16.2 Differences between function and predicate expressions.

	Constant	Variable
	Individual Constant, *Proper Name*	*Individual Variable,* *Variable*
Simple	PIERRE	x
	CARNIVORE	y
	47	z3
	Constant Complex Term	*Variable Complex Term*
Complex	spouse(PIERRE)	spouse(x)
	m-w-m(IGOR, OLGA)	m-w-m(IGOR, x)
	sum-of(47,9)	sum-of(x,y)

Figure 16.3 Examples of constant and variable simple and complex terms, and the terminology used.

Since a function name followed by its arguments is syntactically a term, we will call such expressions **complex terms**, as opposed to the **simple terms** we have met so far – namely the **proper names** such as MARIE and the **variables** such as x and y3. This gives us a two-by-two classification of terms, as in Figure 16.3.

Note that a complex term is variable as long as it contains at least one individual variable, even if it also contains individual constants.

Since a function takes terms as arguments, it can take complex terms as arguments. In this way, we can build up **nested terms** as complicated as we like, as seen in Figure 16.4.

English	*CFL Term*
Olga's spouse's home	home(spouse(OLGA))
x's maternal grandmother	mother(mother(x))
the spouse of the minister who married x's father to y's mother	spouse(m-w-m(father(x),mother(y)))

Figure 16.4 Examples of nested terms.

Exercise 16.2   Translate these between CFL and English:

(a)   Jill meets all her men at her home.
(b)   Jill's spouse is at his home or her home.
(c)   If Jill's home is in (**At**) a port, then the minister who married Jill to her spouse meets her at that port.
(d)   `Meets(JILL,x,y), Port(y) => At(home(x),y)`
(e)   `At(spouse(x),y), Meets(x,JILL,y) =>`
(f)   `At(home(spouse(x)),y), Port(y), Man(JILL,x)`
       `=> Meets(JILL,spouse(x),y)`

Exercise 16.3   In **list theory**, a list $<a_1 a_2 \ldots a_n>$ is a sequence of zero or more elements, for example:

    <CAESAR GREYMALKIN PIERRE 47>   (L1)

Lists can be elements of lists, for example, this list of people-age pairs has six elements, each of which is a list of two elements:

    <<JOHN 34><ANNE 37><PIERRE 44><MARIE 40><IGOR 29><OLGA 51>>   (L2)

The list with no elements, <>, is known as **NIL**, the **null list**.
     For any non-null list l, we call its first (leftmost) element the **head** or **first** of l, written: `first(l)`; and we call what is left over after removing the head, the **tail** or **rest** of l, written: `rest(l)`. For instance, `first(L1)` is CAESAR and `rest(L1)` is the list $<$ GREYMALKIN PIERRE 47 $>$.
     Where L1 and L2 are the lists above, evaluate these terms:

(a)   `first(L2)`
(b)   `rest(rest(L1))`
(c)   `first(rest(L1))`
(d)   `first(first(L2))`
(e)   `rest(first(L2))`
(f)   `rest(rest(rest(L2)))`
(g)   `first(first(rest(rest(L2))))`
(h)   `rest(rest(first(L2)))`
(i)   `rest(rest(rest(rest(L1))))`
(j)   `first(rest(first(rest(L2))))`

16.3   Semantics of functors

The semantics of functors are quite straightforward, and do not require any modification to the proof theory as developed so far. Constant terms still denote objects, and variable terms have objects as values in a given valuation, as always. All we now need to do is to state the denotation rule for functors to guarantee that this is so.

To do this for each n-ary functor f, we have to take each n-tuple of objects in the domain of the interpretation being considered, and suppose that it could be a sequence of objects that are the values of the n arguments of some occurrence of the term $f(t_1, \ldots, t_n)$. (Note that this term may occur inside another term.) Then since f needs to denote a function in the domain, we secure that by setting up, for each of these n-tuples, some object in the domain to be the value of the function with those objects as arguments.

We handle this by taking the existing definition of interpretation and extending it appropriately to cover functors. So we take the Chapter 11 definition and add a new part to the account of a denotation:

Definition Interpretation

An interpretation $\mathcal{I}$ of a knowledge base K is an ordered pair $\langle \mathcal{W}, \mathcal{D} \rangle$, where:

(1) $\mathcal{W}$ (the **domain of discourse**) is a nonempty set of objects; and

(2) $\mathcal{D}$ (the **denotation function**) is a function defined on all constants, functors and predicates occurring in K such that:

(a) $\mathcal{D}(c)$, for each constant c occurring in K, is an object in $\mathcal{W}$, and

(b) $\mathcal{D}(f)$, for each n-ary functor f occurring in K, is a function from each n-tuple of objects in $\mathcal{W}$ to an object in $\mathcal{W}$.

(c) $\mathcal{D}(P)$, for each n-ary predicate P occurring in K, is an n-ary relation in $\mathcal{W}$.

(Def. Interpretation)

(b) is the new part here. It requires us to define a valuation for all terms consisting of an n-ary functor f and its arguments. To do this, we take its n arguments, which are terms, and find out what their values are in this valuation. Then we find the function in the interpretation (see 2(b) above) which f is interpreted as, and apply that function to the sequence of values just found for the arguments. The resulting value is the value we seek. Note in this discussion the crucial distinction between symbols (f and its n argument terms), and the entities those symbols denote in the interpretation (a function and n objects in the domain).

We set that apparatus up as a modification to Def. Valuation in Chapter 11.

Definition Valuation

In any interpretation $\mathcal{I} = \langle \mathcal{W}, \mathcal{D} \rangle$ of a knowledge base K, a **valuation** $\mathcal{V}$ is a function such that:

(1)   For every constant c occurring in K, $\mathcal{V}(c) = \mathcal{D}(c)$.

(2)   For every variable v, $\mathcal{V}(v)$ is an object in $\mathcal{D}$.

(3)   For every complex term $f(t_1, \ldots, t_n)$:

$$\mathcal{V}(f(t_1, \ldots, t_n)) = \mathcal{D}(f)(\mathcal{D}(t_1), \ldots, \mathcal{D}(t_n))$$

(4)   For every predicate occurring P in K, $\mathcal{V}(P) = \mathcal{D}(P)$.

For any term or predicate E, $\mathcal{V}(E)$ is called the **value** of E in the valuation $\mathcal{V}$.

(Def. Valuation)

In part (3) here, $\mathcal{D}(f)$ is the denotation of the symbol f, that is, the function it is interpreted as. That function takes arguments. They are set out in the definition:

$$\mathcal{D}(t_1), \ldots, \mathcal{D}(t_n)$$

The right-hand side of the equation in part (3) applies the function $\mathcal{D}(f)$ to those arguments. (Note this is all happening in the domain – we are no longer talking about the CFL symbols but about the world they denote.) The interpretation defines a value for the function applied to those objects. The left-hand side of the equation, which *is* talking about a term in CFL, says that the value of that term is the object in the domain just found – that is, the value of that function application.

That completes the semantics for functors. A curiosity about these semantics, which can be quite annoying in practical applications, is that a complex term will always have a value, and that value is always in the domain of discourse. Imagine, for example, that you want to set up a small knowledge base about some family relations for a family, and you include the functor `mother-of`, which you want to interpret in the obvious way as a function from each person to their mother. Then two things follow:

(a)   In your intended interpretation (or any model for your knowledge base) each object, whether human, animal, mineral, or vegetable, will have to have the mother function defined for it. (Our functions are **total**.)

You can live with that, for it is not *really* saying that all the non-animals have mothers, just that this function applies to them. You will probably never do any reasoning that applies `mother-of` to some term interpreted as a vegetable anyway.

(b)   The value of the mother function must be something in the domain of the interpretation. (Our functions are **closed** over the domain of discourse.)

So consider Grandpa (denoted by `GP`, say), the oldest person in your intended interpretation. You must include his mother in the interpretation, so that:

```
mother-of(GP)
```

will have a value in the interpretation. And a mother for her mother, and so on. The only way to avoid this rather ridiculous situation is to have more complex semantics for functors that admit partially defined functors. But these can create more paradoxes than they solve, so we will not pursue them here.

SUMMARY

- **Function.** An expression with arguments, whose value is an object and whose arguments are objects.
- **Definition Functor.** A functor consists of a lower-case letter, followed by zero or more lower-case letters, digits, or hyphens.

(Def. Functor)

- **Definition Term.** A term is either:
  - (a) A variable, or
  - (b) A constant, or
  - (c) An n-ary functor ($n > 0$), followed by a left parenthesis, followed by n terms separated by commas, followed by a right parenthesis.

(Def. Term)

- **Definition Interpretation.** An interpretation $\mathcal{I}$ of a knowledge base K is an ordered pair $\langle \mathcal{W}, \mathcal{D} \rangle$; where:
  - (1) $\mathcal{W}$ (the **domain of discourse**) is a nonempty set of objects, and
  - (2) $\mathcal{D}$ (the **denotation function**) is a function defined on all constants, functors and predicates occurring in K such that:
    - (a) $\mathcal{D}(c)$, for each constant c occurring in K, is an object in $\mathcal{W}$, and
    - (b) $\mathcal{D}(f)$, for each n-ary functor f occurring in K is a function from each n-tuple of objects in $\mathcal{W}$ to an object in $\mathcal{W}$.
    - (c) $\mathcal{D}(P)$, for each n-ary predicate P occurring in K, is an n-ary relation in $\mathcal{W}$.

(Def. Interpretation)

- **Definition Valuation.** In any interpretation $\mathcal{I} = \langle \mathcal{W}, \mathcal{D} \rangle$ of a knowledge base K, a **valuation** $\mathcal{V}$ is a function such that:
  - (1) For every constant occurring c in K, $\mathcal{V}(c) = \mathcal{D}(c)$.
  - (2) For every variable v, $\mathcal{V}(v)$ is an object in $\mathcal{D}$.
  - (3) For every complex term $f(t_1, \ldots, t_n)$:

$$\mathcal{V}(f(t_1, \ldots, t_n)) = \mathcal{D}(f)(\mathcal{D}(t_1), \ldots, \mathcal{D}(t_n))$$

(4)   For every predicate occurring P in K, $\mathcal{V}(P) = \mathcal{D}(P)$

For any term or predicate E, $\mathcal{V}(E)$ is called the **value** of E in the valuation $\mathcal{V}$.

(Def. Valuation)

- **Total functions.** Functions in logic are total, that is, defined for all n-tuples of objects in the domain of discourse of an interpretation (where the functor is n-ary).

- **Closed functions.** Functions in logic are closed over a domain of discourse, that is, if the arguments to a function are all in a given domain of discourse, so is the value of the function for those arguments.

Chapter 17
Identity

This chapter explores the very important logical concept of identity. Identity is the dyadic predicate that allows us to say that two things, such as Prince Charles's mother and Queen Elizabeth II, are one and the same.

- We shall begin by noting the relationship of identity to the idea of functions.

- We shall define the two laws of identity – the axioms that govern the use of identity – and learn how to use them in deductions.

- Finally, we shall look at the semantics of the identity predicate.

17.1   Uniqueness and identity

At the beginning of the last chapter, we noted that the clause

$$\text{Mar-to(PIERRE,x), Home(x,y) => At(x,y)} \tag{1}$$

cannot be constrained to mean what it was intended to mean, that Pierre's spouse is at her home. Rather, it means that all Pierre's spouses are at all of their homes.

Then we saw that by using functions, we could say accurately that Pierre's spouse is at her home, unlike (1) above:

$$\text{=> At(spouse(PIERRE),home(spouse(PIERRE)))} \tag{2}$$

The reason why this is a more accurate rendering of what we said in English is that it says, literally, that *the one and only* spouse of Pierre is at *the one and only* home of that unique spouse of Pierre's. On the other hand, (1) is true in a wide range of interpretations: there can be any number of objects to which the relation in the interpretation denoted by Mar-to relates the object denoted by PIERRE, and each of those can be related to any number of objects by the relations denoted by Home and At. There is simply no way of preventing those interpretations from making (1) true.

This illustrates the importance in logic of the fundamental feature of functions, that for a given object a and function f, there is *just one* object $f(a)$. Similarly for a n-ary function, g say, for given objects $a_1, \ldots, a_n$ there is just one object $g(a_1, \ldots, a_n)$. Logicians describe this by saying that the value of a function at given arguments is **unique**. It is functions that allow us to express assertions about uniqueness in logic.

We are familiar with this feature of functions in elementary arithmetic, which abounds with functions. The 'four function calculator' in everyone's pocket computes with functions in our sense – all of them dyadic. For instance, for any two numbers a and b, there is just one number $a+b$. In our notation we can write, for example, $3 + 4$, as sum(3,4). (Division is not quite a function, for it is untrue that for any two numbers a and b there is just one number $a \div b$. Take the case where $b = 0$.)

Since the value of a function at given arguments is unique, it is natural to use **identity** to say what that value is. In arithmetic this is very familiar, where we write statements like $3 + 4 = 7$. In CFL notation we use Eq as the dyadic identity predicate, so we can write this arithmetic statement as:

=> Eq(sum(3,4),7)

That allows us to define values of functions using axioms in a knowledge base. To return to the knowledge base about people's personal lives that we studied in the last chapter, we could use the following as axioms to assert who is the one and only spouse of whom.

```
=> Eq(spouse(JOHN),ANNE)                                    A8
=> Eq(spouse(ANNE),JOHN)                                    A9
```

and so on for the other two couples.

7.1.1   The two laws of identity

The identity relation, Eq, is a central concept of logic, and is governed by two logical laws of its own.

The first is that identity is **reflexive**, or as Aristotle put it, a thing is that it is and not another thing. This gives us an infinity of axioms, such as:

```
=> Eq(JOHN,JOHN)
=> Eq(spouse(ANNE),spouse(ANNE))
=> Eq(sum(x,times(3,y)),sum(x,times(3,y)))
```

We formally define these, the **Eq axioms**, as follows:

Definition   Eq axioms

For any term t expressible in a knowledge base K, => Eq(t,t) is an axiom of K.

(Def. Eq)

Note that since Eq axioms hold in any knowledge base, they are logical axioms.

From now on, we will bow to custom and allow ourselves to rewrite an expression Eq(t_1,t_2) as $t_1=t_2$.

Reflexivity of identity does not seem to be a very powerful logical law, but the second one, **substitutivity of identity**, certainly is. It works like this. Suppose in a deduction we have a line saying that two objects are identical, for example:

```
=> ANNE = mother(MARIE)
```

and another line saying something about one of them:

```
Nationality(mother(MARIE),x) => Nationality(MARIE,x)
```

then we can replace that term by the one Eq to it:

```
Nationality(ANNE,x) => Nationality(MARIE,x)
```

The last line here follows from the other two by substitutivity of identity. Formally stated, it is:

Definition   Substitutivity of identity axioms

Let t_1 and t_2 be any two terms, let $A(t_1)$ be an atom that contains an occurrence of t_1, and let $A(t_2)$ be the result of replacing that occurrence of t_1 in $A(t_1)$ by t_2. Then:

$$t_1 = t_2, \ A(t_1) \ \Rightarrow \ A(t_2)$$

is an axiom of any knowledge base $\mathcal{K}$.

(Def. Sub=)

Here are some examples of Sub= axioms:

```
      x=y, Mar-to(x,z) => Mar-to(y,z)
      Meets(x,y,z), y=x => Meets(x,x,z)
      z=y, m-w-m(x,y)=z => m-w-m(x,y)=y
{m-w-m(x,y)=m-w-m(y,x),
At(m-w-m(x,y), home(x))} => At(m-w-m(y,x), home(x))
```

The second example has the identity atom as the second antecedent, just to remind you that the order in which atoms of an antecedent set are displayed (like the order in which the elements of any set are displayed) is immaterial.

Exercise 17.1   Here are some clauses which are not examples of Sub= axioms. Why not? In each case, can you describe a world in which the clause is false?

(a)   y=x, Home(x,z) => Home(y,z)
(b)   home(x)=home(y),Mar-to(x,z) => Mar-to(y,z)
(c)   home(x)=home(y), Home(x,z) => Home(y,z)
(d)   x=y, Home(x,z), Port(z) => Home(y,z)

EXAMPLE 17.1

Demonstrate the logical law that identity is symmetrical.

For any terms t_1, t_2, we deduce $t_1 = t_2 \Rightarrow t_2 = t_1$ from any axiom set thus:

Sub=	$t_1 = t_2, \ t_1 = t_1 \Rightarrow t_2 = t_1$	(1
Eq	$\Rightarrow t_1 = t_1$	(2
(1),(2) Cut	$t_1 = t_2 \Rightarrow t_2 = t_1$	

This is a **schematic deduction** for any clause of the form of the schema deduced, for example:

$$y=x \Rightarrow x=y \quad \text{and}$$
$$\text{IGOR=m-w-m(PIERRE, MARIE)} \Rightarrow \text{m-w-m(PIERRE, MARIE)=IGOR}$$

From now on we can introduce any such clause in a deduction, and justify it as 'symmetry of $=$'.

---

xercise 17.2 Show that (a) of the previous exercise is a logical law.

XAMPLE 17.2_____

Prove the other version of Sub=:

$$t_2 = t_1, A(t_1) \Rightarrow A(t_2)$$

Sub=	$t_1 = t_2, A(t_1) \Rightarrow A(t_2)$	**(1)**
Symmetry of $=$	$t_2 = t_1 \Rightarrow t_1 = t_2$	**(2)**
(1),(2) Cut	$t_2 = t_1, A(t_1) \Rightarrow A(t_2)$	

From now on we will use Sub= to refer to either this or the original ub=, as appropriate.

---

xercise 17.3 Give a schematic deduction for the logical law that identity is ansitive.

xercise 17.4 Prove:

(a) $x_1 = y_1, x_2 = y_2, P(x_1, x_2) \Rightarrow P(y_1, y_2)$
(b) $x_1 = y_1, x_2 = y_2 \Rightarrow f(x_1, x_2) = f(y_1, y_2)$

7.2   Reasoning with functions and identity

rmed with the apparatus of functions and identity, we can now express and rove a range of new facts in the personal lives knowledge base K as set out bove and in the previous chapter. For a start we can express monogamy:

$$\text{Mar-to(x,y), Mar-to(x,z)} \Rightarrow \text{y=z} \qquad \textbf{A10}$$

Exercise 17.5   Show that the other way of expressing monogamy:

$$\texttt{Mar-to(x,z), Mar-to(y,z) => x=y} \tag{3}$$

is deducible in K from A10.

If we now add an obvious axiom connecting the marriage relation to the spouse function:

$$\texttt{=> Mar-to(x, spouse(x))} \tag{A11}$$

we can easily derive its converse:

$$\texttt{=> Mar-to(spouse(x), x)} \tag{4}$$

and two clauses showing that we have captured much of the meaning of 'spouse':

$$\texttt{Mar-to(x,y) => y=spouse(x)} \tag{5}$$
$$\texttt{y=spouse(x) => Mar-to(x,y)} \tag{6}$$

Exercise 17.6   Deduce (4), (5) and (6) in the personal lives knowledge base.

Another feature of the spouse function is that it is self-reflexive:

$$\texttt{=> spouse(spouse(x))=x} \tag{A1}$$

Exercise 17.7   Prove that spouses come in pairs:

$$\texttt{spouse(x)=y => spouse(y)=x}$$

7.3   Semantics of identity

The semantic explanation of identity is very simple and obvious. The idea is that $t_1 = t_2$ only if t_1 and t_2 denote the same object in the interpretation. Rephrasing that to allow for satisfaction, we get the formal definition:

Definition   Satisfaction for identity

For any terms t_1 and t_2, $\text{Eq}(t_1, t_2)$ is satisfied by a valuation $\mathcal{V}$ in an interpretation $\mathcal{I}$ only if $\mathcal{V}(t_1) = \mathcal{V}(t_2)$.

(Def. Satisfies)

This is the only occasion on which we have taken a predicate and laid down what its satisfaction conditions are to be in any interpretation at all. All other predicates were local to some knowledge base or other, for example, Mar-to, and we usually had specific interpretations in mind for these. For this reason we call Eq a **logical predicate**. We are saying that the concept of identity, unlike the concept of marriage, is a **logical concept** as are implication, truth, mutual exclusiveness, and many others we have studied.

We now need to show that Eq and Sub= axioms are true in any applicable knowledge base.

Proposition 17.1   Reflexivity of identity

Any Eq axiom {} => $\text{Eq}(t_1, t_1)$ is true in any applicable interpretation.

Proof   In any valuation in the interpretation, both arguments of an Eq axiom have the same object in the domain as value. So, by Def. Satisfies for Eq, $\text{Eq}(t_1, t_1)$ is satisfied in that valuation, and hence so is the clause.   □

Proposition 17.2   Substitutivity of identity

Any Sub= axiom $t_1 = t_2, A(t_1)$ => $A(t_2)$ is true in any applicable interpretation.

Proof   Suppose it is not true. Then there is a valuation $\mathcal{V}$ in the interpretation that satisfies both antecedents but does not satisfy the consequent. Since it satisfies the first antecedent, the values of t_1 and t_2 are the same, by Def. Satisfies for Eq. But now, the only difference between $A(t_1)$ and $A(t_2)$ is that $A(t_2)$ has t_2 somewhere that $A(t_1)$ has t_1. But if the satisfaction conditions for t_1 and t_2 are the same (which they are) then there is no way to create a difference in satisfaction conditions between $A(t_1)$ and $A(t_2)$. So our supposition that one is satisfied and the other is not, is impossible.   □

A fully rigorous treatment of this proposition would go into a lot of detail to demonstrate what we claimed in the second-last sentence of this proof. The two exercises below indicate how such a demonstration would be constructed.

Exercise 17.8 Show that, for any valuation $\mathcal{V}$ of any interpretation, if $\mathcal{V}(t) = \mathcal{V}(t')$, then:

$$\mathcal{V}(f(t, t_1, \ldots, t_n)) = \mathcal{V}(f(t', t_1, \ldots, t_n))$$

where the ts are terms and f is an $n + 1$-ary functor $(n \geq 0)$.

Exercise 17.9 Show that, for any valuation $\mathcal{V}$ of any interpretation, if:

$$\mathcal{V}(t) = \mathcal{V}(t')$$

then $P(t, t_1, \ldots, t_n)$ is satisfied in $\mathcal{V}$ only if $P(t', t_1, \ldots, t_n)$ is satisfied, where the ts are terms and P is an $n + 1$-ary predicate $(n \geq 0)$.

SUMMARY

- **Definition Eq axioms**. For any term t expressible in a knowledge base K, $\text{Eq}(t, t)$ is an axiom of K.

  (Def. Eq)

- **Definition Substitutivity of identity axioms**. Let t_1 and t_2 be any two terms, and $A(t_1)$ be an atom that contains an occurrence of t_1, and let $A(t_2)$ be the result of replacing that occurrence of t_1 in $A(t_1)$ by t_2. Then:

  $$t_1 = t_2, \quad A(t_1) \implies A(t_2)$$

  is an axiom of any knowledge base $\mathcal{K}$.

  (Def. Sub=)

- **Definition Satisfaction for identity**. For any terms t_1 and t_2, $\text{Eq}(t_1, t_2)$ is satisfied by a valuation $\mathcal{V}$ in an interpretation $\mathcal{I}$ only if $\mathcal{V}(t_1) = \mathcal{V}(t_2)$.

  (Def. Satisfies)

- **Reflexivity of identity**. Any Eq axiom $\{\} \Rightarrow \text{Eq}(t_1, t_1)$ is true in any applicable interpretation.

- **Substitutivity of identity**. Any Sub= axiom $t_1 = t_2, A(t_1) \implies A(t_2)$ is true in any applicable interpretation.

Chapter 18
Existence

This chapter studies the fundamental logical concept of existence –
the ability that any language should have to express the existence of
some object meeting a given description, without specifying what
the object is. It is necessary to add to our logic, the structures and
processes for handling existence expressions, not just to increase our
expressive power, but for theoretical reasons too. As we shall see,
the incorporation of existence rounds out CFL into a well-integrated
system.

In this chapter we shall:

- Have an informal look at the peculiar logic of existence assertions.

- Introduce the idea of *existential constants*, devices rather
  like ordinary constants which carry the concept of existence.

- Extend that idea to *existential functors* which express the
  idea of dependent existence.

- Set out the semantics of existential terms, that is, the existential constants and functors.

18.1   What there is

One great weakness in our logical system so far, is that we cannot explicitly say that this or that *exists*. We can say that Caesar was murdered, that Brutus murdered Caesar, and that if anyone murdered Caesar, then Caesar was murdered:

$$
\begin{array}{ll}
\texttt{=> Is-murdered(CAESAR)} & \textbf{(1)} \\
\texttt{=> Murdered(BRUTUS, CAESAR)} & \textbf{(2)} \\
\texttt{Murdered(x, CAESAR) => Is-murdered(CAESAR)} & \textbf{(3)}
\end{array}
$$

But we do not have a way of saying these things:

Someone was murdered.	**(4e)**
Someone murdered Caesar.	**(5e)**
If Caesar was murdered then someone murdered him.	**(6e)**

We cannot express (4e) this way:

```
=> Is-murdered(x)
```

for that says that everyone (everything) was murdered – to be true, every value of x must satisfy it. Similarly, this will not do for (5e):

```
=> Murdered(x,CAESAR)
```

for that is true only if everyone (everything) murdered Caesar. And of course:

```
Is-murdered(CAESAR) => Murdered(x,CAESAR)
```

says that if Caesar was murdered then everyone (everything) did the deed.

So, we cannot use variables to express the idea of 'someone' in translating these English sentences. The only other thing to do is to use constants. Why not use SOMEONE? After all, 'Someone was murdered' is syntactically just like 'Caesar was murdered', and in general you can put 'someone' (or 'something') into an English sentence wherever a proper name is appropriate. Then our three English sentences translate as:

```
=> Is-murdered(SOMEONE)
=> Murdered(SOMEONE, CAESAR)
Is-murdered(CAESAR) => Murdered(SOMEONE, CAESAR)
```

But that will not do either. Since SOMEONE is a constant of CFL, it must denote a single thing in the domain of discourse of any given interpretation of the knowledge base. Then, in the first two of these clauses we are saying that both that person was murdered and that person murdered Caesar – one and the same person. That is not what we wanted to say at all, and it was not what the English sentences conveyed. In Shakespeare's world of the Roman Forum on the Ides of March 44 BC, these two someones are, of course, different. One is Julius Caesar, the other could be Brutus or Casca or any of the other three assassins, but not Caesar. But by using a constant to convey the idea of 'someone', we cannot say they are different.

In other words, whatever its syntax might be, 'someone' does not function semantically as a proper name. This is very clear in English. When we say 'Calpurnia is female and Calpurnia is married', we are mentioning the same person twice, and the sentence implies 'Calpurnia is female and married'. But 'Someone is female and someone is married' does not convey that we are talking about the same person twice, and for that reason does not imply 'Someone is female and married'. Think about 'Someone is female and someone is male'!

18.2   Existential terms

Despite the problems in trying to treat 'someone' semantically exactly like a proper name, to do so is essentially on the right track. The only difference is that successive occurrences of 'someone', unlike successive occurrences of a proper name such as 'Calpurnia', need not denote the same object. This type of denotation, when a term denotes a specific object on one occasion of its use and (in general) denotes another object on another occasion, is known as **existential denotation.** That is why 'someone' has the flavour about it of 'a particular definite person but I am not saying who'.

We can capture existential denotation easily in CFL simply by using constants, but we should use *different* constants for each existential denotation unless we really do mean the *same* someone as mentioned previously. A few examples will make this clear.

If we start out by rendering (4e) by:

> => Is-murdered(UNKNOWN)   (4)

then we should use a different constant for the existential denotation in (5e):

> => Murdered(UNKNOWN-1, CAESAR)   (5)

Now we are not making the earlier mistake of equating these two someones. Also, we should add that UNKNOWN and UNKNOWN-1 are persons, as is implied by the use of 'someone'. We will use P(⟨object⟩) for '⟨object⟩ is a person'. Then (4e) is translated jointly by (4) and:

> => P(UNKNOWN)

Finally, we should do the same for the translation of (5e).

What about the translation of (6e)? Are we denoting the same murderer here as in (5e)? (To answer such questions, where the words themselves or the known context do not provide an answer, one must inquire of their author.) In case of doubt, it is best to assume that the denotations are not necessarily the same; so here we will translate by these two clauses:

```
Murdered(CAESAR) => Murdered(UNKNOWN-2, CAESAR)
               => P(UNKNOWN-2)                        (6)
```

Terms that we introduce in this way, as the bearers of existential denotation, we call **existential terms**, because to use them is to assert the existence of something (for example, the existence of a murderer, or of a murderer of Caesar). Historically, they are called **Skolem terms** after their inventor. They can occur as simple terms or as functors, but we will look only at simple existential terms for now.

It is important to note that simple existential terms are subtly but importantly different in their semantics from ordinary constants. It might seem that UNKNOWN behaves semantically just like CAESAR in that it denotes an individual in the world that the knowledge base is about. It might also seem that the only difference between existential and ordinary terms is **pragmatic**: when we use existential terms we might not know, or at least are not telling, what individual the term could be denoting. (Pragmatics as used here is a technical term for a third area of language theory alongside syntax and semantics. It is defined as the study of the *use* of language, thus it considers, as syntax and semantics do not, the relationships between language and its speakers, writers, hearers and readers.)

That there is a significant semantic difference between the two types of constants can be brought out by asking what are the negations of these two clauses:

```
=> P(CAESAR)
=> P(UNKNOWN)
```

The first says that Caesar is a person, so its negation has to say that Caesar is not a person:

```
P(CAESAR) =>
```

Check that the two clauses have opposite truth-values in any interpretation. However, the negation of the other clause, => P(UNKNOWN), cannot be:

```
P(UNKNOWN) =>
```

for that says 'something is not a person'. Remember that => P(UNKNOWN) is representing the claim that something is a person, that is, there exists an object with the property P (being a person). Plainly, to deny that, we say 'There are no people', which is:

```
P(x) =>
```

That is the negation we want.

We will be looking more closely at the formal semantics of existence at the end of this chapter, but it is worth looking a little closer at this, perhaps paradoxical situation about negation, right now. It might seem that despite the above argument, => P(UNKNOWN) and P(UNKNOWN) => are negations of each other, as could be shown by considering the formal semantics of the two clauses. But that is to suppose that UNKNOWN must behave just like an ordinary constant such as CAESAR. What the above informal considerations about negating 'Something is a person' show, is that it *cannot* act in that way. Rather, we have to construe the semantics of UNKNOWN along these lines: if any value of x can be found that satisfies => P(x), then give UNKNOWN that value, which will make => P(UNKNOWN) true. Put crudely, existential terms do not get their denotation when we define the interpretation (unlike ordinary constants). We take the interpretation as given, then try to find values for the existential constants to make the clauses in which they occur come out true. That makes them a little like variables.

From now on, to indicate that a simple term is existential, we will always begin it with the at-sign, @.

Here are some examples of frequently encountered types of existential statement.

(a)   Some women are married:

```
=> Woman(@A)
=> Mar(@A)
```

Translating back, this says there is an individual who is a woman and married. Note that we needed two clauses to say it, and had to use the same existential term in both clauses.

(b)   Some women are not married:

```
          => Woman(@B)
Mar(@B) =>
```

Note that we used a different existential term in this example. If (a) and (b) both belong to the same knowledge base, this is necessary to avoid saying that there is an individual who is a woman, married, and not married.

(c)   Some married women are happy:

```
=> Woman(@C)
=> Married(@C)
=> Happy(@C)
```

When adjectives qualify nouns, as in 'married women', we are picking out those objects that are both married and women; so here we are saying 'There is an individual who is a woman, married, and happy'.

Exercise 18.1   Translate the following:

- (a)   Someone is married to John.
- (b)   Someone's spouse is happy.
- (c)   There are happy married people.
- (d)   There is a place where everyone's spouse is.
- (e)   Pierre and Igor are married to the same person.
- (f)   Jill meets someone at some port.
- (g)   There is a person whom Jill meets at every port.
- (h)   If there is a port Jill is at, Jill's spouse is there.

Exercise 18.2   Translate these into idiomatic English:

(a)
```
                          => Planet(@P1)
                          => Cold(@P1)
                          => Gaseous(@P1)
```
(b)
```
                          => Planet(@P2)
              Cold(@P2) =>
           Gaseous(@P2) =>
```
(c)
```
                          => Mar-to(@A, @B)
                          => P(@A)
                          => P(@B)
```
(d) `P(@C),Mar-to(@C,JILL) =>`

(e)
```
              Port(x) => Meets(@D, JILL, x)
                      => P(@D)
```
(f)
```
                          => Mar-to(JILL, @E)
                          => Mar-to(JILL, @F)
                 @E=@F =>
                          => P(@E)
                          => P(@F)
```
(g)
```
                          => At(home(ANNE),@G),At(spouse(ANNE),@G)
                          => Place(@G)
```
(h)
```
                          => spouse(m-w-m(OLGA, @H)) = @H
                          => P(@H)
```

Here are a couple of surprising translations. The clause:

```
P(x), Mar(x) => Mar(JOHN)                              (7)
```

says that if there exists a married person, John is married. More loosely,
if anyone is married, John is. Why does it say that? Well, the English
translation is plainly false just if both (a) there exists a married person, and
(b) John is not married. And (7) is false only if some valuation satisfies the
antecedent but not the consequent. That will happen (assuming the intended
meaning for the predicates) only if (a) there is a married person (satisfying
the antecedent) but (b) John is not married (consequent not satisfied). So the
truth-conditions for the English and the logic agree. In general, if variables
$v_1, \ldots, v_n$ occur in antecedents of a clause but not in consequents, the clause
can be read as 'If there exist objects $v_1, \ldots, v_n$ of which the antecedents are
true, then a consequent is true.' Another example is:

```
Mar-to(JOHN,x),Mar-to(JOHN,y),
                 Older(x,y) => Bigamist(JOHN)          (8)
```

The use of variables in these examples rather than existential terms seems
more natural if we read the examples not as '*If there exist* two people x and
y ...', but equivalently as '*For any* two people x and y, *if* ...'. In this way,
(7) can be read as 'For any person at all, if s/he is married, so is John'.

18.3   Existential functors

How should we translate 'Everyone knows someone'? The following will not
do (using Knows(⟨knower⟩,⟨known⟩)):

```
P(x) => Knows(x, @A)                                   (9a)
     => P(@A)                                          (9b)
```

for that says that there is a particular person whom everyone knows! To
check that reading, note that the first clause is true only if every valuation
for **x** satisfies it; in which case all of these must be true (assuming Pierre and
friends are in the knowledge base, and using **s** instead of **spouse**):

```
        P(JOHN) => Knows(JOHN, @A)
        P(ANNE) => Knows(ANNE, @A)
     P(s(MARIE)) => Knows(s(MARIE), @A)
  P(s(s(PIERRE))) => Knows(s(s(PIERRE)),@A)
P(m-w-m(IGOR,OLGA)) => Knows(m-w-m(IGOR,OLGA),@A)
```

and an infinity of other ground instances.

Knower	People Known	Function
John	John, Anne, Pierre	@f(JOHN) = PIERRE
Anne	Anne, John, Igor	@f(ANNE) = JOHN
Pierre	Pierre, Marie, Anne	@f(PIERRE) = PIERRE
Marie	Marie, Pierre, Olga	@f(MARIE) = OLGA
Igor	Igor, Olga	@f(IGOR) = OLGA
Olga	Olga	@f(OLGA) = OLGA

Figure 18.1 People in a six-person world, the people they know, and a CFL representation of a function from the people to those they know.

Exercise 18.3 Why an infinity?

The trouble with (9a) is that the existential term **@A** must denote one and the same person, no matter who is being said to do the knowing. However, we are trying to describe a situation in which different knowers may well know different people – the question of who is known depends on who the knower is.

How do we represent that situation, since (9a) will not do? If the question of who is known depends on the knower, we can imagine a function from each knower to *one of* the people they know. (Everyone, remember, is said to know one or more people.) Let us represent that function by **@f** – we will explain the existential flag **@** later. Then supposing that the sets of people whom people know are as in Figure 18.1, we could make **@f** be as shown in that table. There are many other choices we could have made from the people a person knows, in order to construct **@f** ($3^4 \times 2 \times 1$, actually), but any one of these will do.

Exercise 18.4 By realizing that each of the six people in our knowledge base knows him- or herself, give a simple definition of a function **@g** from these people into the people they know.

Now the translation of 'Everyone knows someone' is easily expressed:

$$P(x) \Rightarrow Knows(x, @f(x)) \tag{10a}$$
$$P(x) \Rightarrow P(@f(x)) \tag{10b}$$

This could be read as 'Every person knows someone whose identity depends on that person'. We give the functor the @ sign, since like @A, it carries existential denotation – the person denoted is not made explicit and indeed may not be known by the speaker.

Another example of the same sort is the translation of 'Every married couple have a child'. Using Child(⟨child⟩,⟨parent-1⟩,⟨parent-2⟩) we might try:

```
P(x), P(y), Mar-to(x,y) => Child(@KID,x,y)
```

but that has the same error as (9a) above: it says that a particular person is a child of every married couple. The identity of the child, however, depends on that of both parents, so we need:

```
P(x), P(y), Mar-to(x,y) => Child(@k(x,y),x,y)
```

Exercise 18.5   Translate the following:

- (a) Someone knows everyone.
- (b) Everyone is known by someone or other.
- (c) There's someone whom Jill meets in every port.
- (d) Jill meets someone in every port.
- (e) Everyone meets someone in every port.
- (f) Everyone meets Jill in some port.
- (g) Everyone meets someone in some port.
- (h) Everyone who meets someone in some port is married to someone else.

18.4   The semantics of existential terms

Now, we shall make some formal definitions of the typography and semantics of existential functors and constants.

First, we set up the typography to ensure that they are indeed constants and functors. The way to do that is to say that the earlier definitions of constants and functors were defining a subset of constants and functors call them **individual constants** and **individual functors**). Now we can put an @ sign in front of those to get the existential version, then say that constants and functors are individual or existential constants and functors, respectively. Suitable definitions are in the Summary.

The semantics of existential constants and functors is a little subtle. To begin, we accept the whole of the formal semantics apparatus that we have set up so far, but do not extend it to existential constants and functors. It applies only to individual constants and functors. In particular, an interpretation does not define any denotation or valuation for existential constants or functors.

As we have seen, we cannot say that an existential constant behaves just like an ordinary individual constant, denoting some object in the domain of discourse of a given interpretation $\mathcal{I}$. The reason is, that when we assert a clause containing an existential constant, we are intending the existential constant to refer to some object in the domain of discourse, that will make the clause come out true in the interpretation. For example, if we assert the clause:

    => F(@A)   (11)

we are intending the @A not to refer to just any element in the domain, but to one or another of the elements in the denotation of F. This is because (11) says that *something* Fs. If, in a given interpretation $\mathcal{I}$, there are elements of the domain of discourse that are in the denotation of F, then @A needs to denote one of them. If it did not, then (11) would be false in $\mathcal{I}$, which is not what is intended.

The formal situation then, is this. To begin with a simple case; suppose we have a clause C containing an existential constant e in it somewhere. (Write this as $C(e)$ for explicitness.) The question is, given some interpretation $\mathcal{I}$, is $C(e)$ true in it?

We determine the answer this way. Recall that interpretations are not defined over existential constants, only individual ones. So we will talk of **extended interpretations** which are like ordinary ones but they give a denotation to existential constants (and functors) too. Then we can simply say that $C(e)$ is true in $\mathcal{I}$ only if there is an extension of $\mathcal{I}$ in which $C(e)$ is true.

EXAMPLE 18.1

Take a simple example. Suppose $\mathcal{I} = [\mathcal{W}, \mathcal{D}]$, where the domain of discourse $\mathcal{W} = \{1, 2, 3\}$ and the denotation of a dyadic predicate F is given by $\mathcal{D}(F) = \{\langle 1, 3 \rangle, \langle 2, 2 \rangle, \langle 3, 2 \rangle\}$. That is, 1 Fs to 3, 2 Fs to itself, and 3 Fs to 2. Now, is => F(x,@A) true in $\mathcal{I}$?

No, it is not. For no matter which of the three objects we make @A denote in an extension of $\mathcal{I}$, there is a valuation which does not satisfy the clause in that extension. If, for example, @A denotes 2 in an extension of $\mathcal{I}$, then a valuation giving x a value of 1 will not satisfy the clause.

Exercise 18.6 In the previous example, modify the denotation of F so that the clause is true in $\mathcal{I}$.

Now we have to extend the semantics to cover existential functors. This is an extrapolation of the above in an obvious way. If f is an existential functor, then clause $C(f)$ is true in $\mathcal{I}$ only if there is an extension to $\mathcal{I}$ in which $C(f)$ is true.

Exercise 18.7 With $\mathcal{I}$ as in the previous example, is => F(x,@f(x)) true in $\mathcal{I}$?

There is still more to the semantics, however. We have to allow several existential constants or functors to occur in one clause. Again the extension is straightforward and obvious. If $e_1, \ldots, e_n$ are all the existential functors or constants occurring in a clause C, then we require an extension $\mathcal{I}'$ to $\mathcal{I}$, giving denotations to $e_1, \ldots, e_n$ such that C is true in $\mathcal{I}'$. If, and only if, such an $\mathcal{I}'$ exists, is C true in $\mathcal{I}$.

We can now formally state the definition of the extension of an interpretation.

Definition Extension of an interpretation

Let $\mathcal{I}$ be an interpretation, and let $\{e_1, \ldots, e_n\}$ be a set of existential constants and functors. Then $\mathcal{I}'$ is an **extension** of $\mathcal{I}$ covering $\{e_1, \ldots, e_n\}$ only if it contains $\mathcal{I}$ and if it defines objects in the domain of $\mathcal{I}$ as the denotations of all the existential constants in $\{e_1, \ldots, e_n\}$, and if it defines k-place functions in the domain of $\mathcal{I}$ as the denotations of all k-place existential functors in $e_1, \ldots, e_n\}$, for all k.

(Def. Extend)

The above definition extends an interpretation to cover any set of existential constants and functors. We can now restrict that notion of an extended interpretation so that it just deals with the existential constants and functors occurring in the clauses that concern us, as in, say, a deduction.

Definition Adequate extension of an interpretation

If $\mathcal{I}$ is an interpretation adequate to a clause (or set of clauses) C, then $\mathcal{I}'$ is an extension of $\mathcal{I}$ **adequate** to C if it is an extension covering all the existential constants and functors in C.

(Def. Extend)

The semantic concepts of satisfaction and truth can now be obtained quite easily.

To define satisfaction, note first that for every valuation V in I there is a corresponding valuation V' in I' that agrees with V in the values it gives to variables, and moreover there are plainly no valuations V' other than these. We will call such a valuation V' the **extension** of V in I'.

So, the question is, for a given V in I, can we find an adequate extension I' of I whose V' which extends V, satisfies the clause C in which we are interested? If there is such an I', then we allow C to be satisfied by the original V.

Definition   Satisfaction for existential clauses

A clause C containing existential constants or functors is satisfied by a valuation V in an interpretation I only if there is an extension I' of I adequate to C in which the extension V' of V satisfies C.

(Def. Satisfaction)

Now for truth. We cannot expect our definition of truth in terms of satisfaction to cover existential clauses; we might have a situation in which each valuation of a clause in an interpretation I satisfies an existential clause C, but does so because of different extensions of I. Truth of C in I must be defined in terms of its truth in a single extension of I.

Definition   Truth for existential clauses

A clause C containing existential constants or functors is true in an interpretation I only if there is an extension I' of I adequate to C in which C is true.

(Def. Truth)

18.5   Proof theory for existential terms

We now need to consider how to accommodate existential terms into the proof theory of CFL. We need, for example, to be able to deduce 'John knows someone' from 'John knows Mary'; that is, Knows(JOHN,@A) from Knows(JOHN, MARY).

18.5.1   Introducing existential constants

We handle this inference by a new type of substitution rule, which we will call **existential substitution**. This allows us to replace any *occurrences* of a constant in a clause by a *new* existential constant. Consider, for example, 'Whoever Jill knows, Jill loves':

```
Knows(JILL,x) => Loves(JILL,x)                    (12)
```

Replacing the second JILL gives us 'There is someone who loves everyone Jill knows' (assuming a domain of persons for simplicity):

```
Knows(JILL,x) => Loves(@A,x)                       (13)
```

That certainly follows from (12).

Also, we can replace the first JILL in (12) to infer 'There is someone such that whoever they know, Jill loves':

```
Knows(@B,x) => Loves(JILL,x)                       (14)
```

Did we have to use a new existential constant, @B, here? Yes, if we are in the middle of a deduction in which we have already inferred (13). A new constant has to be new in the deduction in which it is introduced. Note that (14) does not say 'Whoever someone knows, Jill loves', which does not follow from (12). That would be Knows(y,x) => Loves(JILL,x).

Next, we could take (14) and replace the remaining JILL. We must use a new existential constant:

```
Knows(@B,x) => Loves(@C,x)                         (15)
```

This says 'There are two people such that whoever the first knows, the second loves.' That follows from (12) too, since there is no requirement that the two people be different, that is, no requirement that the two existential constants have different denotations.

Finally, we can replace both JILLs in (12) by the same new existential constant, giving 'There is someone such that everyone they know, they love':

```
Knows(@D,x) => Loves(@D,x)                         (16)
```

8.5.2 Introducing existential functors

Existential functors can be introduced in the same non-uniform way as we introduced existential constants, above. Their arguments can be any or all of the different terms in the clause. And like introduced existential constants, they must be new to the deduction.

For example, from (12) above it follows that whoever Jill knows, someone loves:

```
Knows(JILL,x) => Loves(@f(x),x)                    (17)
```

(17) is weaker than (13) since it does not restrict the lovers of the differen
people x to being one and the same person. Consequently, it should be de
ducible from (13) and not just from the stronger (12). We can perform th
deduction by replacing the @A in (12) by @f(x). In other words, when w
introduce an existential term, we can do so by replacing not just individua
constants, but in fact any constant term, that is, any term at all, as long a
it does not contain variables. The closed term could be a constant, like A
or a constant complex term, like sum(product(3,5),2) (that is, $3 * 5 + 2$
or an existential constant, like @B, or a constant existential term, such a
f(@g(A),B).

We can now state the complete rule for existential substitution.

Definition   Existential substitution

Let E be any expression of CFL, let t be a closed term, and let e be an
existential constant or existential term $@f(t_1, \ldots, t_n)$ where f is a functor an
the t_is $(1 \leq i \leq n)$ are terms occurring in E. Then $E[e/t, j_1, \ldots, j_k]$ is th
expression that results from replacing the j_1th ... j_kth occurrences of t in
by e.

(Def. ExSu

Exercise 18.8   Find these expressions:

(a) $P(A,x,A,A)[@B/A, 1, 3]$
(b) $P(A,A) \Rightarrow Q(g(A),x)[@f(x,A)/A, 2, 3]$
(c) $P(f(A,B),f(A,C)) \Rightarrow Q(A,C,f(A,B))[@K/f(A,B), 2]$
(d) $P(@A,x) \Rightarrow Q(@A,y)[@g(x,y)/@A, 2]$
(e) $P(f(A,B)) \Rightarrow Q(f(B,A))[@A/A, 1]$

We can now state the transformation rule for existential substitution
and prove its soundness.

Definition   Existential substitution rule

Let C be a clause occurring in a deduction, let t be a closed term, and let e b
any existential constant or existential term $@f(t_1, \ldots, t_n)$ where f is a functo
and the t_is $(1 \leq i \leq n)$ are terms occurring in C. Then $C[e/t, j_1, \ldots, j$
may be deduced from C, provided that, if e is an existential constant it do
not occur earlier in the deduction, and if e is $@f(t_1, \ldots, t_n)$, then $@f$ does n
occur earlier in the deduction.

(Def. ExSub-Rule

Proposition 18.1   Soundness of ExSub-rule

If a clause C is true in an interpretation $\mathcal{I}$, then so is any clause C' obtained from it by ExSub-Rule.

Proof C' is obtained from C by replacing some occurrences of a closed term by an expression e, which is either (a) an existential constant or (b) a term $f(t_1, \ldots, t_n)$, where $t_1, \ldots, t_n$ are terms occurring in C.

a) We take an applicable extension $\mathcal{I}'$ of $\mathcal{I}$, in which the existential constant e denotes what t does. We can always find such an extension, since e is new to the deduction, so we can give it whatever denotation we like. Then C' is true in $\mathcal{I}'$, and hence, by Def. Truth for existential clauses, it is true in $\mathcal{I}$.

b) Let the variables occurring in e be $v_1, \ldots, v_k$. These all occur in C. We take an applicable extension $\mathcal{I}'$ of $\mathcal{I}$, and we extend each valuation $\mathcal{V}$ in $\mathcal{I}$ to a valuation $\mathcal{V}'$ in $\mathcal{I}'$ by defining $\mathcal{V}'(f(t_1, \ldots, t_n)) = \mathcal{V}(t)$. We can always do this, since @f is new to the deduction, so we can give it whatever valuation we like. Then $\mathcal{V}'(C') = \mathcal{V}(C)$, since where C and C' differ, $\mathcal{V}$ and $\mathcal{V}'$ give the same value to those differing parts. Since C, being true in $\mathcal{I}$, is satisfied by every valuation $\mathcal{V}$, it follows that C' is true in $\mathcal{I}'$. Hence, by *Def. Truth* for existential clauses, it is true in $\mathcal{I}$.   □

Exercise 18.9   Prove all the entailments shown in this 'hexagon of double quanification'. If $L(\langle x \rangle, \langle y \rangle)$ means $\langle x \rangle$ loves $\langle y \rangle$, give translations of each clause.

(a) => L(x,y)

(b) => L(@A,y)   (c) => L(x,@B)

(d) => L(@f(y),y)   (e) => L(x,@g(x))

(f) => L(@C,@D)

SUMMARY

- **Individual constant.** An individual constant consists of a capital letter, followed by any number of capital letters, digits, or hyphens.

- **Individual functor.** An individual functor consists of a lower case letter, followed by any number of lower case letters, digits, or hyphens

- **Existential constant.** An existential constant (or *Skolem constant* consists of an © sign followed by an individual constant.

- **Existential functor.** An existential functor (or *Skolem functor*) consists of an © sign followed by an individual functor.

- **Constant.** A constant is either an individual constant or an existential constant.

- **Functor.** A functor is either an individual functor or an existential functor.

- **Existential term.** A term containing an existential constant or functor. Those that do not are **individual terms**.

- **Pragmatics.** The study of the relationship between language and its users.

- **Pragmatics of existential constants and functors.** Used to indicate that the value of the term is not being explicitly expressed by the user. Similar to English 'something'.

- **Existential denotation.** In English, terms have existential denotation when, though they are constants, they normally denote different objects on different occasions of their use. Example: 'something'. Existential denotation may not occur in logic, so an English term with existential denotation gets translated to different existential terms whenever its occurrences *could* denote different objects.

- **Definition Extension of an interpretation.** Let $\mathcal{I}$ be an interpretation, and let $\{e_1, \ldots, e_n\}$ be a set of existential constants and functors Then $\mathcal{I}'$ is an **extension** of $\mathcal{I}$ covering $\{e_1, \ldots, e_n\}$ only if it contains $\mathcal{I}$ but also defines objects in the domain of $\mathcal{I}$ as the denotations of all the existential constants in $\{e_1, \ldots, e_n\}$, and defines k-place functions in the domain of $\mathcal{I}$ as the denotations of all k-place existential functors in $\{e_1, \ldots, e_n\}$, for all k.

  (Def. Extend

- **Definition Adequate extension of an interpretation.** If $\mathcal{I}$ is an interpretation adequate to a clause (or set of clauses) C, then $\mathcal{I}'$ is an extension of $\mathcal{I}$ **adequate** to C if it is an extension covering all the existential constants and functors in C.

  (Def. Extend

- **Extension of a valuation.** If $\mathcal{I}'$ is an extension of $\mathcal{I}$ adequate for an existential clause C, then the extension $\mathcal{V}'$ in $\mathcal{I}'$ of a valuation $\mathcal{V}$ in $\mathcal{I}$ is the valuation that agrees with $\mathcal{V}$ in the values it gives to all the variables.

- **Definition Satisfaction for existential clauses.** A clause C containing existential constants or functors is satisfied by a valuation $\mathcal{V}$ in an interpretation $\mathcal{I}$ only if there is an extension $\mathcal{I}'$ of $\mathcal{I}$ adequate to C in which the extension $\mathcal{V}'$ of $\mathcal{V}$ satisfies C.

  (Def. Satisfaction)

- **Definition Truth for existential clauses.** A clause C containing existential constants or functors is true in an interpretation $\mathcal{I}$ only if there is an extension $\mathcal{I}'$ of $\mathcal{I}$ adequate to C in which C is true.

  (Def. Truth)

- **Definition Existential substitution.** Let E be any expression of CFL, let t be a closed term, and let e be any existential constant or existential term $@f(t_1, \ldots, t_n)$ where f is a functor and the t_is $(1 \le i \le n)$ are terms occurring in E. Then $E[e/t, j_1, \ldots, j_k]$ is the expression that results from replacing the j_1th $\ldots j_k$th occurrences of t in E by e.

  (Def. ExSub)

- **Definition Existential substitution rule.** Let C be a clause occurring in a deduction, let t be a closed term, and let e be any existential constant or existential term $@f(t_1, \ldots, t_n)$ where f is a functor and the t_is $(1 \le i \le n)$ are terms occurring in C. Then $C[e/t, j_1, \ldots, j_k]$ may be deduced from C, provided that, if e is an existential constant it does not occur earlier in the deduction, and if e is $@f(t_1, \ldots, t_n)$ then $@f$ does not occur earlier in the deduction.

  (Def. ExSub-Rule)

- **Soundness of existential substitution rule.** If a clause C is true in an interpretation $\mathcal{I}$, then so is any clause C' obtained from it by the existential substitution rule.

Chapter 19
Refutation and denial

In the final chapters we shall study a new way of applying the resolution proof procedure to the derivation of deductions of a conclusion from premisses. Instead of working forwards from the premisses until we reach the conclusion, a process known as *forward chaining*, we will *deny* the conclusion we are trying to reach, and apply resolution backwards from that denial until we reach some contradiction with the premisses. While this method, called *backward chaining* or *refutation*, sounds more complex and less obvious as a theory of reasoning, it is in fact simpler and easier to use than forward chaining.

In this chapter we shall introduce the idea of a refutation proof, and concentrate on the slightly tricky business of forming the denials of the conclusions we wish to prove.

19.1   Ground clauses

We begin by considering clauses of the sort discussed in Chapters 8 and 9, clauses with no variables in them, and no existential terms either, that is, ground clauses. Consider an example of a forward-chaining deduction.

EXAMPLE 19.1_____

Use forward chaining to prove:

$$p \Rightarrow s \tag{C}$$

given the premisses

$$p \Rightarrow q, r \tag{P1}$$
$$q \Rightarrow s \tag{P2}$$
$$r \Rightarrow s \tag{P3}$$

Set out in the tree format, to emphasize the forward chaining, this is:

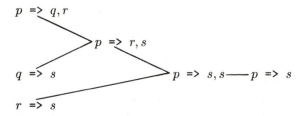

_____

Exercise 19.1   Set this out as a proof in the line-by-line format.

_____

In the backward-chaining approach, we still use the Cut rule to do the work, but we begin with the **negation** (the **denial**) of the conclusion to be proved. In the example above, we are trying to prove $p \Rightarrow s$. A quick check of the informal truth-functional semantics presented in Chapter 8 shows that this is true *unless* its antecedent p is true and its consequent s is false. So to deny that conclusion we assert that p *is* true, and that s *is* false. That is, we deny s.

Now recall that to assert an atom p, we write the clause $\Rightarrow p$, and that to deny an atom s we write the clause $s \Rightarrow$, which asserts its falsity. So now, we have two new assertions:

$$\Rightarrow p \qquad\qquad\qquad\qquad\qquad\qquad \textbf{(D1)}$$
$$s \Rightarrow \qquad\qquad\qquad\qquad\qquad\qquad\quad \textbf{(D2)}$$

We call these (D1) and (D2) to mark that they arise from denying the conclusion. They are not really premises. Together, they comprise the **denial set** for the conclusion.

Now we proceed with a deduction to see where it gets us. In carrying out this deduction, we will begin with the new negative assertion (D2), and always try to resolve using the last resolution product we made. (These are generally two good tactics to use.) We rearrange the ordering of the data slightly to improve the layout of the tree:

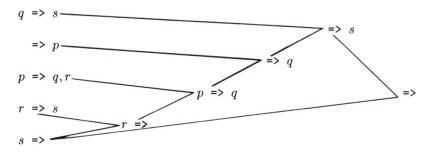

Notice that in this deduction, we have ended up with the **empty clause**, $\Rightarrow$. Recall that it is logically false: it cannot be true in any interpretation at all. So we are in this situation: by applying only the cut rule, which we know is sound (preserves truth), we have deduced something we know to be false. So in any interpretation you choose, one or more of our five premises *must* have been false.

This situation is known as *reductio ad absurdum*, 'I reduce to a contradiction.' If, from any set of assumptions, a contradiction is deducible, then not all of the assumptions are true. In that case, we know we must reject one (or more) of them.

In the example, which can we reject? We cannot reject the premises with which we began, (P1)–(P3), because what we were trying to do was to show that *if* they are true, so is the conclusion. So we are deliberately considering only interpretations that make them all true (if there are any). The assumption we reject is our only real assumption, that the conclusion is false. That, in fact, was split up into two new assertions, (D1) and (D2). In other words, where we accept the premises we cannot accept both (D1) and (D2). But to accept them both is precisely to deny the conclusion (C). That is, we cannot deny the conclusion consistently with accepting the premises. That is, the conclusion must follow logically from the premises.

It is not hard to show that, in general, we deny a non-variable, non-existential clause $p_1, \ldots, p_n \Rightarrow q_1, \ldots, q_m$ by asserting all the antecedents and denying all the consequents. That is, we add to the knowledge base:

$$=> \; p_1$$
$$\ldots$$
$$=> \; p_n$$
$$q_1 \; =>$$
$$\ldots$$
$$q_m \; =>$$

Proposition 19.1   Denial of a ground clause

Let $C = p_1, \ldots, p_n \; => \; q_1, \ldots, q_m (m, n \geq 0)$ be a ground clause. Form the denial set D of C:

$$\{ \; => \; p_1, \ldots, \; => \; p_n, q_1 \; => \; , \ldots, q_n \; => \; \}$$

Then, for any interpretation $\mathcal{I}$, C is true in $\mathcal{I}$ only if not all clauses in D are true in $\mathcal{I}$.

Proof Suppose C is true in $\mathcal{I}$. Then by Def. Truth for ground clauses, either an antecedent p_i is false, or a consequent q_j is true, in $\mathcal{I}$. In that case, either $=> \; p_i$ is false, or $q_j \; =>$ is false, in $\mathcal{I}$.

Conversely, suppose that at least one of the clauses displayed above is false in $\mathcal{I}$. Then either some clause $=> \; p_i$ is false, or some clause $q_j \; =>$ is false, in $\mathcal{I}$. In the first case, p_i is true in $\mathcal{I}$, in which case C is true in $\mathcal{I}$ by Def. Truth for ground clauses. In the second case q_j is true in $\mathcal{I}$, in which case again C is true in $\mathcal{I}$ by Def. Truth for ground clauses.   □

Exercise 19.2 Use the refutation method to do these deductions. List the denial set in each case:

  (a)   Modus Ponens: $=> \; p$; $p \; => \; q$,   therefore $=> \; q$
  (b)   Syllogism: $p \; => \; q$; $q \; => \; r$ therefore $p \; => \; r$
  (c) $p, q \; => \; r$; $s \; => \; q, p$ therefore $p, s \; => \; p, r$

To sum up:

- The aim of a backward-chaining deduction is to deduce the empty clause.

- To do a backward-chaining deduction, we must add to our premisses the negation of the conclusion we wish to prove. This may mean adding more than one clause.

- In the case of ground clauses, we do this by asserting all the antecedents of the clause we wish to prove, and denying all its consequents.

Exercise 19.3   Repeat Examples 14.1 and 14.2 of Chapter 14 (pp. 172–4), using refutation.

19.2   Variable clauses

We now need to consider how to deny conclusions containing variables. A clause containing variables, such as `Inside(x,y) => Smaller(x,y)` is being asserted to hold for all values of the variables, here x and y. So if *that* is not so, there are some values of x and y that do not satisfy the clause. Put another way, if `Inside(x,y) => Smaller(x,y)` is not true for all values of x and y, then there are objects, which we could name @X and @Y say, such that `Inside(@X,@Y)` is true and `Smaller(@X,@Y)` is false.

This makes denying a universal clause very easy. To describe the steps involved, we will first set up some useful terminology. A **unit clause** has just one atom p in it; so its form is either => p, in which case we say it is a **positive unit clause**, or p => , in which case we say it is a **negative unit clause**.

Then the steps involved in forming the denial set of a universal clause are:

(1)   Replace all variables in the clause uniformly by new existential (Skolem) constants, a different one for each different variable.

(2)   Make a positive unit clause out of each of the resulting antecedents.

(3)   Make a negative unit clause out of each of the resulting consequents.

(4)   The denial set comprises all the unit clauses made in (1) and (2).

Note that steps (2)–(4) are just as for ground clauses.

Exercise 19.4   Repeat Examples 14.3 and 14.4 of Chapter 14, pp. 175, 177–8, using refutation.

The justification of our procedure for forming the denial of universal clauses is similar to that for ground clauses.

Proposition 19.2   Denial set of a universal clause

Let $C = p_1, \ldots, p_n$ => $q_1, \ldots, q_m (m, n \geq 0)$ be a universal clause, and let $C' = p'_1, \ldots, p'_n$ => $q'_1, \ldots, q'_m$ be the result of uniformly substituting each variable in C by a new existential constant. Form the denial set D of C:

$$\{ \text{ => } p'_1, \ldots, \text{ => } p'_n, q'_1 \text{ => } , \ldots, q'_n \text{ => } \}$$

Then, for any interpretation $\mathcal{I}$, C is true in $\mathcal{I}$ only if not all clauses in D are true in $\mathcal{I}$.

Proof We first prove that if C is true in $\mathcal{I}$, then not all the clauses in D are true in $\mathcal{I}$. Suppose first that C is true in $\mathcal{I}$. Now, let us hypothesize that, contrary to what we are trying to prove, all the clauses in the denial set D are indeed true in $\mathcal{I}$. That is to say, there exists an extension $\mathcal{I}'$ of $\mathcal{I}$, covering all the new Skolem terms, in which all the clauses in D are true. So take a valuation $\mathcal{V}'$ just like $\mathcal{V}$ except that it assigns to the variables in C the objects denoted by the Skolem terms replacing them. Then $\mathcal{V}'$ satisfies every antecedent of C, and does not satisfy any consequent of C. So it does not satisfy C, so C is not true in $\mathcal{I}$, contrary to our supposition. So our hypothesis that all the clauses in D are true in $\mathcal{I}$ is wrong, and so at least one is false as required.

We now prove the converse: we assume that not all clauses in D are true in $\mathcal{I}$, then show that C is true in $\mathcal{I}$. To do this, let us hypothesize that, contrary to what we are trying to prove, C is not true in $\mathcal{I}$. In that case there is a valuation $\mathcal{V}$ in $\mathcal{I}$ which satisfies all the antecedents and none of the consequents of C. So, there exists an extension $\mathcal{I}'$ of $\mathcal{I}$ covering all the new existential constants, in which all the clauses in D are true. That is to say by Def. Truth for existential terms, they are all true in $\mathcal{I}$, contradicting our supposition. So our hypothesis is wrong, that is, C is true in $\mathcal{I}$ as required.□

19.3   Clauses with Skolem constants

We now need to work out how to deny clauses containing existential (Skolem constants. (We will not look at clauses containing existential functors – that raises a host of problems.) First, we will look at ground existential clauses that is, ones with no variables.

Plainly, the denial of the assertion 'Someone has measles' is the asser tion 'No-one has measles' (in domains of persons; otherwise say 'something 'nothing'). That is, the denial of:

=> Has(@A, MEASLES)

is the clause:

```
Has(x, MEASLES) =>
```

Parallel to this, we deny 'Someone does not have measles', with the assertion 'Everyone has measles'. In clausal form, the denial of:

```
Has(@A, MEASLES) =>
```

is the clause:

```
                    => Has(x, MEASLES)
```

This situation is neatly parallel to the denying of universal clauses where we uniformly replaced the variables by new existential constants, then formed the denial set as for ground clauses. This time we replace the existential constants uniformly by new variables, then form the denial set as for ground clauses. Let us check this method with which a clause has existential constants on both sides. These are not common, since they say very little. But we must still be able to deny them. Take as an example, 'If everyone has measles, someone is inconvenienced.' In clausal form that is:

```
Has(@A, MEASLES) => Incon(@B)
```

which by the above procedure has as its denial set:

```
                    => Has(x, MEASLES)
        Incon(y) =>
```

That is, 'Everyone has measles and nobody is inconvenienced', which is what we would expect.

Now let us look at existential clauses containing variables. A simple case is 'Someone likes everyone', whose denial is 'Everyone has someone they do not like.' That is:

```
                    => Like(@A,x)
```

has as its denial set:

```
Like(y,@f(y)) =>
```

Note that we have replaced existential terms by variables, as above; but we have in addition replaced variables by existential *functors* over the introduced variables.

The next example follows the same pattern. The denial of 'There is someone every woman likes', is 'For every person, there is a woman who does not like him/her.' Assuming a domain of persons (to avoid irrelevant complexity), we have then:

$$\text{Woman}(x) \implies \text{Like}(x, @A)$$

which has as its denial set:

$$\text{Like}(@g(y), y) \implies$$
$$\implies W(@g(y))$$

That is, 'Every person y is not liked by the person who is their g, and their g is a woman.'

Next, let us read the clause:

$$\text{Married-to}(x, y) \implies \text{Married}(@A, x, y), \text{Arrest}(@B, x, y)$$

to mean 'There is a pair of persons (@A and @B) such that for any two people who are married to each other, then either the first of the pair (@A) married them, or the second (@B) will arrest them both.' We deny the existence of that extraordinary pair of wedding monopolists by asserting that there is no pair of people who do that to everyone. Which means that any pair of persons at all have two other people, called say, their f and their g, such that their f is married to their g, the first of the pair did not marry their f and g, and the second of the pair did not arrest their f and g. That is:

$$\implies \text{Married-to}(@f(u,v), @g(u,v))$$
$$\text{Married}(u, @f(u,v),$$
$$@g(u,v)) \implies$$
$$\text{Arrest}(v, @f(u,v),$$
$$@g(u,v)) \implies$$

To bring all the above transformations together, we can state the procedure for forming the denial set of any clause not containing existential functors in this way:

(1)   Replace all existential constants uniformly by new variables, a different one for each constant. (There may, of course, be none.)

(2)   Suppose there are n such new variables. Then replace all the *original* variables uniformly by new existential terms consisting of new n-ary existential functors whose arguments are the n new variables in some fixed order, one such new term for each original variable. If $n = 0$, then we use existential constants.

(3)   Make a positive unit clause out of each of the resulting antecedents.

(4)   Make a negative unit clause out of each of the resulting consequents.

(5)   The denial set comprises all the unit clauses made in (3) and (4).

We will not try to prove the proposition that justifies these rules. It is considerably more complex than the proposition proved above for universal non-existential clauses. Its formulation, and proof, are left as a project for the reader.

We collect here a useful table of common English assertion forms, their causal equivalent, and the denial sets for those clauses and the English reading for the denial sets.

Assertion	Denial
Everything that Fs, Gs	Something Fs and does not G
F(x) => G(x)	=> F(@A); G(@A) =>
Nothing that Fs, Gs	Something Fs and Gs
F(x),G(x) =>	=> F(@A); => G(@A)
If everything Fs everything Gs	Everything Fs and something does not G
F(@A) => G(x)	=> F(x); G(@B) =>
If everything Fs something Gs	Everything Fs and nothing Gs
F(@A) => G(@B)	=> F(x); G(y) =>
If something Fs everything Gs	Something Fs and something does not G
F(y) => G(x)	=> F(@A); G(@B) =>
If something Fs something Gs	Something Fs and nothing Gs
F(y) => G(@A)	=> F(@B); G(y) =>

Exercise 19.5 Form the denial set of these clauses, and give possible readings the clauses and their denial sets. (Take F as father-of, and G as grandfather-.)

```
(a)                => F(A,B),F(B,A)
(b)  F(A,B),G(A,C) => F(B,C)
(c)  F(x,y),F(y,z) => G(x,z)
(d)  F(x,y),F(y,x) =>
(e)        F(x,y) => F(y,x)
(f)                => G(@A,A)
```

```
(g)                    => G(@A,x)
(h)          G(@A,A) =>
(i)          F(x,@A) =>
(j)            G(x,y) => F(@A,y)
```

Exercise 19.6   The clauses => F(x) and F(x) => , together with their denials, form a square of opposition. Draw up the square and prove semantically that the two bottom clauses are jointly exhaustive, that is, in any interpretation at least one of them is true (see Chapter 12).

SUMMARY

- **Unit clauses.** Where p is a single atom, => p is a **positive unit clause** and p => is a **negative unit clause**.

- **Denial set of a clause.** A denial set of a clause C is a set C' of clauses that are all true in any interpretation in which C is false, and not all true in any interpretation in which C is true.

- **Denial set of a ground clause.** The set that comprises the positive unit clauses made from each antecedent in the ground clause, and the negative unit clauses made from each of its consequents. Let C $p_1, \ldots, p_n$ => $q_1, \ldots, q_m (m, n \geq 0)$ be a ground clause. Form the denial set D of C:

$$\{ \text{ => } p_1, \ldots, \text{ => } p_n, q_1 \text{ => } , \ldots, q_n \text{ => } \}$$

  Then, for any interpretation $\mathcal{I}$, C is true in $\mathcal{I}$ only if not all clauses in D are true in $\mathcal{I}$.

- **Denial set of a universal clause.** Let $C = p_1, \ldots, p_n$ => $q_1, \ldots, q_m$ $(m, n \geq 0)$ be a universal clause, and let $C' = p'_1, \ldots, p'_n$ => $q'_1, \ldots, q'_m$ be the result of uniformly substituting each variable in C by a new existential constant. Form the denial set D of C:

$$\{ \text{ => } p'_1, \ldots, \text{ => } p'_n, q'_1 \text{ => } , \ldots, q'_n \text{ => } \}$$

  Then, for any interpretation $\mathcal{I}$, C is true in $\mathcal{I}$ only if not all clauses in D are true in $\mathcal{I}$.

- **Denial of clauses not containing existential functors.** Carry out the following steps:

  (a)   Replace all existential constants uniformly by new variables, different one for each constant.

(b)   Suppose there are n such new variables. Then replace all the *original* variables uniformly by new existential terms consisting of new n-ary existential functors whose arguments are the n new variables in some fixed order, one such new term for each original variable.

(c)   Make a positive unit clause out of each of the resulting antecedents.

(d)   Make a negative unit clause out of each of the resulting consequents.

(e)   The denial set comprises all the unit clauses made in (c) and (d).

- **Backward chaining or refutation.** A proof of this type proceeds by:

(a)   Finding the denial set of the intended conclusion.

(b)   Using resolution on the denial set and the premisses to try to deduce the empty clause.

(c)   The conclusion is deducible from the premisses if and only if the empty clause is deducible by the above process.

Chapter 20
The mechanics of refutation

The purpose of this chapter is to look at some of the more important semantic results underlying the use of resolution refutation as a computer-based proof procedure. This is the widely preferred computer method for doing logic, so its own peculiarities deserve closer study.

In the course of this chapter we shall open up questions about the 'doability' of deductions on the computer. Your experience, earlier in this book, actually doing deductions, may have convinced you that the technique is quite creative; more of an art than a mechanical execution of rules. We shall now explore some fundamental results about the extent to which logic can be mechanized.

First, however, to set the scene, we shall make some less theoretical remarks about why using resolution in a backward-chaining mode, instead of the perhaps simpler and more direct forward-chaining mode, is preferable on a computer.

20.1   The advantages of refutation

The backward-chaining refutation method is the widely preferred approach to doing logic on the computer. The popular PROLOG logic programming language, for example, works entirely by backward chaining. Why is refutation preferred over forward chaining? After all, forward chaining seems to have the following advantages:

(1)   Its method is more straightforward and easier to understand.

(2)   All the difficulties about finding the negation of the desired conclusion are avoided.

(3)   The proofs are usually shorter – indeed all the refutations we did in the previous chapter had more resolution steps in them than in the corresponding forward-chaining proofs of the same inferences in earlier chapters.

The fundamental reason why refutation is preferred as the computational means of doing logic, is that it is more efficient. We will now spell out this rather vague claim in detail. But first, some refutations of the above claims about forward chaining.

(1)   The idea of a *computer* understanding a process or theory is either trivial or meaningless. *You* might need to understand a complex procedure in order to do it right – not just be able to follow mechanically the rules for the process, but know its theory and whys and wherefores – but the computer needs only explicit rules. And as we shall see, backward chaining requires fewer rules than forward chaining, which is a great advantage to the computer. In that sense, refutation is more straightforward.

(2)   This in practice is not a problem. In some resolution refutation systems, the data and desired goal to be proved is entered in the first place, not as clauses, but as pseudo-English, or as predicate calculus (see Appendix A). The procedure that the computer carries out to express these statements in clausal form includes the negating transform at an early stage, and the process of forming the denial set is relatively trivial. But what if the logic system expects input to be in clausal form, and expects the user to figure out and then type in the denial set for the desired conclusion, as essentially does PROLOG? Experience has shown that, in practice, users find the formation of the denial set quite easy, and do not recognize that they are doing it. We will look at this PROLOG situation later.

(3)   The efficiency issue for a computer is not how many steps the final proof took, but how many steps the *search* for that proof took. If, to find a ten-resolution-step proof, the computer needed to carry out

a hundred resolutions in a trial-and-error search for the proof, then that is the measure of the efficiency of the proof system. In general, a refutation proof is much more focussed than a forward-chaining proof, and involves far less backtracking out of unprofitable partial proofs, just because (the denial of) the goal to be proved is in the data, and the system can search backwards from that in an economical way. We will have a closer look at this situation below.

0.1.1   Refutation needs fewer rules

.side from Subst-Rule and Cut-Rule, which are used to make up resolution, orward chaining required:

- Contraction to get rid of repetitions of antecedents or consequents in a clause.

- Id laws, of the form $p \Rightarrow p$, since these logical laws are not provable by forward chaining.

- Weakening to allow the addition of further antecedents or consequents to an already proved clause.

- T/F Contraction which allowed us to remove T from any antecedent and F from any consequent.

Of these, Contraction is the only rule needed in backward-chaining roofs, and as we saw in Chapter 15, we have it trivially available anyway, nd do not need to state it, since we treat our antecedents and consequents s sets. We need T/F Contraction too, if we admit T and F into our logic, for s we saw in Chapter 15, these are the axioms to govern the logical meaning f truth and falsehood.

Id laws and Weakening are not required in refutation proofs. It is easy o see that Id laws are not needed, since they are simple to prove by refutation, s the following exercise shows.

Exercise 20.1 p, q, r are three atoms. Prove $p, q, r \Rightarrow p, q, r$ by forward chaining and by backward chaining.

0.1.2   Factoring

'ontraction, we said, was a trivial rule, needed only for the sake of symbol nanipulation. However there is a useful trick involving Contraction together with Substitution that needs to be applied in some deductions. The process is called **Factoring**.

Consider for example the clause:

```
P(x) => Q(x),Q(y)
```

We cannot quite use Contract here to get rid of the extra Q atom, since they are not identical atoms, but we can after substituting x for y.

EXAMPLE 20.1_____

Use Factoring with the above clause and => P(A) to deduce => Q(A).

Denial	Q(A) =>	(1
Premiss	P(x) => Q(x),Q(y)	(2
Premiss	=> P(A)	(3
(2){x/y}	P(x) => Q(x),Q(x)	(4
(4)*Contract*	P(x) => Q(x)	(5
(5){A/x}	P(A) => Q(A)	(6
(1),(6)*Cut-Rule*	P(A) =>	(7
(3),(7)*Cut-Rule*	=>	

The factoring process here was steps (4) and (5).

_____

Exercise 20.2   Find another way to carry out the above deduction, which delays factoring for as long as possible.

_____

What the previous discussion boils down to, is the claim that the Substitution and Cut rules, together with the Contraction rule, are a complete method for demonstrating the inconsistency of a set S of clauses, that is that S has no model. We say that the set of these three rules is **refutation complete**. (The set is not forward chaining complete.) If amongst S is the denial set of the conclusion we wish to prove, then demonstrating the inconsistency of S amounts to demonstrating the logical validity of the inference of the conclusion from the premisses (that is, from the rest of S).

We will now look more closely at the semantics underlying that situation.

20.2   The semantics of resolution refutation

Resolution refutation is an attempt to find a **model** for a set S of clauses. Recall from Chapter 13, that a model is an interpretation in which all the clauses in the set are true. In the case of resolution refutation, we are hoping to find that there is *no model at all* for our set S. Why? Because S comprises all the premisses of the inference we wish to test for logical validity, and the denial set of the conclusion of that inference. So if S *has* a model, then in that model all the premisses are true and so is the denial of the conclusion; that is, the conclusion is false in that model. So the inference from the premisses to that conclusion is *not* valid. The model could be called a **countermodel** for the validity of the inference: a counterexample to show the inference is not valid.

In that case, what we really want from a refutation deduction technique such as resolution, is that it should find a model for S if there is one, and show it to us; or, if there is no model, determine that there is no model and tell us so. Importantly, we should like all this to happen in a finite number of steps. We want the answer to be settled in a finite time: to wait forever for an answer is not to get the answer.

Unfortunately, it is impossible to satisfy all these requirements. It is the time limit constraint that is impossible. A theorem established by the Princeton logician Alonzo Church in 1936 showed that in areas of logic as rich as the one we are now talking about (CFL), there *cannot* be an **algorithm** (that is, roughly, a specifiable computing procedure) that will decide in a finite number of steps whether or not a given inference is logically valid. This result is known as Church's undecidability theorem.

That is an extremely profound result. Think of what it means. Firstly, we know exactly what we mean by the semantic notion of the validity of an inference. Secondly, we have a precisely stated proof theory, resolution refutation, according to which we may write deductions of conclusions from premisses. Thirdly, we have algorithms in the form of computer programs for doing resolution refutation. Then, thanks to Church's theorem, we know that such an algorithm, when applied to the premisses and conclusion in which we are interested, might never reach a stage where it can stop and deliver the answer about the validity of that inference.

When could the algorithm stop? It could stop when it has found the deduction. Now that might seem hopeful, for we can show that if the number of premisses is finite (as surely it would be in any real-life inference problem), then the number of steps in the proof is finite. But it is not too hopeful, for in general the problem of proof is not one of just marching step by step through the proof, knowing exactly how to start, and at each stage knowing exactly what is the next step to take. The problem is *searching* for the proof, and the search for a finite proof can, in principle, take an infinite time.

But suppose the algorithm is dealing with an inference that, in fact, is not valid. How will it know when to stop looking? The fact that it has not found a proof after a certain number of steps still leaves open the possibility that it will find the proof later. Unless there is some way of enumerating exhaustively, in a finite number of steps, all possible proofs, so that you can come to the end of them all and say 'There, none of them does the job; so there is no proof', you will never know if the proof still lies ahead. What Church's theorem says is that you can never do that, not for proofs in areas as rich as CFL.

20.3   Herbrand's theorem

In the case of refutation techniques for CFL, however, there is some good news. In 1930, Jacques Herbrand proved, in effect, that if a set of clauses S is inconsistent, that fact can be determined in a finite number of steps (though you cannot, in general, tell in advance just how many steps). Just how, we will see in a moment. Its significance is that if you adopt a refutation proof technique for CFL, such as resolution refutation, then that proof technique will determine the validity of valid inferences in a finite time. The price you pay for that result, through Church's Theorem, is that if the inference is invalid, the proof technique might not be able to determine the existence of a counterexample in a finite time. This situation is called **semi-decidability**: if the answer is Yes, that is finitely decidable; but if the answer is No, that is not.

We will not try to give a full proof of Herbrand's theorem here. It will be quite enough to have a look at his methods, which will enable us to give a useful and meaningful statement of this theorem. We will work by way of an example.

Suppose we want to prove:

$$F(x,y) \Rightarrow G(y,x) \tag{1}$$
$$\Rightarrow F(A,B) \tag{2}$$

therefore:

$$\Rightarrow G(B,A) \tag{3}$$

Denying that conclusion gives us:

$$G(B,A) \Rightarrow \tag{4}$$

The set of clauses (1), (2) and (4) (which we will call U) is what we want to prove inconsistent.

Herbrand's approach is to actually construct some interpretations for U, in such a way that if the chosen set U has no model, this series of constructions will show that fact after a finite number of steps.

(1)   To construct the interpretations for a set of clauses S, we look firstly for the constants occurring in it. In our example, U has two A and B. Now, we put these into the domain of discourse of our interpretations. (If S had no constants, we would invent one and put it into the domain. This is to ensure the domain is non-empty, which we have seen is a requirement on our logic.) Putting the constant terms into the domain of interpretation is the main trick of Herbrand's result: domains can be domains of *anything*, so we choose the constant terms of S, then we make each constant term (as term of the language) denote itself (as object in the interpretation). If clauses in S contain existential constants, we treat them as ordinary constants. The resulting domain of discourse is called the **Herbrand universe**.

(2)   Next, we form all possible ground instances of universal clauses in S, made up using only the constants in the Herbrand universe. In the case of U, they are:

$$F(A,A) \Rightarrow G(A,A) \tag{5}$$
$$F(A,B) \Rightarrow G(B,A) \tag{6}$$
$$F(B,A) \Rightarrow G(A,B) \tag{7}$$
$$F(B,B) \Rightarrow G(B,B) \tag{8}$$

We put these ground instances into a set S' along with all the ground clauses from S. So in our example, U' comprises (2), (4), (5), (6), (7) and (8).

(3)   Now, we give each atom that is in set S' of ground clauses a truth-value, and work out the truth-values of all the ground clauses in S' using the truth-functional techniques of Chapter 8. The resulting interpretation of S is called a **Herbrand interpretation**.

In our example, there are eight different atoms, $F(A,A)$, $F(A,B)$, $F(B,A)$, $F(B,B)$, $G(A,A)$, $G(A,B)$, $G(B,A)$ and $G(B,B)$. If we assigned 1 (true) to all these atoms, then the clauses (2) and (5) to (8) are true in this interpretation and (4) is false. Also, (1) is true in this interpretation, since all its possible ground instances, (5) to (8), are true.

(4)   If all the clauses in S' are true under this assignment of truth-values, then we have an interpretation that makes all the clauses in S' true. In that case it can be shown we have constructed a model for S, so we stop.

In the case of U the Herbrand interpretation we have just constructed is this: F and G both denote the relation $\{\langle A, A \rangle, \langle A, B \rangle, \langle B, A \rangle, \langle B, B \rangle\}$, and we already know what A and B denote: themselves. This interpretation is not a model for U.

(5)   If we do not stop on (4), we repeat (3) and (4) for a different assignment of truth-values to the component atoms, until we do find a model and stop, or until we exhaust the possible assignments of truth-values to

the atoms. (For n different atoms, there are 2^n different assignments we can make.) If we exhaust the possible assignments without finding a model, then we have shown that S', the set of ground instances, has no model in the Herbrand universe (and hence, in any universe). That is, it is inconsistent. But, since everything in S' is either a ground clause in S or a ground instance of a clause in S (derived from it by the rule Subst), it follows that S must be inconsistent too, by the soundness of Subst.

A convenient way of setting out these 2^n different valuations is in a truth table, as below.

F(A,B)	F(B,A)	G(A,B)	G(B,A)	(2)	(4)	(6)	(7)
1	1	1	1	1	0	1	1
1	1	1	0	1	1	0	1
1	1	0	1	1	0	1	0
1	1	0	0	1	1	0	0
1	0	1	1	1	0	1	1
1	0	1	0	1	1	0	1
1	0	0	1	1	0	1	1
1	0	0	0	1	1	0	1
0	1	1	1	0	0	1	1
0	1	1	0	0	1	1	1
0	1	0	1	0	0	1	0
0	1	0	0	0	1	1	0
0	0	1	1	0	0	1	1
0	0	1	0	0	1	1	1
0	0	0	1	0	0	1	1
0	0	0	0	0	1	1	1

The headings on the left-hand side are the n different ground atoms, and below them in 2^n rows are the different combinations of truth and falsity they may have. In this example, there are four ground atoms, and so 16 rows. To the right of the vertical line, the headings are ground clauses in S'. Here there are four such ground clauses, the ones numbered (2), (4), (6) and (7). For each of these we enter into the table the value they get in each row, computed from the values given in that row to their component atoms left of the dividing line. Then each row represents a different Herbrand interpretation, and the rows collectively represent all possible Herbrand interpretations. If a set of ground instances (to the right of the line) are all true (get 1) in a given row, the interpretation that row represents is a model for that set of ground instances. Note that in this example, in no row do all the four ground clauses on the right get 1. Hence, in no row are all the ground clauses true.

This table shows only one sixteenth of the full table needed for the S' of the previous example (256 lines). If the full table is set out, it can be seen that in no row are all six ground clauses true. So no Herbrand interpretation is a model for the full S' either, therefore S' is inconsistent.

Exercise 20.3 What is the interpretation for U described in the second row? (Ignore missing ground atoms.) What is the value of (1) in that interpretation?

Now, if that is how to find models for a set of clauses S or show its inconsistency, we would seem to have disobeyed Church's theorem, since in our example set U, the inconsistency of U is quite clearly decidable. Also, any clause set not containing functors will be decidable, and that is perfectly true.

The trouble is that CFL without functors is much weaker than CFL with functors; weak enough for Church's theorem not to apply to it. (Just how strong a logic has to be for Church's theorem to apply, and what is meant by 'strength' here, is well understood, but we will not go into it.)

In fact, what the above example of U shows, is that CFL without functors is really just a shorthand way of writing CFL without variables at all. We can expand CFL clause sets without functors into CFL clause sets without variables, just as U was rewritten as U'. U has a model only if U' does, so as clause sets they are entirely equivalent. In short, we have this very convenient result from the point of view of designing resolution refutation algorithms for a computer:

Proposition 20.1   Decidability of non-functorial CFL

The inconsistency of a set of clauses without functors is decidable. Hence the validity of a CFL inference not containing functors is decidable. $\square$

It is where clauses have functors that Church's theorem bites. For now the Herbrand universe goes infinite. It contains all the constant terms that can be made up out of the constants and functors in the clause set S, and as soon as we admit one functor, we have an infinity of such closed terms constructible.

Take as our example this time the inference:

$$\Rightarrow \text{M}(\text{h}(\text{x}),\text{x}) \tag{9}$$
$$\text{M}(\text{x},\text{y}) \Rightarrow \text{L}(\text{x},\text{y}) \tag{10}$$

therefore:

$$\Rightarrow \text{L(h(A),A)} \tag{11}$$

Denying that conclusion gives us:

$$\text{L(h(A),A)} \Rightarrow \tag{12}$$

We could take this as formalizing: 'A person's husband is married to them, whoever is married to someone loves them, so Ann's husband loves her.' (12) asserts that Ann's husband does not love her.

The set V we wish to test for inconsistency consists of (9), (10) and (12). To test for inconsistency of a set S containing functors, we proceed through steps like those earlier for the constants-only case, but complicated now by the presence of functors.

(1)   The domain of discourse (the Herbrand universe) for our interpretations consists now of all constant terms constructible out of the constants and functors in the set S of clauses. Again, if there are no constants in S, we create one. Any existential constants or functors are treated as ordinary ones.

In the case of V, that is the infinite set $\{\text{A}, \text{h(A)}, \text{h(h(A))}, \ldots\}$.

(2)   Here begins a loop in the procedure (which is re-entered from step (4) below). First time through, construct all ground instances of universal clauses in S by instantiating only to the constants in the Herbrand universe. Add these to any ground clauses in S to form a set S' of ground clauses.

In the example V, that gives us the new ground clauses:

$$\Rightarrow \text{M(h(A),A)} \tag{13}$$
$$\text{M(A,A)} \Rightarrow \text{L(A,A)} \tag{14}$$

With clause (12), they make up V'.

On subsequent passes through, take all the constant terms constructed so far, add to them new ones formed by applying the functors to all of them in as many ways as possible, then add to S' the new clauses obtained by instantiating to the new terms.

For our example, on the second pass through, we add h(A) to A, and so get the new clauses:

```
              => M(h(h(A)),h(A))
              => M(h(h(A)),A)
              => M(h(A),h(A))
M(h(A),h(A)) => L(h(A),h(A))
   M(h(A),A) => L(h(A),A)
   M(A,h(A)) => L(A,h(A))
```

On the third pass through, we add h(h(A)) to h(A) and A, and so on for later passes.

(3)   Now, we give each atom that is in set S' of ground clauses constructed so far, a truth-value, and work out the truth-values of all the ground clauses in S' using the truth-functional techniques of Chapter 8. The resulting interpretation of S is called a **Herbrand interpretation**.

Exercise 20.4   What are the atoms in V' after the first pass through step (2)? Let them all be true. Then what truth-values do the clauses in V' get?

---

(4)   If all the clauses in S' are true under this assignment of truth-values, then we do not yet have an *interpretation* that makes all the clauses in S' true. For we have not yet specified the interpretation to cover objects in the Herbrand universe not occurring in S' so far. So we give up on the present attempt to construct an interpretation not satisfying S', and loop back to step (2).

(5)   If we do not loop on (4) back to (2), we repeat (3) and (4) for a different assignment of truth-values to the component atoms, until we exhaust the possible assignments. (For n different atoms, there are 2^n different assignments we can make.)   If we exhaust the possible assignments without finding one that satisfies all the clauses in S, then we have shown that S', the (current) set of ground instances, has no model in the Herbrand universe (and hence in any universe). That is, it is inconsistent. But, since everything in S' is either a ground clause in S or a ground instance of a clause in S (derived from it by the substitution rule), it follows that S must be inconsistent too, by the soundness of the substitution rule.

Exercise 20.5   Tabulate all the assignments of truth-values to the clauses in V' at the end of the first pass through step (2) of the algorithm. Do any of the assignments verify all the clauses in V'? If so, why is that assignment not a model for V'?

In the case of V', we have found (in the exercise) assignments that do verify all clauses in V' in the first pass through the loop. So we must loop back to (2), enlarge V' accordingly, and see if that larger set avoids getting a model.

That completes the description of a **Herbrand algorithm** which will loop until it constructs an inconsistent set S' of ground instances of a set of clauses S in a finite number of steps, if S is inconsistent itself.

Or will it? Could it be that the inconsistent set of ground instances is not finite? After all, the Herbrand universe is not finite. No, because suppose we replace S with the infinite set of ground instances SS arising from all possible substitutions of variables in S by members of the Herbrand universe. In that case, certainly, SS is inconsistent only if S is. But then, by virtue of a result called the **compactness theorem** which says that an infinite set of clauses is inconsistent only if some finite subset of it is, it follows that SS is inconsistent only if one of our finite S's is.

The compactness theorem ensures that if a (counter-)model to S exists, it will be found in a finite number of passes through the big loop in Herbrand's algorithm.

Having completed that sketch of the Herbrand result, we can now pull the threads together and state Herbrand's theorem.

Proposition 20.2   Herbrand's theorem

A set S of clauses is inconsistent only if there is a finite set of ground clauses S' of S, which is inconsistent.   □

Hence as we have seen, we can state as a corollary the result we are seeking:

Proposition 20.3   Semi-decidability of refutation

If a CFL inference is valid, a refutation technique can be found that will generate its proof in a finite number of steps.   □

If necessary, that technique will be Herbrand's algorithm as described above. In fact, the job is done far faster by using algorithms based on resolution refutation.

SUMMARY

- **Factoring.** The process of making a substitution in a clause to render two antecedents, or two consequents, identical; then removing one by the contraction rule.

- **Refutation completeness.** Resolution as we have defined it, plus the contraction rule, are a complete set of rules for refutations.

- **Decidability.** We say a type of problem is decidable if an algorithm could be guaranteed to solve any problem of that type (or show it has no solution) in a finite number of steps; for example the problem of determining the validity of any inference of CFL.

- **Church's theorem.** The validity problem for CFL is undecidable. (The theorem generalizes to any other problem equivalent to the validity problem for CFL, such as the validity problem for predicate calculus.)

- **Semi-decidability.** A type of problem is semi-decidable if an algorithm will solve all solvable problems of that type in a finite number of steps, but will not, in general, determine the unsolvability of the rest in a finite number of steps.

- **Herbrand universe.** The set of all closed terms (no variables in them) that can be constructed from the constants and functors in some (finite) set S of CFL clauses. If there are any functors, this set is infinite, otherwise finite. The Herbrand universe is used as a domain of discourse for S, enabling many interesting propositions about S to be proved.

- **Herbrand interpretation.** An interpretation for a set S of clauses in which the domain of discourse is the Herbrand universe for S, and each closed term in S is given itself as denotation.

- **Decidability of non-functorial CFL.** The inconsistency of a set of clauses without functors is decidable. Hence the validity of a CFL inference not containing functors is decidable.

- **Compactness theorem.** An infinite set of clauses is inconsistent only if some finite subset of it is. This result is crucial for proving Herbrand's Theorem.

- **Herbrand's theorem.** A set S of clauses is inconsistent only if there is a finite set of ground clauses S' of S, which is inconsistent.

- **Semi-decidability of refutation.** If a CFL inference is valid, a refutation technique can be found that will generate its proof in a finite number of steps.

Chapter 21
Resolution on the computer

In the final two chapters we shall look at some of the problems concerning the use of resolution refutation on the computer. Our purpose is *not* to describe the syntax and use of this or that computer logical reasoning language, such as PROLOG. Our purpose is to look at the logical theory underlying them, and to bring to bear some of the material from earlier in the book, to explain why these systems have the features they do.

In this chapter, we look at ways that are used to make resolution, which is a simple enough rule, more simple and regular, and so more amenable to computer use.

21.1   Unification and resolution

Back in Chapter 14 we gave the name unification to the process of using Subst-Rule on two clauses to prepare them for Cut-Rule. Together, the double step of unification followed by Cut-Rule, is what we called **resolution**.

21.1.1   Standardizing apart

For computational purposes, it is desirable to tidy up this process. For a start, when we have selected two clauses we wish to resolve, we should **standardize apart** their variables. That is, we do not want the two clauses to have variables in common. If they do, we apply Subst-Rule to one of them to replace the variables it has in common with the other, by new variables – variables that occur in neither of the two clauses we wish to resolve.

To see the usefulness of standardizing apart, look at this problem:

EXAMPLE 21.1_____

Prove:

No murderers are saintly,	$M(x,y),S(x)$ =>	**(P1)**
All parents are saintly,	$P(x,y)$ => $S(x)$	**(P2)**
Dad is a parent,	=> $P(D,@X)$	**(P3)**
So Dad didn't murder anyone.	$M(D,x)$ =>	**(C)**

Exercise 21.1   Form the denial (D) of this conclusion, then try to prove the inference using resolution refutation.

That proof method gets stuck. So this time we will standardize apart (P2) from (P1) first:

(P2)$\{u/x,v/y\}$	$P(u,v)$ => $S(u)$	(1)

Now we make the unifying substitution:

(1)$\{x/u\}$	$P(x,v)$ => $S(x)$	(2)
(P1),(2)Cut-Rule	$M(x,y),P(x,v)$ =>	(3)
(3)$\{D/x,@X/v\}$	$M(D,y),P(D,@X)$ =>	(4)
(4),(P3)Cut-Rule	$M(D,y)$ =>	(5)
(5)$\{@B/y\}$	$M(D,@B)$ =>	(6)
(6),(D)Cut-Rule	=>	

21.2   Most general unifiers

The purpose of standardizing apart first, before unifying and resolving, is to make sure that the resolution product is as general as possible. In the answer to the exercise, the resolution product was:

```
M(x,y),P(x,y) =>
```
(1)

but after standardizing apart we obtained:

```
M(x,y),P(x,v) =>
```
(2)

(2) is more general than (1), for note that (1) logically follows from (2) (using Subst), but not conversely. It is very important to ensure that the product of *any* step of reasoning is as general as possible; for more follows from a more general statement, so we are more likely to reach our desired conclusion from it than from a less general version. That is what happened above.

Pursuing the same idea of preserving as much generality as possible, we must aim to ensure that when we unify two clauses, the result is as general as possible.

Exercise 21.2   The two parent clauses to a resolution are:

```
P(x,y) => Q(x,f(y))
Q(u,v) => R(u,v)
```
(1)
(2)

Note they are standardized apart. Find the substitutions that yielded the following resolvents, and discuss which resolvent(s) is/are the most general:

```
P(x,y) => R(x,f(y))
P(u,u) => R(u,f(u))
P(u,y) => R(u,f(y))
```
(3)
(4)
(5)

Unifiers, note, are substitutions. We need to ensure, when unifying two clauses, that the substitution (unifier) we use is as general as possible, in that the result of applying it to the two clauses is to yield two resultant clauses that are as general as possible. We describe that more precisely this way.

Definition   Most general unifier

A substitution $g = \{t_1/v_1, \ldots, t_n/v_n\}$ (where the t_i are terms and the v_i are variables) is a **Most General Unifier** (MGU) of two unifiable clauses C_1

and C_2 only if the following holds. Let s be any unifier of C_1 and C_2. Then we can always find a substitution t such that $C_1gt = C_1s$ and $C_2gt = C_2s$.

(Def. MGU)

In other words, given the results of applying the MGU g to C_1 and C_2, that is, C_1g and C_2g, and given the results of applying any unifier s to C_1 and C_2, that is, C_1s and C_2s, we can make substitutions in C_1g and C_2g, using some substitution t, which results in C_1s and C_2s.

There is a famous algorithm for finding an MGU for any two clauses, called the **unification algorithm**. It is too complex to state and discuss here, and it belongs more properly in a book on computing methods in artificial intelligence. One significant thing about the unification algorithm is this: if a person tries to find an MGU by inspection, in complex cases it can be very hard for to tell intuitively if what they find is an MGU – and it is even harder to apply the unification algorithm by hand. So, the resolution method really is computer-oriented and not very suitable as a hand method of doing symbolic logic.

The tidied-up process of resolution now looks like the following. Each step is something that can be programmed for a computer to perform quite efficiently. We assume that we are resolving in a set S of clauses.

Definition   Resolution algorithm

The algorithm has as input two unifiable clauses C_1 and C_2, and its output is a clause R (the resolvent of C_1 and C_2). The algorithm has the following steps:

(1)   Standardize apart the variables of C_1 and C_2.

(2)   Find a most general unifier for the two clauses (as standardized apart).

(3)   Apply that MGU to the two clauses (as standardized apart).

(4)   Apply the Cut-rule to the result of (4), to give a resolvent R.

(5)   Return R.

(Def. Resolve)

Note that the result of this algorithm is to add a new clause R to S. The process of resolution refutation proof on a set S of clauses amounts to applying the resolution algorithm over and over again to S, each time enlarging it by adding the product R to S, until the algorithm adds the empty clause to S. If it ever does add the empty clause, we know that the *original* S is inconsistent.

What if, on the other hand, the algorithm runs out of clauses to unify, in the ever-growing S? Well, we know from Herbrand's theorem that the algorithm will produce the empty clause if indeed the original S is inconsistent. So if it stops because there is nothing left to do, and has not produced the empty clause, then we know that the empty clause simply is not derivable. That is, the original set S has a model after all. Recall the nature of the semi-decidable status of the unsatisfiability problem for S: if S is inconsistent the algorithm will show that fact in a finite number of steps; if S is consistent the algorithm *could* execute for ever. That does *not* prevent satisfiability (having a model) being shown finitely in some cases. It is shown, for example, wherever S has no functors (and has a model, of course).

However, saying all that assumes that the resolution algorithm just set out is equivalent to Herbrand's, in the sense that it will prove unsatisfiability finitely. Such an algorithm we can call a **complete algorithm**. So, is our resolution algorithm above (together with the use of factoring when needed), complete?

The answer is, it could be, depending on the details of how new clauses are selected for input to the resolution algorithm. This is the topic of the next section.

21.3   Resolution strategies

In this section, we will look at some examples of where a computer programmed with the above resolution algorithm will fail to find a refutation, even though one obviously exists. The problem can be put this way: in the resolution algorithm above, how shall we select two clauses on which to resolve? The algorithm that does this is called the **control algorithm.**

Definition   Control algorithm

(A)   Execute the following loop until success or failure occurs:

  (1) Take the current goal G (a clause), look through the database S in order, with the starting point as the first (top) clause, until a clause C is found with which G will resolve.

  (2) If none is found, report failure, otherwise resolve G and C using the resolution algorithm to produce a resolvent R.

  (3) If R is the empty clause, terminate the algorithm with success.

  (4) Otherwise, enlarge S by adding R at its top, and also change the current goal G to be R.

(B)   If this loop reports failure, remove from S the last (topmost) R added, then repeat the loop but with the starting-point in the database search being the clause after C. If there are no Rs left to delete in this way, terminate the algorithm with failure.

(Def. Control Algorithm)

Note that if in step (B), C is the last clause in the database, then the next call of the loop will fail on step (2).

Step (B) is known as **backtracking**, because at this point the search for a resolution has failed, so the process goes back to the nearest previous point where it could have done something else, and does that instead. But as it moves back to that last choice point, it removes any changes it has made since it was last there. It is a process of throwing away the failed results of one attempt, and trying the next.

We will now, as promised, show how this algorithm can fail to find a refutation.

EXAMPLE 21.2

The database is (where p, q are two ground atoms):

$$=> p \tag{1}$$
$$q => q \tag{2}$$
$$p => q \tag{3}$$

and we wish to prove

$$=> q$$

The denial of the conclusion is

$$q => \tag{4}$$

which we will call the goal.

We begin with the goal as clause (4), that is $q =>$, and look down the database until we find a clause with which to resolve. The first is clause (2), and the resolvent is $q =>$ again. That is now our goal, so we continue with the goal as $q =>$, and look down the database until we find a clause with which to resolve. The first is clause (2), and the resolvent is $q =>$ again. That is now our goal, so we continue .... .

Plainly, the algorithm will loop until the computer runs out of storage. Logically speaking, the algorithm loops forever, yet there is a finite counterexample waiting to be found.

One way to prevent this situation happening is to add a step between (3) and (4) of the algorithm:

(3a)   If R is already in the database, return failure.

This step can be generalized to exclude substitution instances of clauses already in the database. In this form it is known as **subsumption.** Subsumption works this way.

Suppose a database contains a clause C, such as P(x,y) => Q(x,y). Suppose too that resolution on the database yields a clause C' which is a substitution instance of C, such as P(A,B) => Q(A,B) or P(u,x) => Q(u,x). Or, suppose that that C' can be derived using Weak (addition of antecedents and/or consequents) from a substitution instance of C. Then we say C **subsumes** C'. Plainly, the inference from C to C' is logically valid, since we use only Subst and Weak. For purposes of resolution refutation we need not add C' to the database, for if the database with C and C' in it is inconsistent, it is still inconsistent after we remove C'.

The subsumption step can be very expensive however, especially in large databases, so in many computer reasoning systems, such as PROLOG, this check is ignored. Instead, the programmer is expected to order the database in such a way that these loops will not happen. More directly, in this particular example, the programmer is expected not to put in pointless clauses like (2) which could cause trouble. In other words, the philosophy is to accept an efficient but incomplete resolution algorithm and put the onus on the programmer to avoid the pitfalls of incompleteness.

The control algorithm in the above examples exhibits a common control strategy, indeed probably the commonest strategy for cutting down on expensive searches for a proof, and is called the **set of support strategy**. The idea is this. If you are doing a refutation proof, you begin with a set of clauses, some of which are the premisses of your inference, and the rest form the denial set of your conclusion. The set of support strategy says that you should start resolving by taking one of the clauses in the denial set, and afterwards at each resolution step you should still use one of those clauses, or else (next best) one you have derived by resolution and which used a clause in the denial set in some stage of its derivation. In other words, give preference to using clauses in the denial set and their resolution products.

There are many other strategies, most of them involving giving preference in one way or another to the denial set or its descendants by resolution. We will not look at them here, since their discussion is more appropriate to books on computer implementations of logical reasoning systems, rather than having to do with the systems themselves.

Exercise 21.3 A database contains the following clauses, in order, beginning with a two-part definition of ancestors.

(a)   If one person is an ancestor of a second, who is parent of a third, then the first is an ancestor of the third.
(b)   All parents are ancestors.
(c)   Ann is a parent of Bill.
(d)   Bill is a parent of Chris.

Prove, using the above control algorithm without (3a), that Ann is an ancestor of Chris. What goes wrong? Discuss. (Assume the domain is persons.)

SUMMARY

- **Standardizing apart.** If two clauses C_1 and C_2 are to be resolved, they should have no variables in common, in order to ensure we get the most general possible resolvent (see MGU below). If they do, apply the substitution rule to the common variables in one of the clauses, replacing them by variables occurring in neither clause.

- **Definition Most general unifier.** A substitution $g = \{t_1/v_1, \ldots, t_n/v_n\}$ (where the t_i are terms and the v_i are variables), is a **Most General Unifier** (MGU) of two unifiable clauses C_1 and C_2 only if the following holds. Let s be any unifier of C_1 and C_2. Then we can always find a substitution t such that $C_1 g t = C_1 s$ and $C_2 g t = C_2 s$.

  (Def. MGU)

- **Unification algorithm.** A procedure for finding the MGU of any two clauses.

- **Definition Resolution algorithm**. The algorithm has as input two unifiable clauses C_1 and C_2, and its output is a clause R (the resolvent of C_1 and C_2). The algorithm has the following steps:

  (1) Standardize apart the variables of C_1 and C_2.

  (2) Find a most general unifier for the two clauses (as standardized apart).

  (3) Apply that MGU to the two clauses (as standardized apart).

  (4) Apply Cut-Rule to the result of (4), to give a resolvent R.

  (5) Return R.

  (Def. Resolve)

- **Definition Control algorithm.**

  (A) Execute the following loop until success or failure occurs:

    (1) Take the current goal G (a clause), look through the database S in order, with the starting point as the first (top) clause, until a clause C is found with which G will resolve.

    (2) If none is found, report failure, otherwise resolve G and C using the resolution algorithm to produce a resolvent R.

    (3) If R is the empty clause, terminate the algorithm with success.

(4)   Otherwise, enlarge S by adding R at its top, and also change the current goal G to be R.

(B) If this loop reported failure, remove from S the last (topmost) R added, then repeat the loop but with the starting point in the database search being the clause after C. If there are no Rs left to delete in this way, terminate the algorithm with failure.

(Def. Control algorithm)

- **Backtracking.** In the control algorithm, a choice of resolvents may lead to failure to find the empty clause. If so, the proof steps following this choice are thrown away and another choice is made. The steps rejected are the minimum needed to return to a point in the proof where another choice of clauses for resolution can be made.

- **Definition Subsumption.** Clause C subsumes clause C' if C' is a substitution instance of C or a weakening of a substitution instance of C.

(Def. Subsume)

- **Subsumption in resolution refutation.** If C subsumes C' and they are both clauses in an inconsistent database, C' can be removed without affecting the inconsistency of the database. So in a resolution refutation, do not add to the database, resolution products which are subsumed by clauses already in the database.

- **Definition Set of support strategy.** In resolution refutation, call the denial set the **set of support**. Whenever you resolve, ensure that one input to the resolution is in the set of support, and add the output of that resolution to the set of support.

(Def. Set of Support)

Chapter 22
PROLOG

In this final chapter, we look at the PROLOG language, which was described in Chapter 1, as a cut-down logic machine designed to do a certain range of logical deductions simply and efficiently. We shall apply what we have learned in this book to explain the semantics and behaviour of PROLOG, and to explain the logical theory underlying that language.

22.1   The PROLOG language

PROLOG is a language designed to provide for its users a useful and efficien
part of resolution refutation CFL as a programming and knowledge represen
tation device. A PROLOG program consists, more or less, of CFL clauses
which are used both to represent the information or data the program need
to operate on, and also to represent the program itself. In fact, it is rathe
misleading, in PROLOG, to make this traditional program/data distinction
We can look at a set of CFL clauses (a PROLOG program) as a knowledge
base, and the PROLOG interpreter itself as a theorem-proving program which
performs deductions on request from that knowledge base.

In use, PROLOG is very interactive, not unlike a sophisticated hand
calculator. You tell it to store various clauses in its knowledge base, or to
remove them; and you ask it to prove a clause (which you type in) or to find
the satisfiers of a universal clause (which you type in).

So PROLOG is essentially a system for maintaining a CFL knowledge
base and for finding proofs and extracting answers from the knowledge base
This has proved to be a clean and powerful programming paradigm, which is
gaining popularity in artificial intelligence and database work, in particular
It is often described as **declarative programming**, since the statements of
PROLOG are assertions, not commands as is normal in most programming
languages. The concept being urged behind this metaphor is that you tell
PROLOG the facts, and leave it to figure out how to solve the problem you
put to it. It treats the problem as something whose answer is to be proved
using its theorem prover, so it goes ahead and finds the proof.

PROLOG does not contain all the representational richness of CFL, for
every clause in a PROLOG database must contain one and only one conse
quent. Therefore it does not contain all the proving power of resolution refuta
tion CFL, either. Also, its control algorithm is the one set out in the previous
chapter, without the addition of subsumption. So it does not obey Herbrand's
theorem, in the sense that it can miss finding finite counterexamples, and so
cannot be relied on to find finite proofs if they exist. We will look at these
points more closely in a moment.

Moreover, it adds to its fragment of CFL a range of traditional pro
gramming devices that the programmer can employ to instruct the control
algorithm to behave differently. We will not look at those imperative fea
tures, for they are not part of the logic side of PROLOG. 'PROLOG' stands
for 'Programming in logic', but it is important to treat it as meaning 'Pro
gramming plus some unreliable logic'.

22.2   Representation in PROLOG

PROLOG allows you to enter clauses into the database that have exactly
one consequent, and zero or more antecedents. Clauses with zero or one

onsequent are called **Horn clauses**. Ones with no consequent we will call **negative Horn clauses** for obvious reasons, and the other sort, **positive Horn clauses**. This limitation of the PROLOG database to positive Horn clauses imposes two restrictions on its expressive power.

1) We cannot make disjunctive assertions (more than one consequent), for example, that humans are male or female:

    ```
    H(x) => M(x),F(x)
    ```

2) We cannot make negative assertions (no consequents) such as that no human is male and female:

    ```
    H(x),M(x),F(x) =>
    ```

To a certain extent the imperative control devices of PROLOG can be used to relax these restrictions, or we can invent a more complex representation for what we want to say.

We can partially overcome the nonexistence of disjunctive assertions point (1) above), by inventing a new 'disjunctive' predicate. In (1) above, we invent one to mean male-or-female. Then we put into the database:

```
H(x) => M-or-f(x)
M(x) => M-or-f(x)
F(x) => M-or-f(x)
```

But that still leaves us with a problem, as the exercise illustrates:

Exercise 22.1 Show that given the CFL clause in point (1) above, plus data that Shakey is neither male nor female, we can conclude that Shakey is not human. Why will PROLOG not find this proof, even if we add the three clauses just suggested?

Similarly, the PROLOG fix will still not let us prove that if Shakey is human but not male, it is female.

We can overcome the negation problem – (2) above – by saying this:

```
H(x),M(x),F(x) => Have(PIGS, WINGS)
```

or concluding any other obvious falsehood that has nothing to do with the subject matter at hand). Then when we want to prove something, we add its denial to the database and try to prove that pigs have wings.

Why can we add this denial to the database? PROLOG is suppose to accept only positive Horn clauses. The answer is, that when you wan PROLOG to prove something, you trigger off the proof process by trying t enter one negative Horn clause into the database. That sole negative Hori clause is placed at the top of the database, and a procedure resembling th control algorithm described in the last chapter is then invoked to execute th deduction. (We will look closely at that procedure below.) The deductio succeeds when the empty clause is derived, and PROLOG reports the succes back to the user. Finally, the negative Horn clause is removed from th database.

A little thought shows that if PROLOG is to prove things by resolutio refutation, but is restricted to positive Horn clauses, you *have* to add on negative Horn clause to the database if a refutation proof is to be possible For resolving two positive Horn clauses must yield a new positive Horn clause which, while it has one fewer antecedents than the total number of antecedent of its parents, must have one consequent. But in refutation, we are trying t prove the empty clause. We can whittle away the antecedents till none ar left, but we cannot get rid of the consequent, unless we resolve with on consequent-free (negative) clause.

Having two consequent-free clauses is no use; for once we use one, a the resolution products from then on will be negative clauses. These *mus* resolve with positive ones, so we could never use the second negative clause.

So that is why, although PROLOG restricts its database to positiv Horn clauses, we must temporarily let in one single negative Horn clause t allow a proof to happen. That clause is called a **query**, since from the point o view of a PROLOG user, that negative clause seems like a statement of wha he or she wants to prove. The next exercise illustrates this. In the previou exercise, PROLOG's theorem prover will not be triggered into action whe we add clause (1) to the database, since it is not a negative Horn clause, s not a query.

Exercise 22.2   Prove in PROLOG that the human Ann is not male and female.

In PROLOG, the query is not typed in as a negative Horn clause, eve though that is how it functions internally. Instead, the implication sign i removed, and something to indicate querying is added. In micro-PROLO we say is .... For example, we would not say:

```
Have(PIGS,WINGS) =>
```

but instead:

```
is (Have(PIGS,WINGS))
```

We will use an initial question mark to represent the PROLOG query, like this:

```
? Have(PIGS,WINGS)
```

We can see how the PROLOG device of the query as the single negative Horn clause works in practice, by trying to prove a universal conditional. Suppose for example the PROLOG database had in it:

```
A(x) => B(x)
B(x) => C(x)
```

and we wanted to prove:

```
A(x) => C(x)
```

(Check that this is provable.) The negation of this conclusion is:

```
       => A(@K)
C(@K) =>
```

PROLOG does not admit Skolem constants. PROLOG users simulate them by choosing new ordinary constants as needed. In this case, to prove the desired implication, we add to the database:

```
    => A(K)
```

where K is a new constant in the database. Then to trigger off the proof, we add the query ? C(K). Now PROLOG executes the proof (do it for yourself). But when the deduction process is completed, we must remember to explicitly remove => A(K) from the database, since that went in only as a prop to help prove the desired conditional. (The negative clause C(K) => , remember, is automatically removed by PROLOG at the end of the deduction process.)

As another example, suppose the PROLOG database had in it statements that whatever Fs, Gs, and that everything Fs:

```
F(x) => G(x)
    => F(x)
```

and we want to prove that everything Gs:

```
    => G(x)
```

The denial of this is:

        G(@K) =>

where @K is a new Skolem constant. So in PROLOG we should add the quer
? G(K) where K is a new constant. That is, we assert that something doe
not G, and PROLOG then will find a contradiction. Can you? Howevei
the PROLOG user will probably pose instead the query 'Does everything G?
since, naturally, that is what we want to prove. So in goes the query ? G(x
instead, which is wrong. Certainly, a contradiction will be derived, but wha
has in fact been proved is just that *something* Gs, since the negative claus
G(x) => is the denial of => G(@K).

22.2.1   Negation

From the point of view of a person used to working in PROLOG, the ir
admissibility of clauses with two or more consequents makes itself felt as
need to have negated atoms. For example, while we cannot express 'Everyon
is male or female', we might re-express this as 'All non-males are female an
conversely, and all non-females are male and conversely.' That will go straigh
into PROLOG:

$$
\begin{array}{ll}
\text{Non-m(x)} \Rightarrow \text{F(x)} & (3 \\
\text{F(x)} \Rightarrow \text{Non-m(x)} & (3a \\
\text{Non-f(x)} \Rightarrow \text{M(x)} & (4 \\
\text{M(x)} \Rightarrow \text{Non-f(x)} & (4a
\end{array}
$$

Such a move gets us nowhere, since it merely establishes Non-m as a redundar
synonym for F, and Non-f for M. Morever the pairs of clauses just written dow
give PROLOG the possibility of looping fruitlessly forever. For if PROLO(
resolved on (3) to eliminate F(x), it will next try to resolve the resultan
clause, which contains Non-m(x) as an antecedent. So at some stage it ma
resolve that away using (3a), which leaves a clause with F(x) as an anteceden
again, and so we get back to (3) to resolve away.
        So instead of the spurious Non-... predicates, what if we had a genuin
not(...) operator that we could wrap around atoms, to make a **negate**
atom, which is to be true if the atom is false and conversely? That woul
give us multiple disjunctive consequents by the back door. Then, togethe
with the earlier trick for inserting negative Horn clauses, we would have
PROLOG expressively equivalent to CFL.
        So, can we manufacture a working not(...) operator? One way, c
course, would be to have a full CFL system under the surface, and wheneve
PROLOG finds a not(p) antecedent being input, it turns it into a p conse
quent. But then PROLOG might as well come clean syntactically and giv

ıs the CFL syntax. The reason why PROLOG does not do that, is that it is designed to be a very efficient resolution refutation system by *avoiding* multiple consequents, which create great inefficiency. If you really want multiple consequents, choose a non-PROLOG system that gives them to you, and pay the price.

22.2.2   Negation by finite failure

The way PROLOG chooses to implement not(p), is that it tries to prove p, and if it succeeds, then the clause not(p) fails; alternatively if it fails to prove p, then not(p) is taken as proved. This is called **negation by finite failure**.

Semantically, it is certainly not the same as the negation we have studied. To see this, consider a database recording that Victorians and Queenslanders are Australians (forgetting about Tasmanians and the rest) and that if a person is in Australia but not an Australian, they must hold a passport. Prove that Sid, who is a Tasmanian and in Australia, must hold a passport.

We begin the proof this way (with C for 'Citizen'):

Denial	Hold-p(S) =>	(1)
Premiss	=> Tas(S)	(2)
Premiss	=> In(S,OZ)	(3)
Premiss	C(x,VIC) => C(x,OZ)	(4)
Premiss	C(x,QLD) => C(x,OZ)	(5)
Premiss	In(x,OZ),not(C(x,OZ)) => Hold-p(x)	(6)
(1),(6),resolve	In(S,OZ),not(C(S,OZ)) =>	(7)
(7),(3),resolve	not(C(S,OZ)) =>	(8)

We must now try to prove => C(S,OZ).

Exercise 22.3   Show that we finitely fail to prove this.

The exercise shows that we fail, so by negation as finite failure, we can add => not(C(S,OZ)) to the proof:

NFF	=> not(C(S,OZ))	(9)
(8),(9),resolve	=>	

The rule of negation by finite failure is a rule for dealing with negated atoms, those of the form not(p), where p is any ordinary, unnegated atom. It

is a rule stating how to prove a clause `=> not(p)`, namely, you fail to prove
`=> p`.

But it makes a restriction: it requires the `=> not(p)` just proved
to be used in resolution with a clause containing `not(p)` as an antecedent.
So its net effect is to tell us how to eliminate an antecedent of the form
`not(p)`: namely by trying, and failing, to prove `=> p`. The reason for this
restriction is rather obvious. Negation here means failure-to-prove, so a clause of the form A `=> not(p)` would mean 'If A is true, then fail to prove
p.' Or '... then p cannot be proved.' But you cannot instruct PROLOG
to fail to prove something, or tell it that something cannot be proved. On
the other hand, having `not(p)` as an antecedent just means 'p cannot be
proved', and that is something PROLOG can check up on (by trying to prove
p).

There is another restriction on the negation-by-failure rule. It is that
if the negated atom `not(p)` contains variables, then those variables must be
bound by the time PROLOG tries to prove `not(p)`. For example, if PROLOG
has this database about Philip, Charles, and Elizabeth:

Premiss		`=> Parent(P,C)`	(1)
Premiss		`=> Female(E)`	(2)
Premiss	`Parent(x,y),not(Female(x))`	`=> Has-father(y)`	(3)

then in any use of this in a proof, x should be bound in the resolution of
`Parent(x,y)`, before any attempt is made to resolve on `not(Female(x))`. To
take a particular case, if we gave PROLOG the query ? `Has-father(C)`, then
the proof of that will bind the x to P when we resolve the initial antecedent
`Parent(x,y)`. Then the next resolution is, essentially, on `not(Female(P))`.
That means that according to the negation-by-failure rule, PROLOG is asked
to prove `=> Female(P)`. That it fails to do, so the antecedent `not(Female(x)`
with that binding is proved, that is, resolved away.

Exercise 22.4   Carry out this proof.

If alternatively, the x was not bound in `not(F(x))`, as would happen
if we defined `Has-father` not as above, but as:

`not(Female(x)),Parent(x,y) => Has-father(y)`

then the negation-by-failure rule would have us trying to prove `=> F(x)`
with x unbound, so it means 'everything is F'. That is a strong statement to
make, and in our database it certainly fails. So the antecedent `not(F(x))`
is proved (resolved away), but for the wrong reason. For it does not mean

not everything is female', but has a meaning in the context of its clause: 'for any object x, if x *is female*...'. The error is clearly brought out if we take the above database about Charles and his parents, but replace P by E in premiss (1). Then all PROLOG knows is that Charles has a female parent, but is still able to prove that Charles has a father.

Exercise 22.5   Be PROLOG and prove it.

We embody all the above discussion in this definition of the negation-by-failure rule.

Definition   Negation by finite failure

If a clause C in a proof contains an antecedent not (p), and in the course of the proof a resolution is to be carried out on this not (p), and at that time all variables in the p are bound, then attempt to prove => p with those bindings for the variables in p. If, and only if, that proof attempt fails, infer C' which is C without the clause not (p).

(Def. NFF)

One justification given in the literature for the use of NFF is the **closed world assumption**: that we treat a database as saying *all* the truths about the world. More precisely, that the only positive facts about the world described in a database are the database clauses and those that can be deduced from them (without NFF). In that case, if we finitely fail to deduce a particular assertion, it must be false in that world. (So in the passports example, in the world being considered it is false that Tasmania is in Australia, or that the cities Canberra and Melbourne are.) That means we cannot treat the database world as a subworld of the actual state of affairs we are trying to encapsulate in our database; in which case we lose confidence in NFF as a rule that can tell us anything about the world we are trying to encapsulate. It tells us something only about the database.

22.3   Control in PROLOG

The great virtue of PROLOG as a programming language in which to do logic, is that the narrowing of its representational powers allows it to have an efficient control algorithm to govern its resolution refutation steps. Essentially, PROLOG is a resolution refutation machine. It is given a database of positive Horn clauses, then something to prove, and it tries to prove it from the clauses in the database.

22.3.1   Answer extraction

PROLOG actually does more than this. In particular, PROLOG has an inbuilt control feature that will produce all counterexamples to a universal denial $P_1, \ldots, P_n$ => that are provable from the database. This process is called **answer extraction**. To illustrate what it does, and its usefulness, we will look at an example.

EXAMPLE 22.1_____

Given that Philip is a parent of Charles, and that Elizabeth is a parent of Charles, query PROLOG to find all parent-child pairs.

What we want to do is to prove => P(P,C) and => P(E,C). We do not want to just tell PROLOG to prove those two clauses, though; we want PROLOG to find all provable clauses of that form, => P(x,y), and tell us what they are. (Imagine that we have a much larger database, and want to find *all* parent-child pairs provable from the database, and we do not know in advance what they are.)

So what we do is to query PROLOG with a query containing variables, ? P(x,y). Then PROLOG will find *all* answers to that query, that is, all bindings for P(x,y) that satisfy it.

Internally, what happens is that PROLOG temporarily adds the query to the database as the negative Horn clause with variables:

P(x,y) =>

Then PROLOG will *refute* our claim by finding bindings for x and y which give us parent-child pairs. So, it should give us the bindings $\{x \mapsto P, y \mapsto C\}$ and $\{x \mapsto E, y \mapsto C\}$. Either of these pairs of bindings refutes our denial, but PROLOG can be used to find both of them.

The process of answer extraction for this example works in this way. The database is:

Denial	P(x,y) =>	(1)
Premiss	=> P(P,C)	(2)
Premiss	=> P(E,C)	(3)

We apply the control algorithm, only we note the bindings of the variables in the denial, and when we reach the empty clause we report those variables, then backtrack to find another solution. In this simple example, we first reach the empty clause by resolving (1) and (2), in which case x (the parent) was bound to P (Philip) and y was bound to C (Charles). Next, the control algorithm is made to backtrack to the nearest choice point, which in this case is to the resolution of

(1) and (3). The alternative there is to bind x to E and y to C, and the empty clause is derived again. Backtracking again is fruitless, so we have recorded all solutions. So the answer which PROLOG will return is:

x↦P, y↦C
x↦E, y↦C

Exercise 22.6   Given that parents of Elizabeth are Elizabeth B and George, find all parents of parents of Charles.

In the above exercise, we had a two-atom denial. The refutations we found gave us bindings that made *both* atoms provable as assertions. That is, for the first pair of bindings, PROLOG could prove if we asked it:

=> P(EB,E)   and
=> P(E,C)

Proving those is, in fact, trivial.

We can describe this situation by saying that a set of variable bindings discovered in answer extraction will, if we substitute bindings for variables in the atoms of the denial, give us atoms each of which is separately provable as a single assertion. If our denial is $P_1, \ldots, P_n$ => , and the result of substituting the bindings for the variables in each atom P_i $(1 \leq i \leq n)$ is P'_i, then PROLOG can prove => $P'_1, \ldots,$ => P'_n.

22.3.2 PROLOG control strategy

PROLOG's control strategy, the **PROLOG control algorithm**, is very like the control algorithm on p. 265. But in PROLOG, the algorithm always begins execution with the current goal as the query D, which is the negative Horn clause. The algorithm is:

Definition   PROLOG control algorithm

(1)   Begin with D, the negative Horn clause, as the current goal.

(2)   Find the first clause C in the database whose consequent will unify with the leftmost atom of D.

(3)   If there is none, return failure; otherwise resolve D and C, to produce a resolvent R. To make the antecedent of R, put the remaining antecedents of C to the left of the remaining antecedents of D, and in the

order in which they occurred in C and D. (Note that R is another negative Horn clause.)

(4)   If R is the empty clause, return success.

(5)   Otherwise, repeat from step (2), but with R as the current goal.

(Def. PROLOG Control)

Note that D is never actually added to the database, and neither are any of the resolvents. Because of this, PROLOG's algorithm involves a special case of the set of support strategy: the **linear input strategy**. That is, start with the denial as input to the first resolution, then use the resolvent of each resolution as an input to the next.

It also involves another strategy which usually improves efficiency a lot. By virtue of step (2), resolution is performed on the atoms resulting from the cutting away of the leftmost atom in the denial, and similarly on their descendants, until none are left; only then does resolution start on the second atom in the denial. This is known as a **depth-first search** strategy. We search down the descendants of the left atom until all are gone, then down the descendants of the next, and so on. The alternative, **breadth-first search**, would, in (2), put the remaining antecedents of C to the right of those of D, thus ensuring that we resolve next on the next atom in the denial D, then the next one until all are done. At that stage, we would start resolving in a similar fashion, left to right, on all the atoms we collected from the resolutions on the atoms in D; then when finished, on their resolution products and so on until nothing is left (or we get stuck and have to backtrack).

Exercise 22.7   Take the database (2)–(5) of Exercise 22.4, and add (in this order, at the end) clauses that say:

(6)   A person's grandparent is a parent of a parent of theirs.
(7)   Elizabeth B. is female.
(8)   Elizabeth is female.

Then use answer extraction to find bindings in $G(g,C)$, $F(g)$ => , that is, to find all of Charles's grandparents who are female. Do the deduction (a) depth-first, (b) breadth-first.

The final point to note about the PROLOG control strategy, is that it starts a refutation with the only negative clause available, and that has only one atom in it. So by following the linear input strategy, it can be seen that all subsequent resolvents in a proof will have no consequents, only antecedents, as we pointed out earlier. Since the refutation starts from a finite database, the effect of this strategy is to ensure that either all antecedents disappear after a finite number of steps (the empty clause), or a leftmost clause will not unify (backtracking on failure), forcing search for an alternative to the last unification choice made. Those too will be finitely exhausted (unless, that is, a loop occurs). Premisses for a PROLOG deduction (positive Horn clauses with one negative Horn clause) have the property that if they are inconsistent then, with Herbrand, that can be established finitely; but also if consistent then a model can be found finitely. (Where, that is, no function symbols are used. If they are, there might be no finite model for consistent clauses.) That is one reason why PROLOG has the representational (lack of) power that it does. Even so, as we have seen, we cannot be sure that a PROLOG refutation will stop in a finite time with an answer: it can loop forever.

To sum up, PROLOG is an efficient way of doing logic with a restricted representational system. But it can fail to find proofs that exist. Worse, with the addition of negation as finite failure it is unsound, unless the range of possible interpretations is restricted to those for which a closed world assumption holds for the PROLOG database in question.

SUMMARY

- **Horn clauses.** Clauses with zero consequents (negative Horn clauses) or one consequent (positive Horn clauses).

- **PROLOG.** A programming language whose data statements are effectively just positive Horn clauses, and which computes solutions to problems by invoking a resolution refutation theorem prover on those Horn clauses together with one negative Horn clause (the **goal** to be proved). By using a theorem prover, users do not need to write programs of instructions: the prover is a universal program. (This description is somewhat idealized.)

- **Definition Negation by finite failure**. If a clause C in a proof contains an antecedent $not\,(p)$, and in the course of the proof a resolution is to be carried out on this $not\,(p)$, and at that time all variables in the p are bound, then attempt to prove $=>\ p$ with those bindings for the variables in p. If, and only if, that proof attempt fails, infer C' which is C without the clause $not\,(p)$.

  (Def. NFF)

- **Closed world assumption.** The only positive facts about the world that an applied logic is about, are the axioms and theorems of the applied logic. There are no 'omitted' facts.

- **Answer extraction.** The process of finding bindings for variables $v_1, \ldots, v_n$ in a query ? $Q(v_1, \ldots, v_n)$ which amounts to answering the question 'Which $v_1, \ldots, v_n$ are such that $Q(v_1, \ldots, v_n)$?' More precisely, if the denial query is $P_1, \ldots, P_n\ =>$, and the result of substituting the bindings for the variables in each atom P_i $(1 \leq i \leq n)$ is P_i', then PROLOG can prove $=>\ P_1', \ldots,\ =>\ P_n'$.

- **Definition PROLOG control algorithm.**

  (1) Begin with D, the negative Horn clause, as the current goal.

  (2) Find the first clause C in the database whose consequent will unify with the leftmost atom of D.

  (3) If there is none, return failure; otherwise resolve D and C, to produce a resolvent R. To make the antecedent of R, put the remaining antecedents of C to the left of the remaining antecedents of D, and in the order in which they occurred in C and D. (Note that R is another negative Horn clause.)

  (4) If R is the empty clause, return success.

  (5) Otherwise, repeat from step (2), but with R as the current goal.

  (Def. PROLOG Control)

Further reading for Part IV

Functions and identity in logic, and especially their proof theory and semantics, get a close discussion in Chapter 2 of E. Mendelson, *Introduction to Mathematical Logic*, Princeton: Van Nostrand, 2nd edn 1968. While that discussion is in the context of predicate calculus, much of the semantical theory carries across to our CFL approach. J. A. Robinson, in *Logic: Form and Function*, New York: North-Holland, 1979, deals very thoroughly with functions, and particularly the infinitistic trouble they cause in constructing Herbrand Universes. Robinson's discussion of resolution refutation in this book is a classic, partly because he invented the procedure.

Identity is a troublesome notion to admit into mechanical theorem-proving systems, because of the enormous amount of search it can create. The technique of **paramodulation** used to handle identity is discussed in Chapter 5 of D. Loveland, *Automated Theorem Proving*, Amsterdam: North-Holland, 1978. A more straightforward account of it is in L. Wos *et al.*, *Automated Reasoning*, Englewood Cliffs: Prentice-Hall, Chapter 6, 1984.

The idea of handling existence statements by special constants and functors is due to Thoralf Skolem in 1920. His paper, 'Logico-combinatorial Investigations' is reprinted in J. van Heijenoort, *From Frege to Gödel*, Cambridge, MA: Harvard, 1967.

The books on Resolution that were mentioned in Further reading for Part III (p. 197) all cover aspects of the computer implementation of Resolution. Robinson's book (above) is particularly thorough, and contains an implementation in the artificial intelligence language LISP. I. Bratko's book *Prolog Programming for Artificial Intelligence*, Wokingham: Addison-Wesley, 1986, contains PROLOG code for a clean and simple Resolution system, in Chapter 16. Kowalski gives a Horn clause definition of Resolution in Chapter 7, together with a discussion of factoring. Chapter 2 of the same book discusses some of the problems of forming denials of conclusions to be inferred by Resolution refutation.

Alonzo Church's celebrated paper proving the undecidability of logical systems of the power of our CFL, is 'A Note on the Entscheidungsproblem', *Journal of Symbolic Logic*, 1, 40–41, correction on pp. 101–2. It is carefully re-presented in Chapter 3 of Mendelson (above). Its consequences, both for the theory of computability, and more philosophically about the nature of truth and provability, are discussed in E. Beth, *Aspects of Modern Logic*, Dordrecht: Reidel, 1970, Chapter V. A more formal development is in M. Davis, *Computability and Unsolvability*, New York: McGraw-Hill, 1958.

The reference to Herbrand's researches is in Further reading for Part II (p. 153). Robinson (above) has a detailed account, and Loveland (above) sets it out thoroughly in his Chapter 1.

The basics of PROLOG are set out in W. F. Clocksin and C. S. Mellish, *Programming in Prolog*, Berlin: Springer-Verlag, 2nd edn 1984. The micro-PROLOG dialect is set out in K. Clark and F. McCabe, *Micro-Prolog:*

Programming in Logic, Englewood Cliffs: Prentice-Hall, 1984. Bratko (above) is a solid account, and for a very thorough theoretical discussion, see L. Sterling and E. Shapiro, *The Art of Prolog*, Cambridge, MA: MIT Press, 1986. These all contain discussions of the relation of PROLOG to logic, the problems of negation and control, and negation by failure. The fundamental work on negation by failure is in K. Clark, 'Negation as Failure', in H. Gallaire and J. Minker (eds) *Logic and Data Bases*, New York: Plenum Press, 1978. The closed world assumption was developed by R. Reiter in 'On Closed World Data Bases', also in the Gallaire and Minker volume.

In the Appendix, we go on to discuss **First Order Predicate Calculus**, otherwise known as **Quantification Theory**. The logic is set out and discussed in Mendelson (above); W.V.O. Quine, *Methods of Logic*, New York: Holt, 3rd ed 1972; T. J. Richards, *The Language of Reason*, Sydney: Pergamon, 1978; R. Rogers, *Mathematical Logic and Formalized Theories*, Amsterdam: North-Holland, 1971; and in fact just about any book on symbolic logic.

This logic has a much richer set of logical symbols than CFL, and much more complex ways of building formulae out of atoms. This created difficulties for the early attempts to devise theorem proving programs, so various people cast around for **normal forms** – standardized and simplified formats that formulae of first order predicate calculus could be reduced to without sacrificing any of their expressive power. In 1960, M. Davis and H. Putnam, 'A Computing Procedure for Quantification Theory', *Journal of the Association of Computing Machinery*, **7**:3, 201–15, advocated the use of **conjunctive normal form** in their early theorem-proving system. This normal form is essentially identical to the clausal form we are using; and thus, our clausal form has the ability to express any statement expressible in the full first-order predicate calculus. We will look at that in the Appendix.

Appendix
First-order predicate calculus

The purpose of this appendix is to describe briefly the first-order predicate calculus (PC), which is undoubtedly the commonest type of formal logic, and its relation to clausal form logic.

A.1   The symbolism of predicate calculus

We will use the same notation for atoms in PC as in CFL. Atoms are the simplest type of **well-formed formula** (Wff) in PC. Wffs are defined as follows:

Definition   Well-formed formula of PC

(1)   Any atom is a Wff.

(2)   If A and B are Wffs, and v is a variable, then the following are also Wffs:

$\neg A$,

$(A \supset B)$,

$(A \vee B)$,

$(A \wedge B)$,

$(A \equiv B)$,

$\forall v A$

$\exists v A$

(Def. Wff)

Informally, the meaning of these **Wff operators** is as follows:

Name	Example	Meaning
Negation	$\neg A$	A is false
Material Implication	$(A \supset B)$	If A then B
Disjuction	$(A \lor B)$	Either A or B
Conjunction	$(A \land B)$	Both A and B
Material Equivalence	$(A \equiv B)$	A if and only if B
Universal Quantification	$\forall v A$	For all v, A
Existential Quantification	$\exists v A$	there is a v such that A

In the two cases of quantification, the quantified Wff A would normally have in it the **variable of quantification** v, for example:

```
∃x(Person(x) ∧ (Rich(x) ∧ ¬Happy(x)))
```

which can be read as 'There is a thing which is a person and rich and not happy' or more idiomatically as 'Some rich person is not happy'.

As an example of a translation into PC, consider 'Everyone who studies history or philosophy will learn something wise and will do better at any career'. This may be symbolized as:

```
∀x((H(x) ∨ P(x)) ⊃
    (∃y(W(y) ∧ L(x,y)) ∧ ∀y(C(y) ⊃ D(x,y))))        (1)
```

$\forall$ and $\exists$ are called **quantifiers** and the other operators are called **Boolean operators** or (misleadingly) **truth-functions**. Satisfaction-functions would be a better name, as the next section will show. In a quantified Wff of the form $\forall v A$ or $\exists v A$, the subWff A is said to be the **scope** of the quantifier. An occurrence of a variable v inside the scope of a quantifier over v is said to be **bound** by that quantifier, otherwise to be **free**. If it is in the scope of several quantifiers over v, it is bound by the nearest (the innermost). A variable can occur bound and free in the same Wff. In the following, x occurs first bound, then free:

```
∀xF(x) ⊃ G(x)
```

For simplicity, note that we do not count the variable of quantification (the occurrence immediately after the quantifier) as being in the scope of the quantifier (or of any quantifier), hence freedom and bondage do not apply to it. It, so to speak, is part of the quantifier, and not part of what is quantified.

The notion of scope also applies to the Boolean operators. The scope of the negation in $\neg A$ is A, and the scope of any dyadic operator $\circ$ in $(A \circ B)$ is A and B.

A.2   Semantics

We use the same apparatus of interpretations and valuations here as in CFL; in particular we carry over the definitions of valuations and of satisfaction of an atom, that were set out in Chapter 11. We need now to extend that defintion to nonatomic Wffs.

Definition   Satisfaction for Wffs

Let $\mathcal{V}$ be a valuation in some interpretation $\mathcal{I} = \langle \mathcal{W}, \mathcal{D} \rangle$ that is applicable to the Wff A (and, in cases (b) and (c), to Wff B). Then:

(a) $\mathcal{V}$ satisfies $\neg A$ only if it does not satisfy A.

(b) $\mathcal{V}$ satisfies $(A \vee B)$ only if it satisfies at least one of A and B.

(c) $\mathcal{V}$ satisfies $(A \wedge B)$ only if it satisfies both A and B.

(d) $\mathcal{V}$ satisfies $\forall v A$, where v is a variable, just if every valuation $\mathcal{W}$ in $\mathcal{I}$ which is exactly like $\mathcal{V}$ except at most for the value it gives to v, is such that $\mathcal{W}$ satisfies A in $\mathcal{I}$.

(Def. Satisfaction)

The definitions of satisfaction for the remaining connectives can be derived from the above ones by defining those connectives as abbreviations for the above ones, in this way:

Definition   Material implication
$(A \supset B)$ abbreviates $(\neg A \vee B)$.

(Def. $\supset$)

Definition   Material equivalence
$(A \equiv B)$ abbreviates $((A \supset B) \wedge (B \supset A))$.

(Def. $\equiv$)

Definition   Existential quantification
$\exists v A$ abbreviates $\neg \forall v \neg A$.

(Def. $\exists$)

These definitions for material implication and equivalence are arguably rather unsatisfactory as accounts of implication and equivalence, as applicable to reasoning in scientific and ordinary discourse. Certainly, they are different from the other concepts of implication and equivalence defined in most other areas of formal logic, such as modal and relevant logics. Because of the distinctive nature of material implication and equivalence, it is a good idea to retain the traditional $\supset$ and $\equiv$ as their symbols, since these are not used at all for other concepts of implication and equivalence. Similarly one should avoid using $\rightarrow$ and $\leftrightarrow$ as their symbols, since these are also used for other concepts of implication and equivalence, as well as being used informally.

In the case of existential quantification, it can be shown that the satisfaction conditions amount to this:

Proposition A.1   Satisfaction of existential quantification

A valuation $\mathcal{V}$ in an interpretation $\mathcal{I}$ satisfies a Wff $\exists v A$, where v is any variable and A is any Wff, only if there exists a valuation $\mathcal{W}$ in $\mathcal{I}$ which is exactly like $\mathcal{V}$ except at most for the value it gives to v, and which satisfies A in $\mathcal{I}$.   ☐

A.3   Reduction to clausal form

Any Wff may be reduced to a set of one or more clauses, to which it is equivalent in the following sense: there exists a valuation which satisfies the Wff only if there exists one that satisfies all the clauses in the set.

We now state a procedure for carrying out the reduction, following Davis (1963). A PROLOG program carrying out this algorithm is given in Appendix A of Clocksin and Mellish (1984).

A.3.1   Stage 1   Fully quantify the Wff

If the Wff A contains free variables $v_1, \ldots v_n$ then prefix it by $\forall v_1 \ldots \forall v_n$. The order does not matter. For example, the Wff:

$$(F(x,y) \supset \exists y G(y,y)) \tag{2}$$

can be fully quantified in either of these two ways:

$$\forall x \forall y (F(x,y) \supset \exists y G(y,y)) \tag{2.1a}$$
$$\forall y \forall x (F(x,y) \supset \exists y G(y,y)) \tag{2.1b}$$

It is not hard to show that this step of fully quantifying a Wff A yields a Wff which is satisfied in a given interpretation $\mathcal{I}$ only if A is (though not necessarily by the same valuation). We mark this equivalence by saying that A and its fully quantified expansion are **equivalent for satisfiability**, and that the transformation made **preserves satisfiability**.

A.3.2   Stage 2   Relabel clashing variables

If a Wff contains two quantifiers with the same variable of quantification for each, then replace one of those variables of quantification, and all its occurrences bound by that quantifier, with a new variable. For example, (2.1a) can be relabelled as either of these:

$$\forall x \forall y (F(x,y) \supset \exists z G(z,z)) \tag{2.2a}$$
$$\forall x \forall z (F(x,z) \supset \exists y G(y,y)) \tag{2.2b}$$

Wff (1) can be relabelled as:

$$\forall x ((H(x) \lor P(x)) \supset \\ (\exists y (W(y) \land L(x,y)) \land \forall z (C(z) \supset D(x,z)))) \tag{1.2}$$

It can be shown that this step preserves satisfiability.

A.3.3   Stage 3   Eliminate implication and equivalence

We use the abbreviative definitions of $\supset$ and $\equiv$ to eliminate them, leaving Wffs whose Boolean operators are just $\land, \lor$ and $\neg$. Thus (2.2a) becomes:

$$\forall x \forall y (\neg F(x,y) \lor \exists z G(z,z)) \tag{2.3}$$

And (1.2) becomes:

$$\forall x (\neg (H(x) \lor P(x)) \lor \\ (\exists y (W(y) \land L(x,y)) \land \forall z (\neg C(z) \lor D(x,z)))) \tag{1.3}$$

Note that a Wff of the form $(A \equiv B)$ fully expands to the form $((\neg A \lor B) \land (\neg B \lor A))$.

Since these transformations are definitional, satisfiability is preserved.

A.3.4   Stage 4   Move negation inwards

The aim now is to have the negations negating only atoms. (Negated atoms and unnegated atoms are called **literals**.) To do that we make use of the following replacement laws, applied as often as needed. A and B are any Wffs, and v is any variable.

Original Wff	Replacement Wff	Name of Law
$\neg\forall v A$	$\exists v \neg A$	Quantifier-Negation Exchange
$\neg\exists v A$	$\forall v \neg A$	Quantifier-Negation Exchange
$\neg(A \vee B)$	$(\neg A \wedge \neg B)$	de Morgan
$\neg(A \wedge B)$	$(\neg A \vee \neg B)$	de Morgan
$\neg\neg A$	A	Double Negation

Note that each of these laws either eliminates negations or moves them deeper into the Wff, reducing their scope. In this way, the scope of negations can be reduced to single atoms. Note also that each of these laws preserve satisfiability.

This step of moving negations inwards has no effect on Wff (2.3). In the case of Wff (1.3), there is only one application of these laws to make. We obtain:

$$\forall x((\neg H(x) \wedge \neg P(x)) \vee$$
$$(\exists y(W(y) \wedge L(x,y)) \wedge \forall z(\neg C(z) \vee D(x,z)))) \qquad (1.4$$

A more complex transformation, employing all three laws in one form or another, is from a Wff of the form:

$$\neg\forall v(A \wedge (B \vee \neg C))$$

to the form:

$$\exists v(\neg A \vee (\neg B \wedge C))$$

A.3.5   Stage 5   Skolemize

At this stage we need to eliminate all existential quantifiers in favour of Skolem terms. We do it as follows:

(1)   Find an existential quantifier, note its scope and variable of quantification.

In (2.3) we find ∃z, whose scope is G(z,z) and variable of quantification is z.

(2)   Note in the scope of what universal quantifications this existential quantification occurs. Note the variables of those universal quantifications. Suppose they are $v_1, \ldots, v_n$, where $n \geq 0$.

In the present example, ∃zG(z,z) is inside the scope of a universal quantifier over x.

(3)   Delete the existential quantifier with its variable, and replace every occurrence of its variable of quantification in its scope by a new n-ary Skolem functor $@f(v_1, \ldots, v_n)$, where $v_1, \ldots, v_n$ are as in step (2) above. If $n = 0$ (that is, the existential we are deleting is not in the scope of any universal quantifier), then replace the variables by a new Skolem constant @c.

(4)   Repeat the above steps until no existential quantifiers are left.

For Wff (2.3), we end up with:

$$\forall x \forall y (\neg F(x,y) \lor G(@f(x,y), @f(x,y))) \tag{2.5}$$

or the same with any other new two-place Skolem functor.

This transformation captures the point that the identity of the object satisfying an existence assertion must be a function of the instances chosen for any surrounding universal quantifications. For example, in arithmetic, we know that the sum of any two numbers is a number:

$$\forall x \forall y \exists z (z = x + y)$$

The value of z that satisfies this depends on the values chosen for x and y. So we Skolemize this to:

$$\forall x \forall y (@s(x,y) = x + y)$$

where @s is a new Skolem function. We could read @s as 'the sum of' (which shows the triviality of the original arithmetical statement).

When we Skolemize Wff (1.4) we get:

$$\forall x ((\neg H(x) \land \neg P(x)) \lor \\ ((W(@g(x)) \land L(x, @g(x))) \land \\ \forall z (\neg C(z) \lor D(x,z)))) \tag{1.5}$$

or the same with any other new one-place Skolem functor.

Since we bring a new functor or constant into our logic when we Skolemize, we have to define a new interpretation to cover it. Because of that, we do not preserve satisfiability, but we preserve something almost as good. If we make our new interpretation $\mathcal{I}'$ the same as the old one $\mathcal{I}$ plus the following requirement, then it is not hard to prove the proposition that the Skolemized Wff is satisfiable in the new interpretation if, and only if, the original Wff was satisfiable in the old interpretation.

The requirement is this. Take any valuation $\mathcal{V}$ in the original interpretation $\mathcal{I}$ that satisfies the original Wff A. Fix on some existential quantification in A, over v say, and suppose it is inside the scopes of universal quantifications over $v_1, \ldots v_n (n \geq 0)$. Suppose also that d is one of the objects in the domain of discourse which, taken as a value of v by $\mathcal{V}$, would make A be satisfied by $\mathcal{V}$. Then we require that in $\mathcal{V}$ in $\mathcal{I}'$, the value given to $@f(v_1, \ldots v_n)$ is d. (Where $n = 0$ we have a Skolem constant instead of a Skolem functor, and d must be the value given to it by $\mathcal{V}$ in $\mathcal{I}'$.)

That is, very loosely speaking, we make our Skolem term $@f(v_1, \ldots v_n)$ evaluate to the same thing as v does. There is one object which the Skolem term, and the variable of existential quantification, both have as value for given values of the surrounding variables of universal quantification (if any). The proof the proposition just mentioned is essentially a proof that such a Skolem term always exists.

A.3.6   Stage 6   Remove universal quantifiers

This step is easy to perform. We simply delete all universal quantifiers together with their attached variable of quantification. Then Wff (2.5) becomes:

$$(\neg F(x,y) \ \lor \ G(@f(x,y),@f(x,y))) \qquad (2.6)$$

In that case, we deleted initial universal quantifiers, which would appear to be correct. A Wff A is satisfied in an interpretation $\mathcal{I}$ only if $\forall vA$ is satisfied in $\mathcal{I}$ (though not necessarily by the same valuation). But for Wff (1.5) we also remove an internal quantifier:

$$((\neg H(x) \ \land \ \neg P(x)) \ \lor$$
$$((W(@g(x)) \ \land \ L(x,@g(x))) \ \land \ (\neg C(z) \ \lor \ D(x,z))))) \qquad (1.6)$$

The correctness of that step may not be so obvious. We can show, however, that in Wffs like these where the only Boolean operators are disjunction and conjunction, and where clashing variables have been replaced, we can always move universal quantifiers out to the front without disturbing satisfaction. This works only because the other Wffs, that come under the scope of the quantifier when it is shifted out front, do not contain free the variable of quantification. That requirement is automatically satisfied as a result of earlier stages of the reduction to clausal form. The transforms are as follows:

Original Wff	Replacement Wff	Restriction
$(A \wedge \forall v B)$	$\forall v(A \wedge B)$	v not free in A
$(\forall v A \wedge B)$	$\forall v(A \wedge B)$	v not free in B
$(A \vee \forall v B)$	$\forall v(A \vee B)$	v not free in A
$(\forall v A \vee B)$	$\forall v(A \vee B)$	v not free in B

It is easy to show that these transforms also preserve satisfiability.

So, by applying these rules exhaustively, we end up with all quantifiers out front, which may then be deleted. Altogether then, the effect of deleting all universal quantifiers *from a Wff A whose format is as in Stage 5 of these reductions* is to end up with a Wff equivalent for satisfiability to A.

A.3.7   Stage 7   Distribute conjunction over disjunction

By now, our Wffs have no quantifiers, negation only over atoms, and $\wedge$ and $\vee$ are the only dyadic Boolean operators. As a final rearrangement, we want to move conjunction operators *outwards*, and disjunction operators *inwards*, so that we end up with Wffs being conjunctions, like this:

$$(C_1 \wedge C_2 \ldots C_{n-1} \wedge C_n)$$

for $n \geq 1$, where each of these conjuncts $C_i (1 \leq i \leq n)$ is a disjunction of literals:

$$(P_{i_1} \vee P_{i_2} \ldots P_{i_{m-1}} \vee P_{i_m})$$

for $m \geq 1$. Wffs of this shape are said to be in **conjunctive normal form**, hereafter CNF.

To do this we need transforms to distribute $\wedge$ over $\vee$:

Original Wff	Replacement Wff	Name of Law
$(A \vee (B \wedge C))$	$((A \vee B) \wedge (A \vee C))$	Distribution
$((A \wedge B) \vee C))$	$((A \vee C) \wedge (B \vee C))$	Distribution

We also need devices for 'flattening' iterated disjunctions and conjunctions when they occur. We want, for instance, to turn:

$$(A \vee ((B \vee C) \vee D)) \tag{3}$$

into:

$(A \lor B \lor C \lor D)$ **(4)**

To do this we first provide laws that allow us to nest any disjunctions or conjunctions rightward:

Original Wff	Replacement Wff	Name of Law
$(A \lor B) \lor C)$	$(A \lor (B \lor C))$	Associativity
$((A \land B) \land C)$	$(A \land (B \land C))$	Associativity

Applying associativity for disjunction to (3) gives us:

$(A \lor (B \lor (C \lor D)))$ **(5)**

Finally, we provide definitions that allow us to flatten the resulting right associations:

Definition Disjunctive flattening
$(A \lor B \lor C)$ abbreviates $(A \lor (B \lor C))$.

(Def. Flatten)

Definition Conjunctive flattening
$(A \land B \land C)$ abbreviates $(A \land (B \land C))$.

(Def. Flatten)

Applying Flattening to (5) allows us to rewrite it as (4), as required.

It is straightforward to show that all the laws cited here preserve satisfaction, and the definitions do so trivially, hence in this transformation stage satisfaction is preserved.

Wff (2.6) does not change in this stage. It is already in CNF, being a single conjunct containing two disjuncts. Wff (1.6) however undergoes quite a transformation:

```
((¬H(x) ∨ W(@g(x))) ∧
(¬H(x) ∨ L(x,@g(x))) ∧
(¬H(x) ∨ ¬C(z) ∨ D(x,z)) ∧
(¬P(x) ∨ W(@g(x))) ∧
(¬P(x) ∨ L(x,@g(x))) ∧
(¬P(x) ∨ ¬C(z) ∨ D(x,z)))
```
(2.7)

A.3.8   Stage 8   Remove repetitions

At this stage we sometimes find that there are features of our CNF Wffs that allow us to simplify them, preserving satisfiability. We can remove repeated conjuncts or disjuncts:

Original Wff	Replacement Wff	Name of Law
$(A \land B \land B)$	$(A \land B)$	Simplification
$(A \lor B \lor B)$	$(A \lor B)$	Simplification

In these simplification laws, the order or placing of the repetition in the original Wff is irrelevant, since it can easily be shown that disjunction and conjunction are commutative as well as left and right associative, making it possible to reorder conjuncts and disjuncts at will, while preserving satisfiability. Nor do irrelevant conjuncts or disjuncts (A) need to be present in the statement of the simplification laws; or alternatively there can be any number of them.

For example, a Wff of the form:

$$((A \lor A) \land (B \lor A \lor B \lor A \lor A) \land (A \lor A))$$

can be simplified to:

$$(A \land (B \lor A))$$

Wffs (2.6) and (1.7) have no repetitions to remove.

A.3.9   Stage 9   Remove tautologies

A disjunction such as $(A \lor B \lor \neg B)$ is fairly obviously satisfied by any valuation in any interpretation. That is, it is a **tautology**. If that disjunction occurs as one conjunct in a CNF, then since always satisfied it is irrelevant to the determination of whether the CNF is ever satisfied. Consequently, it may be removed from the CNF preserving satisfiability.

That is, we now have the following law:

Original CNF	Replacement CNF	Name of Law
$(A \land (B \lor \neg B \lor C) \land D))$	$(A \land D)$	Tautology

Wffs (2.6) and (1.7) have no tautologies to remove.

If a CNF was just a conjunction of tautologies, for example, $((A \lor \neg A) \land (B \lor \neg B \lor C))$, complete removal of tautologies would give us the empty Wff, which strictly we have not allowed syntactically to be a Wff. You can either define it as a Wff and invent a way of writing it, such as $\odot$ (and realise that it too is a tautology), or you can stop short of removing the last tautology.

A.3.10   Stage 10   Rewrite as clauses

Finally, we rewrite each conjunct in the CNF as a clause, as follows. We remove the negations from the negated atoms and put those atoms to the left of the =>, as antecedents. Then we put the remaining (unnegated) atoms to the right, as consequents.

In this way, Wff (2.6) ends up as the single clause:

$$F(x,y) \Rightarrow G(@f(x,y),@f(x,y)) \qquad\qquad (2.10)$$

A CNF of the form:

$$((A \lor \neg B \lor C \lor \neg D) \land (\neg E \lor \neg F))$$

becomes two clauses:

$$B, D \Rightarrow A, C$$
$$E, F \Rightarrow$$

It is not hard to see why this is the right transform to get a CNF into clausal form. First, as to the conjunction: we can split the conjunction into separate conjuncts since the resulting set of conjuncts will be satisfied by a particular valuation only if the entire conjunction is.

Secondly, looking at each disjunction, for example:

$$(A \lor \neg B \lor C \lor \neg D)$$

we can gather up all the negative literals and apply de Morgan to them, getting for this example:

$$(\neg(B \land D) \lor (C \lor C))$$

By the definition of material implication, this is:

$$((B \land D) \supset (A \lor C))$$

And that, as a comparison of the semantic definitions will confirm, rather obviously has the same satisfaction conditions as:

$B, D \Rightarrow A, C$

The six-conjunct CNF (1.7) ends up as the six clauses:

```
      H(x) => W(@g(x))
      H(x) => L(x,@g(x))
H(x), C(z) => D(x,z)
      P(x) => W(@g(x))
      P(x) => L(x,@g(x))
P(x), C(z) => D(x,z)
```
(2.7)

These can be read (tortuously) as:

For each student of history there is something wise.
Whoever studies history will learn that wise thing related to them.
Whoever studies history and for any career,
    they will do better at that career.
For each student of philosophy there is something wise.
Whoever studies philosophy will learn that wise thing related to them.
Whoever studies philosophy and for any career,
    they will do better at that career.

A.4   Conclusion

A careful study of the reduction procedure to CFL will justify the following important result. We say that a set of Wffs (or CFL clauses) are
simultaneously satisfiable only if there is a valuation in an interpretation
that satisfies all the Wffs (or clauses) in S. Then:

Proposition A.2   Clausal reduction theorem

For every Wff A of PC there can be computed a set S of clauses of CFL which
are simultaneously satisfiable only if A is satisfiable. $\square$

The procedure outlined above computes S, and discussion along the
way provides an outline for a full justification of this proposition.

The significance of this proposition is twofold. First, it shows that CFL
is as expressively powerful as the full PC, that is, whatever can be said in PC
with its rich apparatus of quantifiers and Boolean operators, can be said in
the sparser language of CFL.

Secondly, since resolution is refutation complete for CFL, we can use
resolution as our theorem proving method for PC and know it is refutation

complete. To prove that some PC Wff A follows logically from a set of PC premisses Γ, we:

(1)   Transform all the PC Wffs in Γ to CFL, giving a set of clauses Γ'.

(2)   Transform $\neg A$ into a set of CFL clauses Δ.

(3)   Apply resolution refutation to the set Γ', Δ of clauses. If we deduce the empty clause => , we have succeeded in showing that A logically follows from Γ.

Answers to exercises

Chapter 1

1.1

From (2) and (3)	Piggy did not ride Deety.	(6)
From (6) and (1)	Piggy rode Gay Deceiver.	(7)
From (7) and (1)	Merridew rode Deety.	(8)
From (8) and (4)	Miss Scarlett owns Deety.	(9)
From (5) and (7)	Mrs White did not own Gay Deceiver.	(10)
From (9) and (10)	Col Mustard owns Gay Deceiver.	(11)
From (9) and (11)	Mrs White owns Black Hat.	(12)
From (7) and (3)	Gay Deceiver came last.	(13)
From (11) and (13)	Col Mustard's horse came last.	(14)
From (14) and (2)	Deety came second.	(15)
From (13) and (15)	Black Hat came first.	(16)

So the answer is:

Place	Horse	Jockey	Owner
1	Black Hat	Ralph	Mrs White
2	Deety	Merridew	Miss Scarlett
3	Gay Deceiver	Piggy	Col Mustard

1.2

The premisses are statements (1) – (5) of that exercise. The conclusions we wanted were statements (8), (9), and (11) – (16). The other statements occurring in the deduction – (6), (7) and (10) – can be treated as intermediate conclusions. Conclusions they are; but they are not ones we wanted as results, so much as helpers on the way. Logicians often talk of *the* conclusion of a deduction, meaning the very last statement deduced: number (16) in the horse-race problem.

1.3

(a)   This is the only grammatically incorrect 'sentence'. Since it is ungrammatical, we do not judge it for truth or falsity.

(b)   Grammatically fine, but semantically, it is false.

(c)   Grammatical and true.

1.4

(1) says that one thing is higher than a second if the second thing is lower than the first.

The deduction is:

Premiss	`X higher-than Y if Y lower-than X`	(1)
Premiss	`Stratus lower-than Cirrus`	(2)
(1), Inst	`          X higher-than Stratus`	
	`if Stratus lower-than X`	(3)
(3), Inst	`Cirrus higher-than Stratus`	
	`if Stratus lower-than Cirrus`	(4)
(2), (4) MP	`Cirrus higher-than Stratus`	(5)

Note that when we instantiate a variable to a name in a statement, we replace all occurrences of that variable by the name.

Chapter 2

2.1

Only (a), (c) (f) and (h) do not make statements; (a) asks a question, (c) and (h) issue instructions, and (f) is a subatomic component that doesn't convey any information (state a truth or falsehood) but merely makes a reference. (d) makes a molecular statement, the component atomic statements are that *Antony was an emperor*, and that *Augustus was an emperor*; the glue is conjunction. (e) is molecular: there is a component statement, that *Julius was in danger*, which in turn is stated to be believed by Calpurnia. Treat this sort of molecule as an atom inside an atom, not as two atoms glued together. (g) can also be treated as molecular – the atomic statement that *4 equals 6* is being stated to be false. (i) is plainly a molecule containing two atoms, the statements that *Caesar was an emperor*, and that *Calpurnia was an empress*. The glue is the idea of *if*, usually called **implication**. (j) is not atomic, its component statements are that *Brutus trusted Caesar*, and that *Caesar trusted Brutus*. The glue is conjunction.

2.2

(a) is a conjunction molecule; the rest can all be treated as atomic. (b), (c) and (f) are two-place. (b)'s property is identity, its references are both to Julius Caesar. That same person is referenced twice in (c), the relation is crowning. (d) might look like (b) as a sentence of English, but the statement expressed is structurally different. The relation is obviously not identity: 'is' here means instead something like 'has the property of being'. The straightforward reading of (d) is as expressing a one-place statement, the property of Caesar being described is that of being dead. In (e) there is just one object referenced, Calpurnia. Caesar is not a term in this statement, for the property in the statement (distrusting) is not attached to Caesar but to his wife. Also, *everyone* in (e) is not an object. For now, all we can do is treat the property here as a peculiar one-place one of hating-universally. Similarly (g) is not two-place – *nobody* is not an object. We force this into the atomic mold as the one-place statement that Brutus has the queer property of being universally-not-trusted. Chapter 3 will show us a better mold for both (e) and (g) as types of non-atomic statement. (f) is straightforwardly two-place; the relation is stabbing, the stabber is Brutus, the stabbed is Caesar. Finally (h) is a triadic atomic statement; the objects are Mark Antony, Julius Caesar, and the Roman Forum. The three-place relation is that of one object carrying a second from a place.

2.3

Answers will vary, the author's is this:

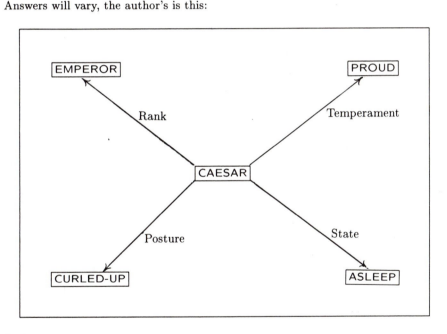

2.4

A disjunctive statement says only that *one or more* of its disjuncts are true. So we can't draw all the disjuncts into a semantic net, for that would be an assertion that they are *all* true. Nor could we just draw in one disjunct, for in general we don't know *which* disjuncts are true. (We could try putting each of the disjuncts into a separate copy of the net, then say that one or more of these disjoint nets is true; but that's a bit like hard work.)

2.5

Symmetrical:

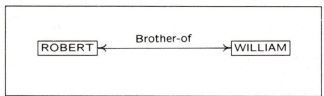

Asymmetrical:

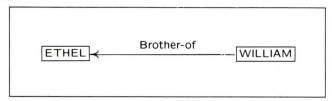

Neither (combine the two worlds above):

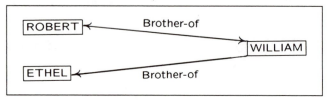

2.6

(a)

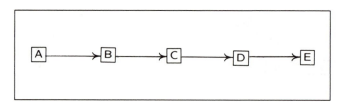

(b)

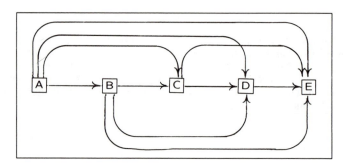

2.7

In the net below, the Likes links have been drawn thick, the Asks-out ones thin. The answers are:

(a)   Asymmetrical.

(b)   C and D.

(c)   No.

(d)   Likes links converse to the existing one-way Likes links, i.e., C to A, E, and F; D to A and C.

(e)   Yes, any looping one, e.g., from A to A.

(f)   Remove B.

(g)   Irreflexive.

(h)   No.

(i)   Yes.

(j)   No.

(k)   A to A, E, and G; B to B, C, and D; E to A, D, E and G; F to D; G to A, C, D, E, and G.

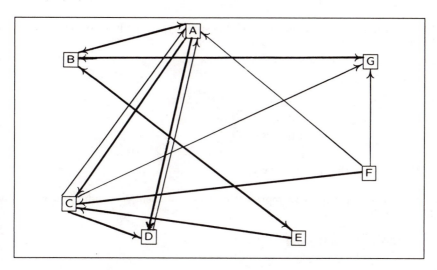

Chapter 3

3.1

You should have added four Knows links, with the same tail and head as each of the four Hates links.

3.2

No, the rules do not. By the new (1) about eye-position we certainly can infer that felines have forward-pointing eyes. But we cannot then invoke that new (1) again to infer that mammals do, for the Ako link is pointing the wrong way. And we have no other route from the only Eye-position link in the diagram to the $\boxed{\text{HORSE}}$ node.

3.3

3, 0, 3.

3.4

(4) Antecedent: Caesar tries to become a dictator

$\boxed{\text{CAESAR}}$ ___Tries-to-become___ ↘ $\boxed{\text{DICTATOR}}$

(4) Consequent: Cassius will conspire with Brutus

$\boxed{\text{CASSIUS}}$ ___Conspires-with___ ↘ $\boxed{\text{BRUTUS}}$

(Note that unless tense is crucial we had best always ignore it or we get into tangles that are not relevant at an introductory level.)

(5) Antecedents: the car's engine is running, the car's gears are engaged, the car's brakes are off:

$\boxed{\text{CAR-1}}$ ___State-of-engine___ ↘ $\boxed{\text{RUNNING}}$
$\boxed{\text{CAR-1}}$ ___State-of-gears___ ↘ $\boxed{\text{ENGAGED}}$
$\boxed{\text{CAR-1}}$ ___State-of-brakes___ ↘ $\boxed{\text{OFF}}$

(5) Consequent: the car will move.

Here are two approaches to representing this statement, depending on what you think of 'will':

$\boxed{\text{CAR-1}}$ ___Next-state___ ↘ $\boxed{\text{MOVING}}$
$\boxed{\text{CAR-1}}$ ___Capability___ ↘ $\boxed{\text{MOVING}}$

Note that when doing logic we always make references explicit: 'its' became 'the car's', etc. You should always do this when writing down statements for use in a logic problem.

3.5

(a)   This is not merely a conditional: *q since p* does not say just *q if p* – it also says that the antecedent *p* is true. Secondly, the component statement that *Calpurnia had a dream that Caesar would die*, is certainly not atomic; and it is hard to see how the other one could be atomic either.

(b)   This fails the second restriction. Its consequent is non-atomic, containing a conjunction of two statements, that *Caesar is evil* and that *Caesar is ambitious*. You can overcome this problem, however, by devising two acceptable conditionals with the original antecedent and each with one of the two conjuncts of the consequent: 'If Caesar killed Pompey then Caesar is ambitious', and 'If Caesar killed Pompey then Caesar is evil'. You can always perform this splitting trick when the consequent is a conjunction.

(c)   This is fine. The author's vectors are:

SOOTHSAYER	_Warned_ →	CAESAR
CALPURNIA	_Warned_ →	CAESAR
CAESAR	Danger-rating →	PERIL

(d)   is a conjunction not a conditional. If you split the conjunction, the first conjunct is a two-place atom and so could go straight into the semantic net. The second statement is an acceptable conditional.

3.6

Here is one way of doing it:

If Greymalkin is a cat and a cat is a kind of a feline,
then Greymalkin is a feline.   (1)

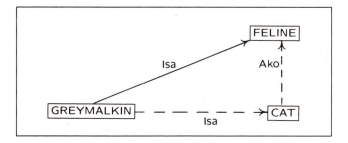

If Greymalkin is a feline and felines are a kind of carnivore,
then Greymalkin is a carnivore.   (2)

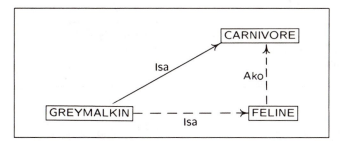

(1) matches in the main net (Figure 3.1), so we add:

$$\boxed{\text{GREYMALKIN}} \underline{\quad\text{Isa}\quad}_{\rightarrow} \boxed{\text{FELINE}}$$

to that net. Then (2) matches, so we add:

$$\boxed{\text{GREYMALKIN}} \underline{\quad\text{Isa}\quad}_{\rightarrow} \boxed{\text{CARNIVORE}}$$

to the main net.

Chapter 4

4.1

It will match:

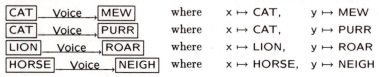

		where		
CAT — Voice → MEW		where	$x \mapsto$ CAT,	$y \mapsto$ MEW
CAT — Voice → PURR		where	$x \mapsto$ CAT,	$y \mapsto$ PURR
LION — Voice → ROAR		where	$x \mapsto$ LION,	$y \mapsto$ ROAR
HORSE — Voice → NEIGH		where	$x \mapsto$ HORSE,	$y \mapsto$ NEIGH

and that is all.

4.2

If x is a kind of y, and y is a kind of z, then x is a kind of z.

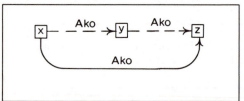

    The series of matches of that conditional in the main net, and the variable bindings and conclusion reached at each stage (which is added to the main net) are shown in this table:

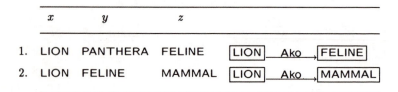

	x	y	z	
1.	LION	PANTHERA	FELINE	$\boxed{\text{LION}}\underline{\quad\text{Ako}\quad}_{\rightarrow}\boxed{\text{FELINE}}$
2.	LION	FELINE	MAMMAL	$\boxed{\text{LION}}\underline{\quad\text{Ako}\quad}_{\rightarrow}\boxed{\text{MAMMAL}}$

4.3

(a)

(i)   There is really only one way to do this:

> If x is a kind of y, and y has a docile temperament,
> then x has a docile temperament.

(You might have used different variables, as long as you repeated them in the same positions as the xs and ys here.)

(ii)

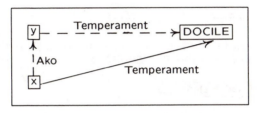

(iii)   The conditional in this net matches into Figure 4.1 in only one way, with $x \mapsto$ CAT and $y \mapsto$ DOMESTIC-ANIMAL. Then the conclusion:

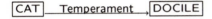

is immediate.

(b)

(i)   This is the most obvious way:

> If an x's diet is meat and a y is a kind of an x,
> then a y's diet is meat.   (1)
> If an x's diet is meat and y is an x, then y's diet is meat.   (2)

(ii)

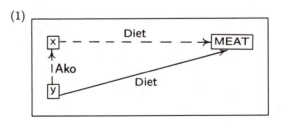

(2)

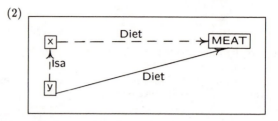

(iii)   We match (1) to the main net first. It matches in only one way, with
        x ↦ CARNIVORE and y ↦ FELINE. Then the conclusion:

$$\boxed{\text{FELINE}}\underline{\quad\text{Diet}\quad}\!\!\rightarrow\!\boxed{\text{MEAT}}$$

can be added to the net. We can now re-match (1) to the net, this time with
x ↦ FELINE and y ↦ PANTHERA, giving a new conclusion:

$$\boxed{\text{PANTHERA}}\underline{\quad\text{Diet}\quad}\!\!\rightarrow\!\boxed{\text{MEAT}}$$

This allows a third match of (1), with x ↦ PANTHERA and y ↦ LION. We
can now add a third conclusion:

$$\boxed{\text{LION}}\underline{\quad\text{Diet}\quad}\!\!\rightarrow\!\boxed{\text{MEAT}}$$

Finally we can now match (2) to the net, with x ↦ LION and y ↦ LEO.
The final conclusion now emerges:

$$\boxed{\text{LEO}}\underline{\quad\text{Diet}\quad}\!\!\rightarrow\!\boxed{\text{MEAT}}$$

4.4

Their auxiliary nets are:

(2)

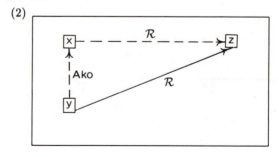

(3)

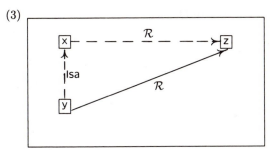

The order of application of those conditionals to the main net, and the variable bindings and conclusion reached at each stage, are shown in this table. In each application, $\mathcal{R} \mapsto$ Covering.

	x	y	z			
(2)	MAMMAL	EQUINE	HAIR	EQUINE	Covering	HAIR
(2)	EQUINE	HORSE	HAIR	HORSE	Covering	HAIR
(3)	HORSE	BUCEPHALUS	HAIR	BUCEPHALUS	Covering	HAIR

4.5

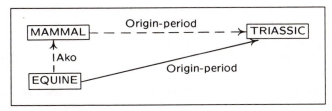

$\mathcal{R} \mapsto$ Origin-period , $x \mapsto$ MAMMAL , $y \mapsto$ EQUINE , $z \mapsto$ TRIASSIC

4.6

The Ako relation itself is collective, and by definition it does obey rule (2). Isa is also a collective property of the group at the head of an Isa link. It does not obey rule (2). For example, Hodge is a feline, but he is not a panthera.

Chapter 5

5.1

In all cases the denotation of R is fixed since there is only one relation for it to denote.

(a)   An interpretation of world W2:

Label	Denotes
R	is less than
A	2
B	4
C	5
D	7

(b)   There are many interpretations that meet the requirements on $\mathcal{J}$. A simple one is where R is as in (a) (of course), and all four constants denote the number 2.

(c)   Again, many interpretations can be found, namely all those that will not do for $\mathcal{I}$ or $\mathcal{J}$. One solution is to take (a) above and interchange the denotations of A and B.

5.2

(a)   This is true in $\mathcal{I}$. This can be seen without even looking at the antecedents, since the consequent is true in $\mathcal{I}$. So, by the definition of truth-conditions of ground conditionals, this is not the case that makes the conditional false.

(b)   This is false in $\mathcal{I}$. Both antecedents are true in $\mathcal{I}$, and the consequent is false in $\mathcal{I}$. So the falsity of the conditional follows by the definition of truth for ground conditionals.

(c)   In this case we note that the consequent is true in $\mathcal{I}$. This, by the definition of truth for ground conditionals, is not the case that makes a conditional false, so (c) is true in $\mathcal{I}$.

5.3

(a)   Let x denote 7. Then since in $\mathcal{I}$, B denotes 4 and R denotes the less-than relation, the conditional has a true consequent under this valuation (it says that $4 < 7$). By the definition of truth for conditionals, a conditional is true if it has a true consequent, so under this valuation the conditional is true. That is, the valuation satisfies the conditional in $\mathcal{I}$.

(b)   Let x denote 2, y denote 4, and z denote 5. Then under this valuation both antecedents are true and the consequent is false, so by the definition of truth for conditionals, the conditional is false under this valuation, that is, the valuation does not satisfy the conditional in $\mathcal{I}$.

5.4

Yes, it is false in $\mathcal{I}$. We have already seen, in Exercise 5.3 (b), a valuation that did not satisfy the conditional in $\mathcal{I}$. So the conditional is false in $\mathcal{I}$, by the definition of truth for universal conditionals.

5.5

A simple interpretation $\mathcal{I}$ in the domain of natural numbers is to let R denote $\leq$ (is less than or equal to), and let S denote $=$, that is, equality, and let A denote 0. Then the conditional asserts the **antisymmetry** of $\leq$: that if two numbers are less than or equal to each other, they are equal to each other. The vector in the other set asserts that $0 \leq 0$. All these statements are true in $\mathcal{I}$.

The inference proceeds thus: bind x and y both to A; then both antecedents match the vector in the second net. In that case, the consequent, with the bindings replacing the variables, that is, $\boxed{\text{A}} \underline{\quad\text{S}\quad}_{\blacktriangleright}\boxed{\text{A}}$, can be added to the second net. It asserts that $0 = 0$, which is true. (If a relation $\mathcal{R}$ is such that, wherever $x\mathcal{R}y$ and $y\mathcal{R}x$ both hold, then $x = y$, we say that $\mathcal{R}$ is **antisymmetric**.)

Chapter 6

6.1

It is denying that *both* the antecedents are true; that is, it is saying that at least one antecedent is false. For, if the conditional is true in an interpretation, then since its consequent is false, not all its antecedents can be true in the interpretation (by Def. Truth for ground conditionals). Conversely, if both antecedents were true in an interpretation, then the conditional would be false.

6.2

Suppose the conditional is *satisfied* by the valuation. Then by Def. Satisfaction, if we treat the variables as constants denoting their values in the valuation, the conditional would be true in $\mathcal{I}$. In that case, by Def. Truth for ground conditionals, the antecedent S would be false. So, by Def. Satisfaction again, S is not satisfied by that valuation.

Conversely, suppose the conditional is *not satisfied* by the valuation. Then by Def. Satisfaction, if we treat the variables as constants denoting their values in the valuation, the conditional would be false in $\mathcal{I}$. In that case, by Def. Truth for ground conditionals, the antecedent S would be true. So, by Def. Satisfaction again, S is satisfied by that valuation.

6.3

If the sex of x is male and the sex of x is female, then falsum.

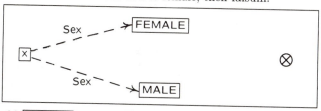

We add $\boxed{\text{HODGE}} \underline{\quad\text{Sex}\quad}_{\blacktriangleright}\boxed{\text{FEMALE}}$ to Figure 4.1; then the conditional in the above auxiliary net will match, with $x \mapsto$ HODGE. So the conclusion falsum can be deposited into the main net.

6.4

(a)

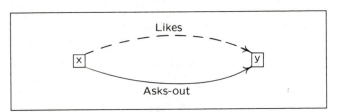

The conditional is false: any valuation for x and y that satisfies x̲ ̲Likes̲ →y̲ does not satisfy x̲ ̲Asks-out̲ →y̲ .

(b)

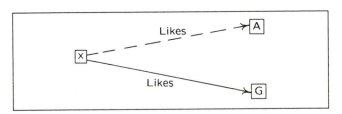

True. For could we find a valuation that satisfies the antecedent but not the consequent? The only valuation that satisfies the antecedent is where x has the value Bill, but that valuation satisfies the consequent.

(c)

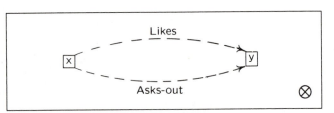

True. If it were not, we could find a valuation for x and y that satisfies both the antecedents. But there is no such valuation.

(d)

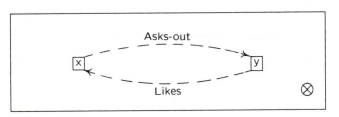

This is false. A valuation not satisfying it is where x has Charlie as value and y has Alf.

(e)

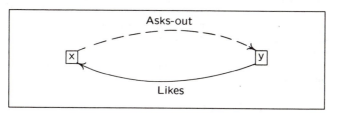

This too is false. A valuation not satisfying it is where x has Alf as value and y has Bill.

6.5

The net is:

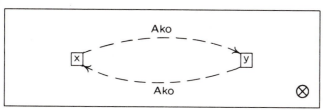

Assume that equines are a kind of horse, that is, add an Ako link from EQUINE to HORSE . Then the antecedent of the above conditional matches in the resulting net, so falsum can be added to it.

Chapter 7

7.1

(a)	neither	(f)	constant
(b)	constant	(g)	constant
(c)	neither	(h)	predicate
(d)	constant or predicate	(i)	constant
(e)	predicate	(j)	neither

7.2

a)   The sonship relation is dyadic. The author chose to represent it as:

Son-of($\langle$son$\rangle$, $\langle$parent$\rangle$)

giving as translation:

Son-of(HAM, NOAH)

The other way round is equally acceptable, of course.

(b)   The sonship relation here is different from the one in (a). Here we are expressing the relation that holds between a son and *both* his parents, not just one. So it is three-place. In this example, the author did not distinguish between father and mother, since the English sentence did not specify the sexes of the parents. And he used 'Son-of-parents' not 'Son-of', just to avoid possible confusion with the different predicate in (a). The schema for the predicate was:

Son-of-parents(⟨son⟩, ⟨parent⟩, ⟨parent⟩)

so the translation was:

Son-of-parents(CAIN, ADAM, EVE)

As far as the specification of the predicate goes:

Son-of-parents(CAIN, EVE, ADAM)

is equally acceptable.

(c)   With the schema:

Built(⟨builder⟩, ⟨thing built⟩, ⟨material⟩)

the translation is:

Built(NOAH, THE-ARK, GOPHER-WOOD)

(d)   Remembering that we must give the ladder a name, the schema:

Climbed(⟨climber⟩, ⟨thing climbed⟩, ⟨from⟩, ⟨to⟩)

gives the translation:

Climbed(JACOB, LADDER-1, EARTH, HEAVEN)

(e)   A suitable property is a group journey, with a leader, a group, start and finish places, and time taken. Capture that in the predicate:

Journey(⟨leader⟩, ⟨group⟩, ⟨origin⟩, ⟨destination⟩, ⟨years duration⟩

and then the translation is:

Journey(MOSES, HEBREWS, EGYPT, ISRAEL, 40)

7.3

(a)	false	(f)	false
(b)	false	(g)	false
(c)	false	(h)	false
(d)	false	(i)	false
(e)	false	(j)	true

Chapter 8

8.1

(a) No: lacks the implication arrow and braces.

(b) No: the braces enclose the whole clause; there should be one set enclosing just the antecedents and another enclosing the consequents.

(c) Yes.

(d) No. There is a capital letter in the middle of the predicate `Will-Conquer`. Otherwise it is correct.

(e) Yes.

8.2

(a)   `{Spies-for(P-G, SMERSH)} => {Traitor(P-G)}`

(b)   `{Not-in(B-P, CAKE-1)} => {Flat(CAKE-1)}`

(c)   `{Borders(HOLLAND, BELGIUM),`
        `Borders(FRANCE, BELGIUM)} => {Same-land-mass(HOLLAND, FRANCE)}`

(d)   `{Weather(RAINY),`
             `Waterlogged(PITCH)} => {State-of(C-MATCH-1, CANCELLED)}`

(e)   `{Phylum(CR-1, CHORDATE),`
         `Chromos(CR-1, NORMAL)} => {Female(CR-1), Male(CR-1)}`

8.3

In the first row, the clause has a true consequent, so by Def. Truth (a) for clauses, the clause is true. In the second row, it has all antecedents true (all one of them) and all consequents false (all one of them), so by Def. Truth (a) for clauses, the conditional is false.

8.4

Suppose the clause is true. Then there are two possible reasons for that, by Def. Truth (a) for clauses. The first is that the clause has a true consequent. Adding a false one does not change that. The second is that it has a false antecedent; and adding a false consequent does not change that either. (Actually, in both those cases, it does not matter what is the truth-value of the consequent you add; the clause stays true.)

Suppose alternatively that the clause is false. Then by Def. Truth (a) for clauses it has no true consequents and no false antecedents. Adding a false consequent changes neither of those facts, so the clause stays false.

8.5

There are no false antecedents, since there are no antecedents at all. That is, condition (a) of Def. Truth (a) for clauses holds. (If you are not happy about that, see the note just following Def. Truth (a) for clauses which *stipulates* how to read (a) when there are no antecedents.) Similarly, there are no true consequents, that is, condition (b) holds too. Hence, by Def. Truth (a) for clauses, the clause is false.

Note that since all antecedents are true, we could add T as an antecedent without disturbing that fact; similarly we could add F as a consequent. So the empty clause could also be written as {T} => {F}.

8.6

The author's choice of atoms here may differ from your representations, but aside from that the clauses should be the same.

(a)   {} => {In(AUSTRIA, EUROPE)}

(b)   {} => {In(TURKEY, EUROPE),
                              In(TURKEY, ASIA)}

(c)   {In(AUSTRIA, ASIA)} => {}

(d)   {In(TURKEY, EUROPE),
            In(TURKEY, ASIA)} => {}

(e)   {Touches(RUSSIA, TURKEY)} => {In(RUSSIA, EUROPE),
                                     In(RUSSIA, ASIA)}

(f)   {In(RUSSIA, EUROPE),
            In(RUSSIA, ASIA)} => {Straddles(RUSSIA, URALS),
                                  Borders(RUSSIA, CASPIAN)}

Chapter 9

9.1

(a)   {} => {Obeys(ANNE, LAW),
                              Arrested(ANNE)}

(b)   {Arrested(BILL),
                Obeys(BILL, LAW)} => Made-mistake(POLICEMAN)

(c)   {Taps(CATHIE, PHONES),
                Obeys(CATHIE, LAW),
        Job-type(CATHIE, CIVILIAN)} => {}

(d)   Compromises(DICK, DIPLOMATS) => {Clothes-type(DICK, MAN),
                                        Has-vices(DICK),
                                        Woman(DICK), Spy(DICK)}

(e)   A three-stage approach makes this one easy. The intuitive reading as a clause is 'not–(either Ernie is a spy or Fyodor is a spy) => not–(Ernie is trying to expose Fyodor and Fyodor is trying to expose Ernie)'. Switch both sides using the transfer rule for negation, and the clause now is 'Ernie is trying to expose Fyodor and Fyodor is trying to expose Ernie => either Ernie is a spy or Fyodor is a spy.' That will now go cleanly into CFL:

> T-t-e(E,F), T-t-e(F,E) => Spy(E), Spy(F)

9.2

(a)   This ends up as three clauses:

> {} => Wearing(ANNE, JEANS)
> {} => Wearing(ANNE, SHIRT)
> {} => Wearing(ANNE, SHOES), Wearing(ANNE, BOOTS)

(b)   In(BOBBIE, ROOM) => In(BOBBIE, ROOM)

(c)   Using N for the number being discussed:

> Positive-integer(N) => Odd(N), Even(N)
> Real(N) => {}
> => Positive(N)
> => Less(N, 10), Equal(N, 10)

(d)   The disjunctive antecedent creates three clauses:

> Fails(CAROL, MATHS) => Leaves(CAROL, UNIVERSITY)
> Fails(CAROL, LOGIC) => Leaves(CAROL, UNIVERSITY)
> Fails(CAROL, COMP-SCI) => Leaves(CAROL, UNIVERSITY)

(e)   This representation needs to be built in two stages. First we split up the disjunctive antecedent, giving 'If Diane visits London she will find culture and beauty', and 'If Diane visits Paris she will find culture and beauty'. Next we split the conjunctive consequents of these two assertions, giving the result:

> Visits(DIANE, LONDON) => Finds(DIANE, CULTURE)
> Visits(DIANE, LONDON) => Finds(DIANE, BEAUTY)
> Visits(DIANE, PARIS) => Finds(DIANE, CULTURE)
> Visits(DIANE, PARIS) => Finds(DIANE, BEAUTY)

Alternatively we could have split the conjunctive consequent first, with the same final result.

9.3

Schema	Formula
Isa(⟨act⟩, ⟨act type⟩)	Isa(G-1, GIVING)
Donor(⟨act⟩, ⟨donor⟩)	Donor(G-1, GOD)
Recipient(⟨act⟩, ⟨recipient⟩)	Recipient(G-1, MOSES)
Gift(⟨act⟩, ⟨gift⟩)	Gift(G-1, COMMANDMENT-1)

9.4

The author used this schema to define his 'selling' predicate:

Sells(⟨seller⟩, ⟨buyer⟩, ⟨item sold⟩, ⟨price paid⟩)

The relationship vectors and corresponding dyadic atoms can be defined in this way:

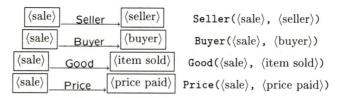

⟨sale⟩ — Seller → ⟨seller⟩		Seller(⟨sale⟩, ⟨seller⟩)
⟨sale⟩ — Buyer → ⟨buyer⟩		Buyer(⟨sale⟩, ⟨buyer⟩)
⟨sale⟩ — Good → ⟨item sold⟩		Good(⟨sale⟩, ⟨item sold⟩)
⟨sale⟩ — Price → ⟨price paid⟩		Price(⟨sale⟩, ⟨price paid⟩)

The author used 'sale' as the predicational term, and for instance terms used 'S_1' for the sale in (a), and 'S_2' for that in (b). He called the trader 'Trader-1' and used obvious abbreviations for 'Sydney Harbour Bridge' and 'Joseph's older brother'. Then the vectors for (a) are:

S-1 — Isa → SALE
S-1 — Seller → CON
S-1 — Buyer → HYLAS
S-1 — Good → S-H-B
S-1 — Price → DOLLARS-1000

The vectors for (b) are:

S-2 — Isa → SALE
S-2 — Seller → J-O-B
S-2 — Buyer → TRADER-1
S-2 — Good → JOSEPH
S-2 — Price → SHEKELS-20

In CFL the 4-ary formulae are:

(a)   Sold(CON, HYLAS, S-H-B, DOLLARS-1000)

(b)   Sold(J-O-B, TRADER-1, JOSEPH, SHEKELS-20)

The 2-ary formulae for (a) are:

```
Isa(S-1, SALE)
Seller(S-1, CON)
Buyer(S-1, HYLAS)
Good(S-1, S-H-B)
Price(S-1, DOLLARS-1000)
```

The 2-ary formulae for (b) are:

```
Isa(S-2, SALE)
Seller(S-2, J-O-B)
Buyer(S-2, TRADER-1)
Good(S-2, JOSEPH)
Price(S-2, SHEKELS-20)
```

9.5

The assertion of (a) is straightforward:

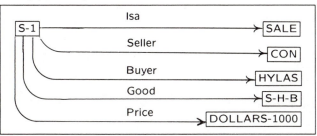

To deny (b), we first note that (b) is represented by several vectors, that is, if it is true they are all true, and conversely if they are all true so is (b). That is, (b) is equivalent to the conjunction of its representing vectors. To deny (b) must then be to deny the conjunction of its representing vectors. In CFL this is:

```
{Isa(S-2, SALE),
 Seller(S-2, J-O-B),
 Buyer(S-2, TRADER-1),
 Good(S-2, JOSEPH),
 Price(S-2, SHEKELS-20)} => F
```

As an auxiliary net this is:

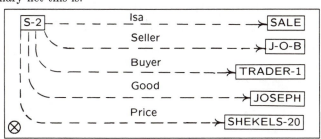

9.6

We start with this main net:

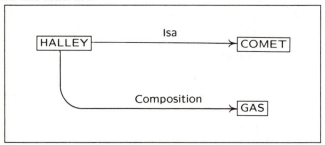

One auxiliary net we need is Figure 9.3. Applying it to this main net we get these two new main nets:

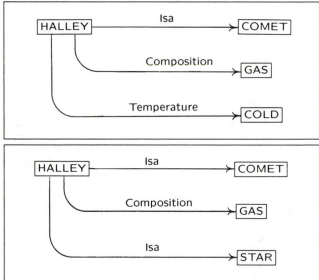

The new conditional gives us this second auxiliary net:

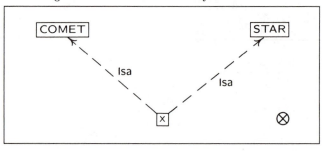

It can be matched only in the second of the new main nets above. Doing so extends that main net to this:

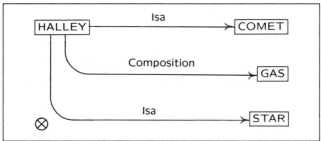

The world that net is trying to represent is impossible, since it contains falsum. We reject it. The only main net we are left with is the first of the pair above; there is now no alternative to it. It contains the assertion that Halley is cold, so we have deduced that assertion.

Chapter 10

10.1

See the Summary.

10.2

Your answers should be the same as these, except perhaps for using SOCRATES instead of S, etc. and except that in each example you might have different variables. But if, in a particular example, you use y, say, where the author uses x, you must use it wherever he uses x in that example, and not use it elsewhere in that example.

(a)   => Listens(S,P)

(b)   => Listens(S,x)

(c)   Listens(P,x) =>

(d)   Listens(S,x) => Listens(x,S)

(e)   Listens(x,S) => Listens(x,P)

(f)   Listens(x,P) => Listens(S,x)

(g)   Listens(x,S) =>   and
       Listens(x,P) => . Note that since variables are places for matching terms within one clause, xs within one clause have nothing to do with xs in another. So we could have used different variables in these two clauses.

(h)   Listens(x,S),Listens(x,P) => Listens(S,x)   and
       Listens(x,S),Listens(x,P) => Listens(P,x)

(i)   Listens(x,S) => Listens(A,x)   and
       Listens(x,P) => Listens(A,x)

(j)   Listens(x,y) => Listens(x,Socrates)

(k)   => Listens(x,y)

(1)   `Listens(x,S) => Listens(y,x)`   and
       `Listens(x,P) => Listens(y,x)`

10.3

In quasi-English 'For any objects x and y, if x is capital of y and x is in Australia, then y is a state or a territory, or x is Canberra.' Idiomatically, 'Any capital in Australia is capital of a state or territory, or else is Canberra.' The auxiliary net is:

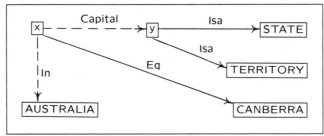

10.4

There is no variation on these answers:

(a)   `P(A,y) => P(y,A)`
(b)   `P(x,x) => P(x,x)`
(c)   `P(x,y) => P(y,x)`
(d)   `P(A,z) => P(z,A)`
(e)   `P(B,B) => P(B,B)`

The last two, note, make a substitution on the result of a substitution.

10.5

The problem is to avoid assimilating different variables by substituting one of these three for another. To do that we introduce a new variable to get (say) x out of the way while we replace z by x. The answer is (try it):

$$F(y,z,x) \;=\; F(x,y,z)\{w/x\}\{x/z\}\{z/y\}\{y/w\}$$

10.6

If (3) was deduced by consistent rules from the knowledge base, then since those rules are consistent, we know that (3) is true in every interpretation in which all the premisses used to deduce it are true. So it is true in every model of the knowledge base. (If you cannot see that, do not go on to the next chapter yet, but do some more revision.) We saw in the previous chapter that a clause with no consequent, like (3), is equivalent to one with F as the sole consequent, that is, treat it as having a false consequent. But then, by the definition of truth (a) for clauses, a true clause with all its consequents false, must have a false antecedent. So for (3), its antecedent must be false in the interpretations in question, that is, in all the models for the knowledge base.

Chapter 11

11.1

(a)   {1, 3, 5}. You may, of course, have the three members stated in any order you like. Sets are not ordered.

(b)   {⟨1, 1⟩, ⟨2, 4⟩}. The angle brackets indicate *ordered sets* (also called *tuples*), so you may not rearrange their contents. Here, you may not have ⟨4, 2⟩ as a member of the relation.

(c)   {⟨1, 1, 1⟩, ⟨1, 2, 3⟩, ⟨3, 2, 1⟩, ⟨1, 3, 5⟩, ⟨5, 3, 1⟩, ⟨2, 2, 2⟩,
        ⟨2, 3, 4⟩, ⟨4, 3, 2⟩, ⟨3, 3, 3⟩, ⟨3, 4, 5⟩, ⟨5, 4, 3⟩, ⟨4, 4, 4⟩, ⟨5, 5, 5⟩}

   Note how these triples sometimes come in twos: this is because, for example, 4 is the average of 3 and 5 (in that order) as well as of 5 and 3 (in that order).

11.2

In any valuation, each variable can have one of six different values, giving $3 \times 6 = 18$ different valuations. All valuations agree on all constants and predicates, so these 18 are all there are.

   In the general case, there are $n_v \times n_w$ different valuations. This number is always independent of the number of constants and predicates in the knowledge base, since all valuations agree on them.

11.3

Only two, where $\mathcal{V}(\mathbf{x}) =$ Rome, and $\mathcal{V}(\mathbf{x}) =$ the slave.

11.4

There are many possible valuations in most cases. The ones selected here were chosen for their simplicity; but yours may well differ from these.

(a)   *Satisfaction.* Any value for **x** not satisfying the antecedent will satisfy the clause. There is only one of these: $\mathcal{V}(\mathbf{x}) =$ Rome.

   Non-satisfaction. **x** must have as value a person who does not love Rome; then antecedent is satisfied and consequent is not, that is, $\mathcal{V}(\mathbf{x}) =$ the slave.

(b)   *Satisfaction.* This is satisfied if the consequent is satisfied. In that case **x** must have as value an object u in the domain such that $\langle u, u \rangle$ is in $\mathcal{D}_R(\textbf{Stabbed})$. There is no such object. So no valuation satisfies (b).

   Non-satisfaction. From the preceding, it follows that every valuation will not satisfy (b).

(c)   *Satisfaction.* We need to satisfy the consequent. Valuations in which $\mathcal{V}(\mathbf{x}) =$ Caesar and $\mathcal{V}(\mathbf{y}) =$ Rome, will do.

   Non-satisfaction. (c) is not satisfied by a valuation if its consequent is not. The pair ⟨Rome, Calpurnia⟩ is not in $\mathcal{D}_R(\textbf{Loves})$, so we choose the valuation in which $\mathcal{V}(\mathbf{x}) =$ Rome and $\mathcal{V}(\mathbf{y}) =$ Calpurnia.

(d)   *Satisfaction.* We seek a valuation that does not satisfy the antecedent. Ones in which $\mathcal{V}(\mathbf{x})$ = Rome will do, since $\langle$Rome, $\mathcal{V}(\mathtt{C})\rangle$ is not in the relation $\mathcal{V}(\mathtt{Stabbed})$.

   Non-satisfaction. We seek a valuation that does satisfy the antecedent. The one where $\mathcal{V}(\mathbf{x})$ = Brutus will do.

(e)   *Satisfaction.* We need to satisfy one consequent (at least). We satisfy the first consequent in any valuation where $\mathcal{V}(\mathbf{x})$ = Brutus and $\mathcal{V}(\mathbf{y})$ = Rome.

   Non-satisfaction. We need a valuation not satisfying either consequent. Ones in which $\mathcal{V}(\mathbf{x}) = \mathcal{V}(\mathbf{y})$ = Caesar will do.

(f)   *Satisfaction.* We need a valuation that fails to satisfy at least one of the antecedents. Ones in which $\mathcal{V}(\mathbf{x}) = \mathcal{V}(\mathbf{y})$ = Caesar will do, satisfying neither antecedent.

   Non-satisfaction. We need a valuation that satisfies both antecedents, but there is none in $\mathcal{I}_R$ that does.

(g)   *Satisfaction.* There are no variables here, so all interpretations will agree with each other. And they all agree on satisfying both consequents, and hence the clause.

   Non-satisfaction. By the preceding, there is no such valuation.

(h)   *Satisfaction.* This is satisfied by any valuation that does not satisfy the antecedent. Any in which $\mathcal{V}(\mathbf{x})$ = Caesar will do.

   Non-satisfaction. We need a valuation that satisfies the antecedent but does not satisfy the consequent. Taking valuations in which $\mathcal{V}(\mathbf{x})$ = Brutus will satisfy the antecedent, so now we seek a value for $\mathbf{y}$ which will leave the consequent not satisfied, given that value for C. Any of the valuations just selected in which $\mathcal{V}(\mathbf{y})$ = Brutus will do, since $\langle$Brutus, Brutus$\rangle$ is not in the relation $\mathcal{D}_R(\mathtt{Loves})$.

(i)   *Satisfaction.* This is satisfied if the consequent is; so we can choose any valuation where $\mathcal{V}(\mathbf{x})$ = Caesar.

   Non-satisfaction. We need a valuation that satisfies the antecedent but not the consequent. We fail to satisfy the consequent only by taking valuations in which:

   (a) $\mathcal{V}(\mathbf{x})$ = the slave, or

   (b) $\mathcal{V}(\mathbf{x})$ = Rome.

   For type (a) interpretations, we are seeking a value u for $\mathbf{y}$ such that the pair $\langle$the slave, $u\rangle$ is in the relation $\mathcal{D}_R(\mathtt{Stabbed})$, but there is none such. So no type (a) valuation will do.

   For type (b) interpretations, we are seeking a value u for $\mathbf{y}$ such that the pair $\langle$Rome, $u\rangle$ is in the relation $\mathcal{D}_R(\mathtt{Stabbed})$, but there is none such. So no type (b) valuation will do either. Hence, there is no valuation that fails to satisfy clause (i).

(j)   *Satisfaction.* Any valuation that satisfies the consequent will do, which means we can ignore the value given to $\mathbf{y}$. Any valuation in which $\mathcal{V}(\mathbf{x})$ = Caesar and $\mathcal{V}(\mathbf{y})$ = Rome will do.

   Non-satisfaction. We seek a valuation that satisfies both antecedents but not the consequent. $\mathbf{z}$ must evaluate to Rome in order to satisfy the second antecedent, and $\mathbf{y}$ must evaluate to Caesar to satisfy the first antecedent. Fortunately on that value for $\mathbf{y}$, the second antecedent does get satisfied. So now, to complete the satisfaction of the first antecedent, $\mathbf{x}$ must evaluate to

Brutus or Casca; but whichever of these we take, the consequent *is* satisfied. So there is no valuation in $\mathcal{I}_R$ that fails to satisfy clause (j).

Chapter 12

12.1

(a)　False. It says 'Every person loves Rome.'

(b)　False. 'Everything stabbed itself.'

(c)　False. 'Everything loves everything.'

(d)　False. 'Nothing stabbed Caesar', or more literally 'If anything stabbed Caesar then falsehood follows.'

(e)　False. 'For any two objects at all, either the first loves the second or the second loves the first.' More idiomatically, 'Everything loves, or is loved by, each thing.'

(f)　True. Literally: 'For any two objects (possibly the same), if one stabbed the other and the other stabbed the first, then falsehood follows.' Better English: 'No two things stabbed each other', (though perhaps this does not allow that the two could be the same).

(g)　True. 'Caesar is a person, or Calpurnia is.'

(h)　False. 'Whatever stabbed Caesar, loves everything.' Literally, 'For any objects x and y, if x stabbed Caesar, then the x loves y.' Where, as here, a variable such as y occurs in the consequent but not the antecedent, it is often more understandable to read it as 'For all ⟨the other variables⟩, if ⟨antecedents⟩, then for all objects y, ⟨consequents⟩.' So we can read this one as 'For any object x, if x stabbed Caesar, then for all objects y, x loves y.'

(i)　True. 'Whatever stabbed anything, loves Rome.' Literally, 'For any objects x and y, if x stabbed y, then the x loves Rome.' Where, as here, a variable such as y occurs in the antecedent but not the consequent, it is often more understandable to read it as 'For all ⟨the other variables⟩, if there is a y such that ⟨antecedents⟩, then ⟨consequents⟩.' So we can read this one as 'For any object x, if there is an object y that x stabbed, then x loves Rome.'

(j)　True. 'Everything that stabbed something that loves anything, loves that thing.' Better English: 'All stabbers love the beloved of those they stabbed.'

12.2

For satisfiability of a clause of a given type, its satisfaction condition must hold for *some* valuation; for truth it must hold for *every* valuation.

　　For falsity of a clause of a given type, its non-satisfaction condition must hold for *some* valuation; for unsatisfiability it must hold for *every* valuation.

12.3

(b) is the only unsatisfiable clause in the interpretation; the rest are satisfiable.

12.4

Once you have realized that these four sets of clauses say:

(1) p and q are both true,
(2)   either p or q (or both) are true,
(3) p and q are both false, and
(4) p and q are not both true;

then it is easy to see that the square must be arranged either like this:

(1)   (3)

(2)   (4)

or as its mirror image about a vertical axis. That is, as:

(3)   (1)

(4)   (2)

But since squares of opposition always occur in such pairs, it is usual to consider just one of them and ignore the other.

12.5

Suppose an interpretation $\mathcal{I}$ has a valuation that satisfies p. Then Id is satisfied by that valuation since its consequent is. Now suppose that $\mathcal{I}$ has a valuation that does not satisfy p. Then Id is still satisfied by that valuation since its antecedent is not. Hence every valuation in $\mathcal{I}$ satisfies Id, so Id is true in $\mathcal{I}$. But $\mathcal{I}$ was arbitrary, so Id is true in *any* interpretation $\mathcal{I}$.

12.6

Only the empty clause.

12.7

Only T can be. Any other, $P(t_1, \ldots, t_n)$, can be shown to have a valuation in an interpretation that does not satisfy it. Simply give denotations to the constants among $t_1, \ldots t_n$, and give values to the variables among $t_1, \ldots t_n$, and then define the denotation of the predicate P to exclude $\langle d_1, \ldots, d_n \rangle$, where d_i is the value given to t_i. That gives you an interpretation, and a valuation in that interpretation, which do not satisfy the atom.

Chapter 13

13.1

You cannot use (1){y/x}{z/y}{x/z}, as it yields P(x,x,x) => F(x,x),F(x,x).
However this will work: (1){x1/x}{x/z}{z/y}{y/x1}.

13.2

You can deduce:

$$p, p \Rightarrow r, r$$

which is just the same clause as:

$$p \Rightarrow r$$

The reason is that antecedents and consequents are *sets* of atoms, and you cannot have repeated elements in a set. If you write '$\{p, p\}$' with the braces, as you should if you are being very correct about writing clauses, then the braces should remind you that you are just writing down a set, which thus has but a single element, p, even though you wrote its name twice. That is, $\{p, p\} = \{p\}$.

13.3

$s = 1$ and $r = 0$, to make the conclusion $= 0$. Then $p = q = 1$ or $p = q = 0$ will make both premisses $= 1$.

13.4

Note first that there is no valuation in which these two conclusions can both be satisfied; for in any given valuation, either p is satisfied (making the second clause unsatisfied) or p is not satisfied (making the first clause unsatisfied).

Now, if there were an interpretation in which the axioms (clauses in K) were all true, then since the premises for deducing these two conclusions are axioms in K, it must follow by soundness that the two conclusions are both true in that interpretation – which they cannot be. So there is no such interpretation.

If there can be no interpretation in which all axioms in a knowledge base (or any other set of clauses for that matter) are true, we say they form an **inconsistent set** of clauses.

Chapter 14

14.1

The axiom A6 is `F(x,y) => Par(x,y)`. We need to prove that A4 is deducible from
A6 and the other axioms:

Premiss, A2	`=> F(P,C)`	**(1)**
Premiss, A6	`F(x,y) => Par(x,y)`	**(2)**
(2){P/x}{C/y}	`F(P,C) => Par(P,C)`	**(3)**
(1),(3) Cut-Rule	`=> Par(P,C)`	**(4)**

14.2

The formula (1){y/x}{z/y} is `F(z,z) => Par(z,z)`, which is not what we wanted.

14.3

Tree for deduction of T1:

```
A1: F(x,y) => M(x)───────F(P,C) => M(P)
                                          ──────── {} => M(p)
A2: {} => F(P,C)────────────────────────
```

Note how it helps to use `{}` in sideways tree deductions. The tree for T2 has
this structure (we show line numbers instead of the clauses, to save space):

```
(1)───────(2)
              ──(4)───────(5)
(3)─                          ──(7)
(6)───────────────────────────
```

14.4

Compare this with the answer just above.

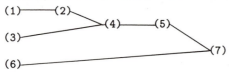

14.5

(a)   Anyone who is someone's parent, and male, is their father.

(b)   It says that one person is another's father if the first person is male and the
       other person is their child. (Isn't English clumsy?) The deduction is:

Premiss, A10	`Par(x,y),M(x) => F(x,y)`	(1)
Premiss, A8	`Ch(x,y) => Par(y,x)`	(2)
(1){w/y}{y/x}	`Par(y,w),M(y) => F(y,w)`	(3)
(2){w/x}	`Ch(w,y) => Par(y,w)`	(4)
(3),(4) Cut-Rule	`Ch(w,y),M(y) => F(y,w)`	(5)
(5){x/w}	`Ch(x,y),M(y) => F(y,x)`	(6)

14.6

Premiss, A3	`Par(x,y),Par(y,z) => Gpar(x,z)`	(1)
Premiss, A8	`Ch(x,y) => Par(y,x)`	(2)
(1){v/x,u/y}	`Par(v,y),Par(u,z) => Gpar(v,z)`	(3)
(2){u/x,v/y}	`Ch(u,v) => Par(v,u)`	(4)
(3),(4) Cut-Rule	`Par(u,z),Ch(u,v) => Gpar(v,z)`	(5)
(5){y/u,z/v,x/z}	`Par(y,x),Ch(y,z) => Gpar(z,x)`	(6)
(2),(6) Cut-Rule	`Ch(x,y),Ch(y,z) => Gpar(z,x)`	(7)

Note that Sim-Subst-Rule gave us an advantage over Subst-Rule only in line (6), where its use allowed us to avoid a temporary variable.

14.7

This deduction inserts the deductions of the two theorems in their place, and renumbers the lines.

Premiss, A10	`Par(x,y),M(x) => F(x,y)`		(1)
Premiss, A8	`Ch(x,y) => Par(y,x)`		(2)
(1){w/y}{y/x}	`Par(y,w),M(y) => F(y,w)`		(3)
(2){w/x}	`Ch(w,y) => Par(y,w)`		(4)
(3),(4) Cut-Rule	`Ch(w,y),M(y) => F(y,w)`	T5 =	(5)
(5){x/w}	`Ch(x,y),M(y) => F(y,x)`		(6)
Premiss, A1	`F(x,y) => M(x)`		(7)
(7){P/x}{C/y}	`F(P,C) => M(P)`		(8)
Premiss, A2	`=> F(P,C)`		(9)
(8),(9) Cut-Rule	`=> M(P)`	T1 =	(10)
(6){P/y}	`Ch(x,P),M(P) => F(P,x)`		(11)
(10),(11) Cut-Rule	`Ch(x,P) => F(P,x)`		(12)
Premiss, A11	`=> Ch(A,P)`		(13)
(12){A/x}	`Ch(A,P) => F(P,A)`		(14)
(13),(14) Cut-Rule	`=> F(P,A)`		(15)

Chapter 15

15.1

(a)

A1, {A/x/,x/y}	`F(A), G(A) => H(A,x)`	(1)
(1),A2 Cut	`F(A), F(A), G(A) => I(x,y)`	(2)
(2), Contract	`F(A), G(A) => I(x,y)`	

(b)

B2 {y/x}	H(y) => F(y)	**(1)**
B1,(1) Cut	F(x), G(x,y) => F(y)	**(2)**
(2) {x/y/,y/x}	F(y), G(y,x) => F(x)	**(3)**
(3),B3 Cut	F(y), G(x,y) => H(x), F(x)	**(4)**
B2, (4) Cut	F(y), G(x,y) => F(x),F(x)	**(5)**
(5), Contract	F(y), G(x,y) => F(x)	

15.2

All we need to do is to find one example of the two clauses and one interpretation for them with the desired property. Let us look for a simple example, by supposing P and Q are empty, and so we can ignore them. And let us take p as the atom P(x).

(a)   We need to find an interpretation $\mathcal{I} = \{W, \mathcal{D}\}$ in which P(x) => P(x) is true and {} => P(x) is false. This will not be hard, for plainly P(x) => P(x) will be true in every interpretation.

A good trick when looking for an example interpretation is to choose some very simple one from arithmetic. Here, let W = the natural numbers, that is $\{0, 1, 2, \ldots\}$ and let $\mathcal{D}(P)$ = the odd numbers. Then any valuation that gives x an even number as value will not satisfy {} => P(x), so the clause is false in that interpretation. (It says 'Everything is odd.')

(b)   Now we are looking for an interpretation in which P(x) => {} is false. The same one will do, for now any valuation that gives x an odd number as value will not satisfy P(x) => {}, so the clause is false in this interpretation. (It says 'Nothing is odd.')

15.3

We need to find a counterexample, that is, an interpretation in which the premiss is true and the conclusion is false. As in the previous exercise, we will choose one from elementary arithmetic of natural numbers. We let F mean 'is odd', and we let G mean that the sum of its two arguments is even. (We could set this out in terms of interpretations, denotation, etc. if we wanted to, but that seems like overkill and may obscure a simple example.) Then the premiss is certainly true: the sum of any two odd numbers is even. But the conclusion is false: it says that an odd number, when summed with any number, gives an even number.

15.4

Take any predicate you like in the knowledge base, such as K( ) from the knowledge base about Scandinavian royalty. Then since there is an infinite supply of variables, we can fill the argument place of that predicate in an infinite number of ways, for example, K(y), K(x374), giving an infinite number of atoms.

Strictly, we do not need to add that infinity of axioms, because Subst-Rule will allow us to add all Ids of the form K( ) => K( ), for example, K(x) => K(x).

15.5

Define the valuation and interpretation we want in this way: let A have the value 0, x the value 1, and y the value 2. Let F denote the set {0}, and let G denote the set

$\{\langle 1, 2 \rangle\}$. Then in this valuation, every antecedent is satisfied and no consequent is satisfied, so the clause is not satisfied, and hence is false in this interpretation.

15.6

Proof of (5)

Id	$\mathtt{T \Rightarrow T}$	**(1)**
(1), T/F Contract	$\mathtt{\{\} \Rightarrow T}$	

Proof of (6)

Id	$\mathtt{F \Rightarrow F}$	**(1)**
(1), T/F Contract	$\mathtt{F \Rightarrow \{\}}$	

15.7

(a) If $\mathtt{T}, A \Rightarrow C$ is true in an interpretation $\mathcal{I}$, so is $A \Rightarrow C$. For if $\mathtt{T}, A \Rightarrow C$ is true in $\mathcal{I}$, then every valuation $\mathcal{V}$ in $\mathcal{I}$ satisfies $\mathtt{T}, A \Rightarrow C$, in which case, by Def. Truth for clauses, it either fails to satisfy an antecedent, or it satisfies a consequent, in C. But it cannot fail to satisfy $\mathtt{T}$, so it fails to satisfy an antecedent in A, or it satisfies a consequent in C. In which case, by Def. Truth for clauses, it satisfies $A \Rightarrow C$. Since this holds for every $\mathcal{V}$ in $\mathcal{I}$, $A \Rightarrow C$ is true in $\mathcal{I}$.

(b) If $A \Rightarrow \mathtt{F}, C$ is true in an interpretation $\mathcal{I}$, so is $A \Rightarrow C$. For if $A \Rightarrow \mathtt{F}, C$ is true in $\mathcal{I}$, then every valuation $\mathcal{V}$ in $\mathcal{I}$ satisfies $A \Rightarrow \mathtt{F}, C$, in which case, by Def. Truth for clauses, it either fails to satisfy an antecedent, or it satisfies a consequent, in C. But it cannot satisfy $\mathtt{F}$, so it fails to satisfy an antecedent in A, or it satisfies a consequent in C. In which case, by Def. Truth for clauses, it satisfies $A \Rightarrow C$. Since this holds for every $\mathcal{V}$ in $\mathcal{I}$, $A \Rightarrow C$ is true in $\mathcal{I}$.

15.8

A1,Weak	$p, p, q_1 \Rightarrow r_1$	**(1)**
(1),A2 Cut	$p, q_1, q_2 \Rightarrow r_1, r_2$	**(2)**
(2),A3 Cut	$q_1, q_2, q_3 \Rightarrow r_1, r_2, r_3$	

15.9

We are asked to show that any theorem of the form $p, p \Rightarrow p, p$ is a logical theorem. We can deduce any such theorem from the corresponding Id axiom in this fashion:

Premiss, Id	$p \Rightarrow p$	**(1)**
(1), Weak	$p, p \Rightarrow p$	**(2)**
(2), Weak	$p, p \Rightarrow p, p$	

We call this display a **deduction schema** since it is the schema or pattern to follow in any actual deduction of a particular clause, for example, of $\mathtt{K(x), K(x) \Rightarrow K(x), K(x)}$.

15.10

Suppose $P \Rightarrow Q$ is true in an interpretation $\mathcal{I}$. Then it follows that in any valuation $\mathcal{V}$ in $\mathcal{I}$, there is either an atom in the antecedent not satisfied by $\mathcal{V}$, or one in the consequent that is. Then that is also true in both $P, p \Rightarrow q$ and $P \Rightarrow p, Q$.

15.11

Using an obvious lexicon, the deduction can be done this way:

Premiss	=> Paid(S, F)	(1)
(1), Weak	=> Paid(S, F),Spy(P-M)	(2)
Premiss	Paid(S, F) =>	(3)
(2),(3) Cut	=> Spy(P-M)	

Chapter 16

16.1

With an obvious lexicon:

        Man(JILL,x),Port(y),At(JILL,y) => Meets(JILL,x,y)

16.2

(a)   Man(JILL,x) => Meets(JILL,x,home(JILL))

(b)   => At(spouse(JILL),home(spouse(JILL))),
            At(spouse(JILL),home(JILL))

(c)   At(home(JILL),x),Port(x) => Meets(m-w-m(JILL,spouse(JILL)),JILL,x)

(d)   If Jill meets someone at a port, then that is their home.

(e)   Nobody meets Jill at a place where their spouse is.

(f)   If the home of the spouse of any of Jill's men is a port, then Jill meets the spouse at that port.

16.3

(a)	<JOHN 34>	(f)	<<MARIE 40><IGOR 29><OLGA 51>>
(b)	<PIERRE 47>	(g)	PIERRE
(c)	GREYMALKIN	(h)	NIL or <>
(d)	JOHN	(i)	NIL or <>
(e)	<34>	(j)	37

Chapter 17

17.1

(a) The definition of Sub= effects the replacement of the left-hand term in an identity atom (here, **y**) in the other antecedent atom (which here must be **Home(x,z)**). But **y** does not occur there. However, (a) is nevertheless a logical law – which we will shortly demonstrate by using the symmetry property of identity – so no counter-example world is describable.

(b) The first antecedent expresses the identity of **home(x)** and **home(y)**. Those terms are not what get substituted in the rest of (b), which is why (b) is not a case of Sub=. An interpretation falsifying (b) is this: the objects in it are just two people, called A and B, say, who are married to each other and not to themselves; and one home, which is the home of both of them. We take **home(⟨person⟩)** to be that one home, and we take **Mar-to** to denote the relation of being married to.

In this interpretation consider the valuation in which **x** has A as value, and **y** and **z** both have B as value. Then both antecedents are satisfied, but the consequent is not. So the clause is not true in this interpretation.

(c) This case is exactly the same as (b), except that **Home** occurs instead of **Mar-to**. But that is an irrelevant difference. The letters you choose for a predicate do not fix its meaning – the interpretation does. So we can take exactly the same counter-example world here as in (b) above, and we say that **Home** denotes the relation of being married to. Then the previous counterexample holds.

This example (c) is important as a reminder that however perverse and unhelpful to a reader it might be to choose the word **Home** to use as a predicate meaning 'married to', doing so offends no principle of logic. If we wanted to tie in the predicate **Home** in its expected meaning of **Home(⟨person⟩,⟨house⟩)** as true in a world if ⟨house⟩ is a home of ⟨person⟩ in that world, with the expected meaning of **home(⟨person⟩)** as referring to the house which is ⟨person⟩'s home, then we must do so with an explicit axiom, for example:

```
=> Home(x,home(x))
```

In English that sounds like a tautology – 'the home of a person is their home' – but only because in English the first, functional use of 'home' already has the same meaning as the second, predicational use. In logic such an equivalence cannot be assumed.

(d) This would be a Sub= axiom if **Port(z)** were not there. Nevertheless it is a logical law, and so has no counterexample. To prove it we take the Sub= axiom

```
x=y,  Home(x,z) => Home(y,z)
```

and use Weak to get (d).

17.2

The deduction, from any knowledge base, is:

Symmetry of $=$	y=x => x=y	(1)
Sub$=$	x=y, Home(x,z) => Home(y,z)	(2)
(1),(2) Cut	y=x, Home(x,z) => Home(y,z)	

17.3

We wish to prove, for any terms t_1, t_2, t_3, that:

$t_1 = t_2, t_2 = t_3$ => $t_1 = t_3$

is deducible from any knowledge base. The deduction is:

Sub$=$	$t_2 = t_1$, $t_2 = t_3$ => $t_1 = t_3$	(1)
Symmetry of $=$	$t_1 = t_2$ => $t_2 = t_1$	(2)
(1),(2) Cut	$t_1 = t_2$, $t_2 = t_3$ => $t_1 = t_3$	

17.4

(a)

Sub$=$	$x_1 = y_1, P(x_1, x_2)$ => $P(y_1, x_2)$	(1)
Sub$=$	$x_2 = y_2, P(y_1, x_2)$ => $P(y_1, y_2)$	(2)
(1),(2) Cut	$x_1 = y_1, x_2 = y_2, P(x_1, x_2)$ => $P(y_1, y_2)$	

(b)

Sub$=$	$x_1 = y_1, f(x_1, x_2) = f(x_1, x_2)$ => $f(x_1, x_2) = f(y_1, x_2)$	(1)
Eq	=> $f(x_1, x_2) = f(x_1, x_2)$	(2)
(1),(2) Cut	$x_1 = y_1$ => $f(x_1, x_2) = f(y_1, x_2)$	(3)
Sub$=$	$x_2 = y_2, f(x_1, x_2) = f(y_1, x_2)$ => $f(x_1, x_2) = f(y_1, y_2)$	(4)
(3),(4) Cut	$x_1 = y_1, x_2 = y_2$ => $f(x_1, x_2) = f(y_1, y_2)$	

17.5

The deduction is:

A7 {x/y,y/x}	Mar-to(y,x) => Mar-to(x,y)	(1)
(1),A10 Cut	Mar-to(y,x), Mar-to(x,z) => y=z	(2)
A7 {z/x,x/y}	Mar-to(z,x) => Mar-to(x,z)	(3)
(2),(3) Cut	Mar-to(y,x), Mar-to(z,x) => y=z	(4)
{x/y,z/x,y/z}	Mar-to(x,z), Mar-to(y,z) => x=y	

17.6

The deductions are (using **s** instead of **spouse**):

(4)

A7 {s(x)/y}	Mar-to(x,s(x)) => Mar-to(s(x),x)	(1)
(1),A11 Cut	=> Mar-to(s(x),x)	

(5)

```
A10, {s(x)/z}  Mar-to(x,y),Mar-to(x,s(x)) => y=s(x)        (1)
(1),A11 Cut                     Mar-to(x,y) => y=s(x)
```

(6)

```
Sub=        Mar-to(x,s(x)),y=s(x) => Mar-to(x,y)           (1)
(1),A11 Cut             y=s(x) => Mar-to(x,y)
```

17.7

The deduction is (using s instead of **spouse**):

```
Sub=        s(x)=y, s(s(x))=s(s(x)) => s(y)=s(s(x))        (1)
Eq                             => s(s(x))=s(s(x))          (2)
(1),(2) Cut             s(x)=y => s(y)=s(s(x))             (3)
Sub=        s(y)=s(s(x)), s(s(x))=x => s(y)=x              (4)
A12                             => s(s(x))=x               (5)
(4),(5) Cut        s(y)=s(s(x)) => s(y)=x                  (6)
(3),(6) Cut             s(x)=y => s(y)=x
```

17.8

Since $\mathcal{V}(t) = \mathcal{V}(t')$:

$$\mathcal{V}(f)(\mathcal{V}(t), \mathcal{V}(t_1), \ldots, \mathcal{V}(t_n)) = \mathcal{V}(f)(\mathcal{V}(t'), \mathcal{V}(t_1), \ldots, \mathcal{V}(t_n))$$

Hence by Def. Valuation:

$$\mathcal{V}(f(t, t_1, \ldots, t_n)) = \mathcal{V}(f(t', t_1, \ldots, t_n))$$

17.9

Since $\mathcal{V}(t) = \mathcal{V}(t')$, we have:

$$\langle \mathcal{V}(t), \mathcal{V}(t_1), \ldots, \mathcal{V}(t_n) \rangle = \langle \mathcal{V}(t'), \mathcal{V}(t_1), \ldots, \mathcal{V}(t_n) \rangle$$

Consequently, $\langle \mathcal{V}(t), \mathcal{V}(t_1), \ldots, \mathcal{V}(t_n) \rangle$ is an $n + 1$-tuple belonging to the relation $\mathcal{V}(P)$ only if $\langle \mathcal{V}(t'), \mathcal{V}(t_1), \ldots, \mathcal{V}(t_n) \rangle$ does. In that case, by Def. Satisfies, $P(t, t_1, \ldots, t_n)$ is satisfied in $\mathcal{V}$ only if $P(t', t_1, \ldots, t_n)$ is.

Chapter 18

18.1

You might not have the same existential terms as here, but at least yours must be different from each other where these ones are.

```
(a)                          => Mar-to(@X, JOHN)
                             => P(@X)
(b)                          => Happy(spouse(@WHO))
                             => P(@WHO)
(c)                          => Happy(@GUESS)
                             => Married(@GUESS)
                             => P(@GUESS)
(d)                          => At(spouse(x), @Y)
                             => Place(@Y)
(e)                          => Mar-to(PIERRE, @Z)
                             => Mar-to(IGOR, @Z)
                             => P(@Z)
(f)                          => Meets(JILL, @U, @P)
                             => P(@U)
                             => Port(@P)
(g)              Port(x)     => Meets(JILL, @W, x)
                             => P(@W)
(h)  At(JILL, x), Port(x)    => At(spouse(JILL), x)
```

That last one was a bit of a false friend – an example of 'there is' in English that is universal not existential in its meaning.

18.2

Variations will occur, but check that your answers say the same as these.

(a)   Some planets are cold and gaseous. (Or: there is a cold gaseous planet. Some people worry that 'some' with a plural noun means more than one; if you do, choose a clearly singular translation.)

(b)   Some planet is neither cold nor gaseous.

(c)   There is a married couple.

(d)   There is someone who is not married to Jill (or is not a person).

(e)   There is someone who meets Jill at every port.

(f)   Jill is married to two different people.

(g)   There is a place where either Anne's home or Anne's spouse is.

(h)   There is a certain person who is the spouse of the minister who married Olga to that person. Or, Olga is married to the spouse of the minister who married them. (Almost impossible to express a reasonably literal translation easily in English. But note that, assuming no bigamy, it amounts to saying that Olga performed her own marriage ceremony. The minister was the bride.)

18.3

Once we allow functors in, we can create an infinity of new terms, for example, spouse(MARIE), spouse(spouse(MARIE)), spouse(spouse(spouse(MARIE))), ... Each of these generates a new ground instance of (9a) when substituted for x.

18.4

We add the axiom:

```
=> @g(x) = x
```

18.5

(a)
```
                    => P(@A)
         P(x) => Knows(@A,x)
```

(b)
```
         P(x) => Knows(@f(x),x)
         P(x) => P(@f(x))
```

(c)
```
      Port(x) => Meets(JILL, @B, x)
              => P(@B)
```

(d)
```
      Port(x) => Meets(JILL, @g(x), x)
      Port(x) => P(@g(x))
```

(e)
```
   P(x),Port(y) => Meets(x,@h(x,y),y)
   P(x),Port(y) => P(@h(x,y))
```

(f)
```
         P(x) => Meets(x,JILL,@i(x))
         P(x) => Port(@i(x))
```

(g)
```
         P(x) => Meets(x,@j(x),@k(x))
         P(x) => P(@j(x))
         P(x) => Port(@k(x))
```

(h)
```
   P(x),Meets(x,@l(x),@m(x)),
         P(@l(x)), Port(@m(x)) => Mar-to(x, @n(x))
   P(x),Meets(x,@l(x),@m(x)),
         P(@l(x)), Port(@m(x)) => P(@n(x))
```

18.6

We need 1, 2, and 3 all to F to one object. So $\mathcal{D}(F) = \{\langle 1,3,\rangle, \langle 2,3\rangle, \langle 3,3\rangle\}$ will do. The clause says 'There is something that everything Fs to', and in $\mathcal{I}$, 3 is just such a thing. With this interpretation $\mathcal{I}$, there is an extension of it that makes the clause true, so the clause is true in $\mathcal{I}$.

18.7

Yes. We take as an extension of $\mathcal{I}$, an assignment to @f of the function f such that $f(1) = 3, f(2) = 2, f(3) = 2$. What this clause says is 'Everything has something it Fs to', and that is true in $\mathcal{I}$. 1 Fs to 3, 2 Fs to 2, and 3 Fs to 2.

18.8

(a)   P(@B,x,A,@B)

(b)   P(A,@f(x,A)) => Q(g(@f(x,A)),x)

(c)   P(f(A,B),f(A,C)) => Q(A,C,@K)

(d)   P(@A,x) => Q(@g(x,y),y)

(e)   P(f(@A,B)) => Q(f(B,A))

18.9

The translations are:

(a)   Everyone loves everyone.
(b)   There is someone who loves everyone.
(c)   There is someone who is loved by everyone
(d)   Everyone is loved by someone (or other).
(e)   Everyone loves someone (or other).
(f)   Someone loves someone.

(a) entails (b)

Premiss (a)	=> L(x,y)	(1)
(1){@A/x}	=> L(@A,y)	(2)

(a) entails (c)

Premiss (a)	=> L(x,y)	(1)
(1){@B/y}	=> L(x,@B)	(2)

(b) entails (d)

Premiss (b)	=> L(@A,y)	(1)
(1)[@f(y)/@A]	=> L(@f(y),y)	(2)

(c) entails (e)

Premiss (c)	=> L(x,@B)	(1)
(1)[@g(x)/@B]	=> L(x,@g(x))	(2)

(d) entails (f)

Premiss (d)	=> L(@f(y),y)	(1)
(1){A/y}	=> L(@f(A),A)	(2)
(2)[@C/@f(A)]	=> L(@C,A)	(3)
(3)[@D/A]	=> L(@C,@D)	(4)

(e) entails (f)

Premiss (e)	=> L(x,@g(x))	(1)
(1){A/x}	=> L(A,@g(A))	(2)
(2)[@C/A]	=> L(@C,@g(A))	(3)
(3)[@D/@g(A)]	=> L(@C,@D)	(4)

Chapter 19

19.1

Premiss P1	$p \Rightarrow q, r$	(1)
Premiss P2	$q \Rightarrow s$	(2)
(1),(2),Cut-Rule	$p \Rightarrow r, s$	(3)
Premiss P3	$r \Rightarrow s$	(4)
(3),(4),Cut-Rule	$p \Rightarrow s, s$	(5)
(5)Contract	$p \Rightarrow s$	

19.2

Note that in each proof, we start with the negative denial. This is nearly always the best place to start.

(a)   The denial set comprises just $q \Rightarrow$.

Denial	$q \Rightarrow$	(1)
Premiss	$p \Rightarrow q$	(2)
(1),(2) Cut-Rule	$p \Rightarrow$	(3)
Premiss	$\Rightarrow p$	(4)
(3),(4) Cut-Rule	$\Rightarrow$	(4)

(b)   The denial set comprises $\Rightarrow p$ and $r \Rightarrow$.

Denial	$r \Rightarrow$	(1)
Premiss	$q \Rightarrow r$	(2)
(1),(2) Cut-Rule	$q \Rightarrow$	(3)
Premiss	$p \Rightarrow q$	(4)
(3),(4) Cut-Rule	$p \Rightarrow$	(5)
Denial	$\Rightarrow p$	(6)
(5),(6) Cut-Rule	$\Rightarrow$	

(c)   The denial set comprises $\Rightarrow p$ and $\Rightarrow s$ and $p \Rightarrow$ and $r \Rightarrow$.

Denial	$p \Rightarrow$	(1)
Denial	$\Rightarrow p$	(2)
(1),(2) Cut-Rule	$\Rightarrow$	

19.3

Example 14.1. The denial set contains just `M(P) =>`.

Denial	`M(P) =>`	(1)
Premiss	`F(x,y) => M(x)`	(2)
(2){P/x,C/y}	`F(P,C) => M(P)`	(3)
(1),(3)Cut-Rule	`F(P,C) =>`	(4)
Premiss	`=> F(P,C)`	(5)
(4),(5)Cut-Rule	`=>`	

Example 14.2. The denial set contains just `Gpar(P,W) =>`.

Denial	`Gpar(P,W) =>`	(1)
Premiss	`Par(x,y),Par(y,z) => Gpar(x,z)`	(2)
(2){P/x,W/z}	`Par(P,y),Par(y,W) => Gpar(P,W)`	(3)

(1),(3)Cut-Rule	Par(P,y),Par(y,W) =>	(4)
Premiss	=> Par(P,C)	(5)
(4){C/y}	Par(P,C),Par(C,W) =>	(6)
(5),(6)Cut-Rule	Par(C,W) =>	(7)
Premiss	=> Par(C,W)	(8)
(7),(8)Cut-Rule	=>	

19.4

Example 14.3: The denial set comprises:
=> F(@X,@Y); => F(@Y,@Z) and Gpar(@X,@Z) => .

Denial	Gpar(@X,@Z) =>	(1)
Premiss	Par(x,y),Par(y,z) => Gpar(x,z)	(2)
(2){@X/x,@Z/z}	Par(@X,y),Par(y,@Z) => Gpar(@X,@Z)	(3)
(1),(3)Cut-Rule	Par(@X,y),Par(y,@Z) =>	(4)
Premiss	F(x,y) => Par(x,y)	(5)
(5){@X/x}	F(@X,y) => Par(@X,y)	(6)
(4),(6)Cut-Rule	Par(y,@Z),F(@X,y) =>	(7)
Denial	=> F(@X,@Y)	(8)
(7){@Y/y}	Par(@Y,@Z),F(@X,@Y) =>	(9)
(8),(9)Cut-Rule	Par(@Y,@Z) =>	(10)
(5){@Y/x,@Z/y}	F(@Y,@Z) => Par(@Y,@Z)	(11)
(10),(11)Cut-Rule	F(@Y,@Z) =>	(12)
Denial	=> F(@Y,@Z)	(13)
(12),(13)Cut-Rule	=>	

Example 14.4: The denial set comprises => Par(@X,@Y); => F(@Y) and
Dtr(@Y,@X) => .

Denial	Dtr(@Y,@X) =>	(1)
Premiss	Ch(x,y),F(x) => Dtr(x,y)	(2)
(2){@Y/x,@X/y}	Ch(@Y,@X),F(@Y) => Dtr(@Y,@X)	(3)
(1),(3)Cut-Rule	Ch(@Y,@X),F(@Y) =>	(4)
Denial	=> F(@Y)	(5)
(4),(5)Cut-Rule	Ch(@Y,@X) =>	(6)
Premiss	Par(x,y) => Ch(y,x)	(7)
(2){@Y/y,@X/x}	Par(@X,@Y) => Ch(@Y,@X)	(8)
(6),(8)Cut-Rule	Par(@X,@Y) =>	(9)
Denial	=> Par(@X,@Y)	(10)
(9),(10)Cut-Rule	=>	

19.5

(a)   F(A,B) =>
       F(B,A) =>

(b)   => F(A,B)
                 => G(A,C)
       G(B,C) =>

(c)   => F(@X,@Y)
                 => F(@Y,@Z)
       G(@X,@Z) =>

(d)   => F(@X,@Y)
                       => F(@Y,@X)

(e)   => F(@X,@Y)
          F(@Y,@X) =>

(f)   G(a,A) =>

(g)   G(a,@f(a)) =>

(h)   => G(a,A)

(i)   => F(@f(a),a)

(j)   F(a,@g(a)) =>
                       => G(@f(a),@g(a))

Possible readings are:

(a)   Abel is father of Bob or Bob is father of Abel.

Denials:
Abel is not father of Bob, and
Bob is not father of Abel.

(b)   If Abel is father of Bob and grandfather of Cat, then Bob is father of Cat.

Denials:
Abel is father of Bob, and
Abel is grandfather of Cat, and
Bob is not father of Cat.

(c)   If one person is father of a second who is father of a third, then the first is grandfather of the third.

Denials:
There are three people such that:
the first is father of the second, and
the second is father of the third, and
the first is not grandfather of the third.

(d)   No two people are fathers of each other.

Denials:
There are two people who are fathers of each other.

(e)   If one person is father of a second, the second is father of the first.

Denials:
There are two people, the first of whom is father of the second,
but not conversely.

(f)   Someone is Abel's grandfather.

Denials:
Nobody is Abel's grandfather.

(g)   Someone is everyone's grandfather.

Denials:
Everyone has someone they are not grandfather of.

(h)   Someone is not Abel's grandfather.

Denials:
Everyone is Abel's grandfather.

(i)   Someone has no father.

Denials:
Everyone has a father.

(j)   There is somebody such that, for everyone who has a grandfather, they are their father.

Denials:
There are functions f, g on people such that for any given person a:
a is not father of their g-er, but
a's f-er is grandfather of their g-er.

More freely: For any person at all, there is a grandfather and his grandchild such that the person is not father of the grandchild.

19.6

The square is:

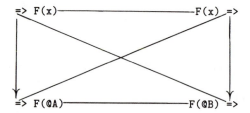

Suppose, contrary to what we are trying to prove, there is an interpretation $\mathcal{I}$ in which the bottom clauses are both false. Then, by Def. Truth for existential terms, there is no extension of $\mathcal{I}$ that makes either of them true. So in any extension $\mathcal{I}'$ of $\mathcal{I}$, (looking at the bottom left clause) no value for **x** will satisfy **F(x)**, and (looking at the bottom right clause), every value of **x** satisfies **F(x)**. But that gives us a contradiction, so our supposition is false.

Chapter 20

20.1

Forward chaining.

Id	$p \Rightarrow p$	(1)
(1),Weak	$p, q \Rightarrow p$	(2)
(1),Weak	$p, q, r \Rightarrow p$	(3)
(1),Weak	$p, q, r \Rightarrow p, q$	(4)
(1),Weak	$p, q, r \Rightarrow p, q, r$	

Backward chaining. Let $\Rightarrow p'$ be the clause in the denial set made from the antecedent p. Then the clause made from the consequent p is $p' \Rightarrow$. The deduction is:

Denial		=> p'	(1)
Denial	p' =>		(1)
(1),(2)Cut-Rule		=>	

Note the irrelevance of the other clauses in the denial set. This is symmetrical with their introduction via Weak in forward chaining. In each proof we deduced something stronger to begin with. In forward chaining we need to go on to infer the weaker result from the stronger; but in refutation the proof of the stronger result *is* a proof of all its weakenings.

20.2

Denial	Q(A) =>	(1)
Premiss	P(x) => Q(x),Q(y)	(2)
Premiss	=> P(A)	(3)
(2){A/x}	P(A) => Q(A),Q(y)	(4)
(3),(4)Cut-Rule	=> Q(A),Q(y)	(5)
(5){A/y}	=> Q(A),Q(A)	(6)
(6)Contract	=> Q(A)	(7)
(1),(7)Cut-Rule	=>	

Note that in this case we could have avoided contraction by resolving twice on Q.

20.3

The denotations for A and B we know: themselves. For F it is $\{\langle A, B\rangle, \langle B, A\rangle\}$. For G it is $\{\langle A, B\rangle\}$. Clause (1) is false, since where x gets value A and y gets value B, (as with clause (6)), the clause is not satisfied.

20.4

They are L(A,A); L(h(A),A); M(A,A); M(h(A),A). If they are all true, (13) and (14) are true but (12) is false.

20.5

There are three assignments (starred) where all clauses in V' are true. The first of them defines a partial interpretation $\mathcal{I} = \langle \mathcal{W}, \mathcal{D}\rangle$, where the universe $\mathcal{W} = \{A, h(A)\}$ and the denotations of the predicates are: $\mathcal{D}(L) = \{\langle A, A\rangle\}; \mathcal{D}(M) = \{\langle A, A\rangle, \langle h(A), A\rangle\}$. However it does not define fully the interpretation of the functor h. By the way the Herbrand Universe was set up, we know that h(A) denotes h(A), but we also need to know the denotation of h(h(A)). That is, suppose the denotation of the functor h is some total function h in the domain, that is, a function defined for every object in the domain. Now we know that $h(A) = h(A)$ but we do not know $h(h(A))$. And that matters. For when we evaluate (7) we have to take the case where the value of x is h(A), that is, we must find the value of $h(h(A))$.

L(A,A)	L(h(A),A)	M(A,A)	M(h(A),A)	(12)	(13)	(14)	
1	1	1	1	0	1	1	
1	1	1	0	0	0	1	
1	1	0	1	0	1	1	
1	1	0	0	0	0	1	
1	0	1	1	1	1	1	*
1	0	1	0	1	0	1	
1	0	0	1	1	1	1	*
1	0	0	0	1	0	1	
0	1	1	1	0	1	0	
0	1	1	0	0	0	0	
0	1	0	1	0	1	1	
0	1	0	0	0	0	1	
0	0	1	1	1	1	0	
0	0	1	0	1	0	0	
0	0	0	1	1	1	1	*
0	0	0	0	1	0	1	

In this way, we can see that no valuation in which all the (ground) clauses in V' are true, defines an interpretation for V. Hence it certainly does not define a model for V.

Chapter 21

21.1

The denial of (C) is:

Dad murdered someone.	=> M(D,@B)	**(D)**

Did you get this?

(P1),(P2)Cut	M(x,y),P(x,y) =>	**(1)**
(1),(P3), resolve	M(D,@X) =>	**(2)**
... Stuck!		

21.2

The unifications needed are:

(3) $\{x/u, f(y)/v\}$

(4) $\{u/x, u/y, f(u)/v\}$

(5) $\{u/x, f(y)/v\}$

(3) and (5) are more general that (4), since (3)$\{u/x,u/y\}$ = (4), and (5)$\{u/y\}$ = (4), but no substitution in (4) will give the other two. (3) and (5) are equally general, since (3)$\{u/x\}$ = (5), and (5)$\{x/u\}$ = (3).

21.3

We deny that Ann is a parent of Chris, which gives us the denial set. We need to prove inconsistent (1)–(5) below.

Denial	`A(A,C) =>`	(1)
Premiss	`A(x,y),P(y,z) => A(x,z)`	(2)
Premiss	`P(x,y) => A(x,y)`	(3)
Premiss	`=> P(A,B)`	(4)
Premiss	`=> P(B,C)`	(5)
(1),(2),resolve	`A(A,y),P(y,C) =>`	(6)
(6),(2),resolve	`A(A,y),P(y,u),P(u,C) =>`	(7)
(7),(2),resolve	`A(A,y),P(y,v),P(v,u),P(u,C) =>`	(8)

and so on. Adding step (3a) to the control algorithm will not help since these are all new clauses. Nor can we factor (7) to get anything useful: we just get `A(A,C),P(C,C) =>`. Nor will subsumption work, since (6) does not subsume (7). The only alternative is to reorder the database so that (3) comes before (2).

Chapter 22

22.1

CFL:

Denial	`=> H(S)`	(1)
Premiss	`H(x) => M(x),F(x)`	(2)
Premiss	`M(S) =>`	(3)
Premiss	`F(S) =>`	(4)
(1),(2),resolve	`=> M(S),F(S)`	(5)
(5),(3),resolve	`=> F(S)`	(6)
(6),(4),resolve	`=>`	

In a PROLOG proof, we reject line (2) above, since the clause has a multiple consequent, and put in the three clauses suggested. An attempt to carry out the proof on that basis would then proceed thus:

Denial	`=> H(S)`	(1)
Premiss	`H(x) => M-or-f(x)`	(2)
Premiss	`M(x) => M-or-f(x)`	(3)
Premiss	`F(x) => M-or-f(x)`	(4)
Premiss	`M(S) =>`	(5)
Premiss	`F(S) =>`	(6)
(1),(2),resolve	`=> M-or-f(S)`	(7)

There is now no further resolution to make, so the deduction will fail. But anyway, PROLOG could not even get that far, since we still have two negative Horn clauses in the database, which is not legal in PROLOG. A third reason for PROLOG failing here will emerge immediately in the main text.

22.2

Denial	`Have(PIGS, WINGS) =>`	(1)
Premiss	`=> H(A)`	(2)
Premiss	`=> M(A)`	(3)
Premiss	`=> F(A)`	(4)
Premiss	`H(x),M(x),F(x) => Have(PIGS, WINGS)`	(5)
(1),(5),resolve	`H(x),M(x),F(x) =>`	(6)
(6),(2),resolve	`M(A),F(A) =>`	(7)
(7),(3),resolve	`F(A) =>`	(8)
(8),(4),resolve	`=>`	

22.3

We deny it, `C(S,OZ) =>` , call this denial (1a), and add it to the current database, (1)–(6). It resolves with (4) which yields `C(S,VIC) =>` , which fails to resolve. So (following the control algorithm), we resolve (1a) with (5) which yields `C(S,QLD) =>` , which fails to resolve. There is now nothing left for (1a) to resolve with, so we have finitely failed to prove `=> C(S,OZ)`.

22.4

Denial	`Has-father(C) =>`	(0)
Premiss	`=> Parent(P,C)`	(1)
Premiss	`=> Female(E)`	(2)
Premiss	`Parent(x,y),not(Female(x)) => Has-father(y)`	(3)
(0),(3),resolve	`Parent(x,C),not(Female(x)) =>`	(4)
(1),(4),resolve	`not(Female(P)) =>`	(5)

Now PROLOG tries to prove `=> Female(P)` but fails.

(5),NFF	`=>`	

22.5

Denial	`Has-father(C) =>`	(0)
Premiss	`=> Parent(E,C)`	(1)
Premiss	`=> Female(E)`	(2)
Premiss	`not(Female(x)),Parent(x,y) => Has-father(y)`	(3)
(0),(3),resolve	`not(Female(x)),Parent(x,C) =>`	(4)

Now PROLOG tries to prove `=> Female(x)` but fails.

(4),NFF	`Parent(x,C) =>`	(5)
(5),(1),resolve	`=>`	

22.6

We remove (1) from the the above database and add:

Denial	`P(x,y),P(y,C) =>`	(1)
Premiss	`=> P(P,C)`	(2)
Premiss	`=> P(E,C)`	(3)
Premiss	`=> P(EB,E)`	(4)
Premiss	`=> P(G,E)`	(5)

We carry out one refutation, carefully noting all variable bindings on the way.

`(1){EB/x,E/y}`	`P(EB,E),P(E,C) =>`	(6)
`(6),(4),Cut`	`P(E,C) =>`	(7)
`(3),(7),Cut`	`=>`	(8)

We have completed one refutation. Note the variable bindings. Now backtrack to the point in the proof where we can do something different, and try again. That is, to the point after line (5).

`(1){G/x,E/y}`	`P(G,E),P(E,C) =>`	(6)
`(6)(5)Cut`	`P(E,C) =>`	(7)
`(3),(7),Cut`	`=>`	(8)

That completes a second refutation. We note the bindings. There is now no way of performing another refutation, so we are finished. The variable bindings in each refutation were:

$x \mapsto EB,\ y \mapsto E$
$x \mapsto G,\ \ y \mapsto E$

The bindings of x give us the parents of parents of Charles, so the answer is EB and G, that is, Elizabeth B. and George.

22.7

The negative Horn clause and premisses are:

Denial	`G(g,C), F(g) =>`	(1)
Premiss	`=> P(P,C)`	(2)
Premiss	`=> P(E,C)`	(3)
Premiss	`=> P(EB,E)`	(4)
Premiss	`=> P(G,E)`	(5)
Premiss	`P(x,y),P(y,z) => G(x,z)`	(6)
Premiss	`=> F(EB)`	(7)
Premiss	`=> F(E)`	(8)

(a) The depth-first search is:

`(1),(6),resolve`	`P(x,y),P(y,C),F(x) =>`	(9)

resolution of (9) with (2) leads to failure, so next does resolution of (9) with (3). The next try is:

(9),(4),resolve	`P(E,C),F(EB) =>`	**(10)**
(10),(3),resolve	`       F(EB) =>`	**(11)**
(11),(7),resolve	`            =>`	**(12)**

The ultimate binding here is **g↦EB**. Success. Backtrack to after (9). resolution of (9) with (5) leads to failure. There are no alternative resolutions, so the procedure terminates. The only binding found gives that Elizabeth B. is Charles's only female grandparent.

(b) The breadth-first search is:

(1),(6),resolve	`F(x),P(x,y),P(y,C) =>`	**(9)**
(9),(7),resolve	`P(EB,y),P(y,C) =>`	**(10)**
(10),(4),resolve	`P(E,C) =>`	**(11)**
(11),(3),resolve	`=>`	**(12)**

The ultimate binding here is **g↦EB**. Success. Backtrack to after (9). Resolution of (9) with (8) leads to failure. There are no alternative resolutions, so the procedure terminates. The only binding found gives that Elizabeth B. is Charles's only female grandparent. Note that in this example, breadth-first search has been more efficient than depth-first search.

Index

6392   7290